AF328685

SUSTAINABLE FINANCE FOR RETURNS AND IMPACT

Wiley Finance Series

SUSTAINABLE FINANCE FOR RETURNS AND IMPACT

MATTHEW DEARTH, JAMES CHEO

WILEY

Contents

PART THREE

Regulations and Companies

PART FOUR

Sustainable Investing

PART FIVE

Incorporating Sustainability into Your Portfolio

Acknowledgments

We could not have completed this book without a lot of help from people around us. Throughout our careers, our colleagues and clients have been a source of inspiration and perspiration, whose help and encouragement (and tough questions) have helped make us who we are today. Thank you all for the journeys we have shared together.

We thank Valencia Sie, Koh Wen Yu, and Zhu Jiayu for their valuable research assistance. We also received comments and feedback from Lynette Lee, Wilson Tan, Daniel Lee, and Yuxia Zou, and an exceptional proofreading from Judd Labarthe. Thank you all very much for your help.

One of the defining elements of this book is the opportunity to hear directly from practitioners. We extend our deepest appreciation to our interviewees who made time in their schedules to share their insights with us: Griet Cattaert, Trista Chen, Fang Eu-Lin, Jeremy Hall, Mitch Reznick, Mervyn Tang, Michael Tang, Emily Woodland, and Heidi Yip.

The Wiley team have been great to work with, especially Syd Ganaden who brought us together in the first place, and Venkat who helped keep the train running close to schedule.

Finally, none of this would have been possible—our careers and our lives, let alone this book—without the love and support from our families, here in Singapore and around the world.

About the Authors

Matthew Dearth, PhD
Associate Professor of Finance (Practice)
Nanyang Business School
Singapore

Dr. Matthew Dearth is Associate Professor of Finance (Practice) at Nanyang Business School (NBS) where he holds appointments as Assistant Dean (Undergraduate) and Co-Director of the Centre for Sustainable Finance Innovation.

Before transitioning to academia full-time, Dr. Dearth was Managing Director at Silvercrest Asset Management (Singapore) and head of the Singapore office. Earlier, he was founder of TRQ Advisors, a boutique consultancy serving clients in the investment management industry. His 30+ years of finance industry experience also includes leadership roles at Marshall Wace, Goldman Sachs, and Booz Allen & Hamilton.

Since 2023, Dr. Dearth has been a full-time faculty member at NBS where he teaches undergraduate, postgraduate, and executive courses in sustainable finance and impact investing. In 2024, he was named Program Director for the NBS Global Leaders program, the newest signature program at Nanyang Technological University (NTU). From 2016 to 2023, Dr. Dearth taught postgraduate finance courses at Singapore Management University in subjects such as sustainable investing, alternative investments, and asset management. He was recognized on the Dean's Teaching Honor

List for Top Adjunct Faculty (Postgraduate) between 2019–2023. Dr. Dearth is a co-author of *Getting Started in Alternative Investments* (Wiley, 2023) and has published multiple case studies on investment management topics.

Dr. Dearth holds a PhD (General Management) from Singapore Management University, an MBA from Massachusetts Institute of Technology (MIT), and a Bachelor of Science in Civil Engineering and Operations Research from Princeton University.

James Cheo, CFA, CAIA, FRM
Chief Investment Officer
Global Investment Bank

James Cheo is the Chief Investment Officer of a global bank and a leading voice on macroeconomics, investing, and portfolio strategy.

With more than two decades of experience, Mr. Cheo has advised institutional investors, private clients, and family offices across Asia on asset allocation and sustainable finance. His research and thought leadership focus on structural economic shifts, long-term capital flows, and the integration of ESG principles in multi-asset portfolios.

Mr. Cheo has established a strong media profile, with appearances on notable financial media including Bloomberg, CNBC, Channel News Asia, and Channel 8; and in printed publications such as the *Financial Times*, *Straits Times*, and *Business Times*. He has been recognized among the Top 20 Most Influential LinkedIn Voices in Singapore and the Top 30 Global Voices in Financial Markets, with his posts reaching over 11 million views annually.

He currently serves on the Council of the Economic Society of Singapore and is a faculty member at the Wealth Management Institute of Singapore, where he teaches courses on wealth strategy and sustainable investing.

Mr. Cheo graduated with First Class Honours in Finance from Nanyang Technological University and was awarded the Chartered Financial Analyst in 2007. He also holds the Chartered Alternative Investment Analyst and Financial Risk Manager designations.

Introduction

Before the Industrial Revolution, the discovery of fossil fuels as an energy source, and the invention of the steam engine, human beings lived in relative harmony with the environment. This is not to say that there weren't problems, e.g., clear-cutting forests for wood, overhunting or overfishing, slavery and systematic oppression of Indigenous peoples in the era of colonization. But the relatively small scale of humanity and manual nature of most activities limited the absolute amount of damage that we could do.

But the Industrial Revolution brought an irreversible increase in productivity. We could dig deeper, harvest more quickly, travel further faster, kill each other more efficiently. We also increased access to food and developed medicines, extending the average lifespan, and improved quality of life. Technology amplified the good and the bad until we reached the point where today we have a problem.

The same technology that helped increase lifespans and lifted hundreds of millions out of poverty is eroding the conditions we take for granted. There is a framework of "planetary boundaries,"[1] first proposed by scientists in 2009, a quantitative assessment of safe limits for human pressure on nine natural processes (Figure I.1). In 2023, scientists concluded that two-thirds of the boundaries have been crossed, increasing the risk of large-scale environmental changes. The framework doesn't predict what will break, when, or how bad things will be—but we shouldn't need that precision[2] to appreciate the risk and to want to change.

More of us need to be aware of these issues and to feel comfortable talking about them with others. To paraphrase the Canadian climate scientist, speaker, and author Katherine Hayhoe, even if you don't believe everything people say about climate change, odds are you or someone you know has been affected in some way. Maybe someone you know was impacted by a flood or fire, or as a scuba diver you were saddened to see the bleaching of coral reefs, or you complain that snow conditions aren't what they used to be at your favorite ski resort, or the game birds that you hunt in the fall show up later each year and in smaller numbers, or its harder to grow your vegetable garden due to the increasing heat. All of these are real for someone, somewhere, and while scientists cannot attribute individual environmental

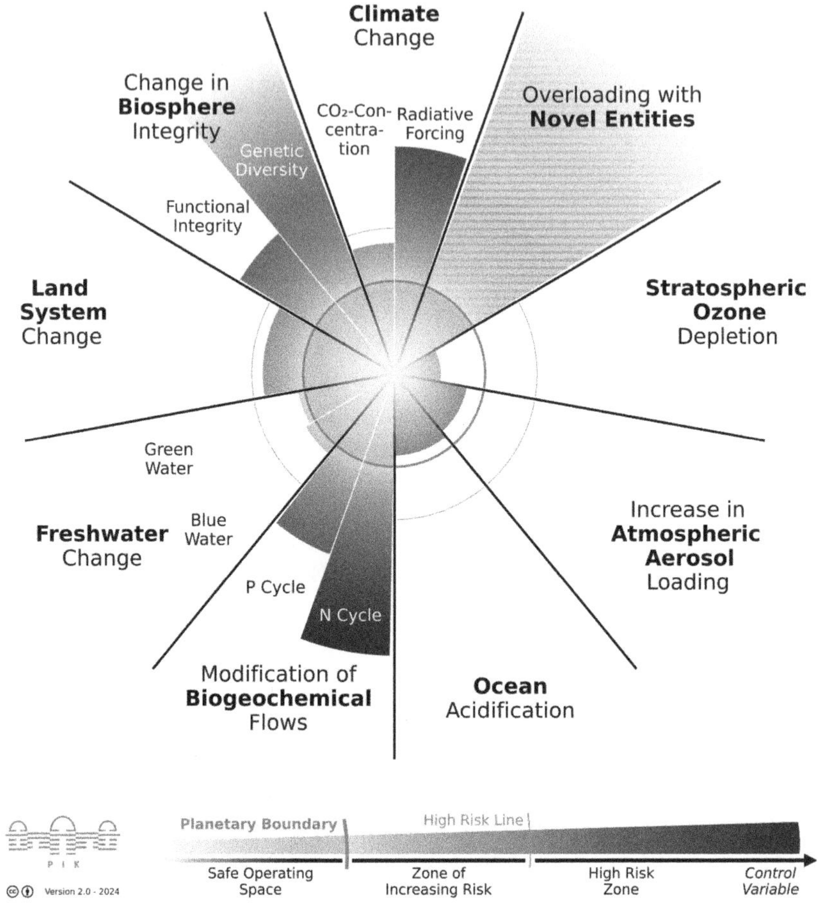

FIGURE I.1   Framework of planetary boundaries, 2023.
Source: https://www.pik-potsdam.de/en/output/infodesk/planetary-boundaries.

events or conditions to climate change with 100% accuracy, they can estimate the *increase in probability* that those events or conditions happen. The good news is that if one of the primary causes is human activity, then we humans can decide to change our activity. The bad news is that it will require systems change more than individual change. Thinking about the importance of finance and investing to the overall systems change is the subject of this book.

WHAT IS DIFFERENT ABOUT THIS BOOK?

We wrote this book to fill a gap in the market: an introductory book that covers the whole topic of sustainable investing from challenges to solutions, including a healthy mix of insights from both theory and practice. Many of the books we could identify focus on either the corporate sustainability perspective or the investor perspective, but not both. Most books do not include discussions of the environmental, social, and governance (ESG) issues to help readers acclimate to the topic if this is their first exposure. And perhaps because the space is changing rapidly, most books do not incorporate the regulatory perspective that is critical to the smooth functioning of the ecosystem overall. We believe readers should appreciate all of these aspects of the problem, not just a subset. The same holds for true for students in the classroom as for experienced professionals contemplating a career change. Solving sustainability problems requires a well-rounded perspective that starts with an appreciation of the stakeholders—especially companies, investors, and governments—and their incentives and motivations.

This is not a "math-y" textbook; rather the emphasis is on critical thinking about why and what kinds of changes in behavior are needed across the ecosystem—more like a "liberal arts course in finance." Readers looking for detailed material on sustainability accounting standards or how to adjust investment valuation for stranded asset risk will be better served by other works focused on these more specialized topics. That said, like other books in the field we include many references to academic research. Scientific inquiry builds a strong foundation that helps us understand how things should work. As current and former practitioners, however, we also wanted to balance the academic perspective with a practical one, capturing the relationship between sustainability and finance/investing as it actually exists. These practical insights are brought to life through transcribed interviews with experienced market practitioners. We are grateful for the time and insights[3] shared by these busy professionals:

In alphabetical order:

Practitioner	Organization	Role
Ms. Griet Cattaert	United Nations Global Compact (UNGC)	Formerly, Head of Social Initiatives at UNGC. Since the interview was conducted, she has moved into a new role as *Regional head of Western Europe and North America* for UNGC
Ms. Trista Chen	LGIM	Head of Investment Stewardship, Asia ex-Japan

(Continued)

(*Continued*)

Practitioner	Organization	Role
Ms. Fang Eu-Lin	PwC Singapore	Sustainability and Climate Change Practice Leader
Mr. Jeremy Hall	Brookfield	Managing Director and Head of Asia Pacific, Brookfield Oaktree Wealth Solutions
Mr. Mitch Reznick, CFA	Federated Hermes	Head of Sustainable Fixed Income
Mr. Mervyn Tang	Schroders	Head of Sustainability Strategy, APAC
Mr. Michael Tang	SGX	Head, Listing Policy and Product Admission and Head, Sustainable Development Office, Singapore Exchange Regulation
Ms. Emily Woodland	BlackRock	Head of Sustainable and Transition Solutions, APAC
Ms. Heidi Yip	BlackRock	Head of Sustainable and Transition Solutions, Southeast Asia

Finally, as the title suggests, we want our readers to finish this journey well-equipped to incorporate sustainability into their investment portfolios. This is by no means one of those "follow our trading system and retire early!" books. Instead we offer practical suggestions for investors regardless of whether you are a student, an early-career individual just starting out, or a finance professional well-versed in wealth management techniques.

WHAT IS INSIDE?

We break the book into five distinct parts, beginning with the underlying issues, to the implications for companies and investment managers, the role of government, and finally the opportunity for individual investors.

- *Part One* sets the scene by describing the challenges we face across ESG factors, as well as a recap of some of the major multinational responses.
- *Part Two* presents the corporate perspective, starting with why companies should care about people and planet in addition to profit. If companies are expected to care, they need to measure and disclose the

current state of their sustainability practices. For firms that decide to make changes to their current practices, there are specialized instruments available to finance sustainable activities.

- *Part Three* introduces the role of government in regulating companies and markets. Three specific roles are explored in these chapters: regulations for measurement and disclosure of sustainability information, minimizing corporate greenwashing through taxonomies and other regulations, and putting a price on pollution through carbon taxes and market-based solutions.
- *Part Four* switches to the investor perspective. In many ways, the bridge between corporate sustainability and investors is what's known as ESG ratings, so we start there before describing the primary strategies that investors use to incorporate sustainability into their investment decisions. One of these strategies, impact investing, is different enough to get its own chapter, followed by a review of how sustainable investing can be applied to a wide variety of asset classes, public and private. Part Four concludes with a review of investor greenwashing, and the regulatory response in select jurisdictions around the world.
- *Part Five* brings the book to its conclusion by synthesizing all this material into suggestions for how investors—especially individual investors—can incorporate sustainability into an investment portfolio. Issues of asset selection and portfolio construction are discussed in the context of potentially very different investor preferences and objectives.

HOW TO READ THIS BOOK

If you read this far into the Introduction you should consider reading the book straight through, but there are other options. For readers with some sustainability or investing experience, we break the book into thematic Parts for easy consumption. Each Part opens with a brief introduction to the material covered in the Chapters contained in that Part. Skimming the Part introduction will give you a sense for what's inside so you can decide which Parts/Chapters to prioritize first. For example, Part One describes the challenges facing society today—environmental (Chapter 1), social (Chapter 2), and governance (Chapter 3)—and some of the major initiatives launched in response (Chapter 4). Those readers less familiar with the United Nations Environment Programme (UNEP) may wish to read Chapter 4 before going back to refresh on the ESG issues in Chapters 1–3. A similar thought process applies to Parts—Two to Five: if you read each Part introduction in order and see something you're not very familiar with, that might be a good place to start.

HOW WE WROTE THIS BOOK

It may or may not quite be our "Skynet" moment,[4] but the arrival of ChatGPT in 2022 has had a profound impact on the act of writing. Lest readers question the provenance of the words to follow, let us share a bit about our work process. Both authors have decades of experience in this and related fields. Dr. Dearth teaches sustainable finance at Nanyang Technological University in Singapore; Chapters 1–15 are closely tied to his course outline and include many of the same structural elements and reference materials he uses in the classroom. Throughout his career, Mr. Cheo has spoken with colleagues and clients about how to make investment decisions; Chapters 16 and 17 are based on his years of professional experience.

Both authors used various large language models (LLMs; including ChatGPT, Claude, STORM, NotebookLM, and Gemini) to identify appropriate and/or additional material to complement their professional knowledge of these topics. For example, when contemplating the "Skynet" reference earlier in this section, Dr. Dearth gave Claude the following prompt: "During all the Terminator movies, when is the best short introduction to the history of Skynet and what happened when it became self-aware? Please direct me to specific scenes (by minute) in specific movies." Being familiar with the movies, Dr. Dearth was unsatisfied with the response he received. Rather than using the material Claude provided, he decided to direct the reader to the original movie in the footnote below. In all cases, LLM output was carefully read and edited; in very rare instances the LLM output was sufficiently well phrased that the authors incorporated some of the text directly. Finally, it should be noted that Dr. Dearth has been a fan of the long "em dash" for many years—long before ChatGPT. In no way should the presence of an em dash be taken as a sign that the text originated in an LLM.

Challenges Ahead

Why does it seem that we care about "sustainability" so much more today compared to a few short decades ago? And what does "sustainability" mean, anyway? The root of the word is *sustain*, which the Oxford English Dictionary defines as "to keep in existence, maintain." In our context, the term sustainability means "the degree to which a process or enterprise is able to be maintained or continued while avoiding the long-term depletion of natural resources."[1] But today we live in a time of contrast. Sustainability appears to be rising. Life expectancies are higher than they have ever been. For many people around the world, quality of life—which itself is a subjective term but generally captures a standard of living including health, comfort, safety, and even happiness—is increasing rapidly.

The development of modern technology from the printing press to electricity and beyond has transformed what it means to be human, from the Indigenous/hunter-gatherer lifestyle to GLP-1 drugs and lattes and laptops and everything else. Our longer life expectancies and perceived quality of life today are tied to those innovations.

On the other hand, there are signs that our ability to sustain that high quality of life for a long time to come comes at a cost. Those costs fall into different categories. Throughout the book we will use the term "ESG"—Environmental, Social, and Governance—to organize our thinking. Setting aside the post-COVID debate about whether ESG is "good" or "bad," the term captures three important dimensions of sustainability. Part One uses this framework to present those costs as challenges facing humanity today (see Table P1.1).

We begin in Chapter 1 with environmental issues, especially climate change, but also including biodiversity loss, deforestation, pollution, and access to clean water. The physical world is the realm of "hard sciences," and while we know a lot about how our planet works there is more that we don't know.

TABLE P1.1 Examples of Environmental, Social, and Governance (ESG) Issues[2]

Environmental Issues	Social Issues	Governance Issues
Climate change and carbon emissions	Customer satisfaction	Board composition
Air and water pollution	Data protection and privacy	Audit committee structure
Biodiversity	Gender and diversity	Bribery and corruption
Deforestation	Employee engagement	Executive compensation
Energy efficiency	Community relations	Lobbying
Waste management	Human rights	Political contributions
Water scarcity	Labor standards	Whistleblower schemes

Source: Hayat et al. 2015, p. 4.

Chapter 2 shifts our attention from the physical world to the people living in it, and to what are referred to collectively as social issues: treatment of people by gender, race, and religion, as well as access to basic needs such as food, shelter, education, and opportunity. This collection of issues presents a different sort of challenge. These issues are less about "hard science" and more subject to debate depending on context. In Singapore or Toronto, for example, we may take for granted the ability to meet our basic needs (food, water, shelter). But even in large, developed cities—not to mention life for hundreds of millions in emerging markets—many people still do not know where their next meal will come from.

In Chapter 3 we address what are referred to as governance issues; things that are associated with the ways in which organizations are managed. Here we include topics such as voting rights and compensation that are indeed very different from the environmental and social issues, and also important in understanding the relative sustainability of modern life.

For decades, people have been hard at work building initiatives and organizations, e.g., various United Nations agencies, that would address these issues; these efforts are the topic of Chapter 4. That the issues persist is perhaps less a statement about the effectiveness of their efforts and more about the difficulty of creating change on a global scale and the "tragedy of the commons."

Finally, a brief note for context: detailed examination of these issues is beyond the scope of this text, but the high-level overview presented here in Part One is important to set the stage for the rest of the book. Indeed, "sustainable investing" may be narrowly focused on a single issue or more broadly constructed to address a wide range of issues. By presenting a variety of ESG issues here at the beginning of the book we hope to focus the reader on the wide-ranging implications for companies, investors, and regulators in the chapters that follow.

CHAPTER 1

Environmental Issues

In the mid-2020s, the state of the environment is marked by myriad challenges across multiple ecological systems. The systemic nature of environmental issues means that addressing one problem can influence another, making it imperative to appreciate these connections—on a global scale. From rising global temperatures and deforestation to lost biodiversity and ocean acidification, the long list of issues challenges us to think holistically about our relationship with the environment.

CLIMATE CHANGE AND GLOBAL WARMING

At the core of climate change is the accumulation of greenhouse gases (GHGs) like carbon dioxide (CO_2), methane (CH_4), and nitrous oxide (N_2O). These gases trap heat in Earth's atmosphere, creating what scientists call the "greenhouse effect." This effect is essential for maintaining temperatures that support life, and natural occurrences, such as volcanic and sunspot activity, lead to variation in temperatures over time, e.g., periods of much colder temperatures lead to the ice ages. More recently, however, GHG concentrations have risen far beyond observable historical levels, leading scientists to conclude[1] that human activity, such as burning fossil fuels, deforestation, and industrial agriculture, are the major drivers.

The resulting rise in global average temperatures—already exceeding 1.1°C above pre-industrial levels—is affecting our climate.[2] Extreme events, like hurricanes, droughts, increased precipitation, heatwaves, and wildfires, are becoming more frequent and severe, affecting millions of people and costing billions of dollars in damages across the world. At the same time, increases in average temperatures contribute to the melting of glaciers and polar icecaps, leading to sea-level change that threatens coastal cities and many island nations. Some forecasts suggest that by the end of the century, sea level may rise at least 0.3 meters above year 2000 levels,[3] endangering hundreds of millions of people living in coastal regions.

It should be noted that complex interrelationships across the climate system make it difficult to forecast what the future climate will look like under different scenarios. For example, temperature rise leads to melting of the Arctic permafrost which releases methane, a very potent GHG, which further increases GHG concentration in the atmosphere. This is a positive feedback loop since it accelerates the underlying process. Actions may have unforeseen negative relationships as well. For example, large segments of the maritime shipping industry burn an oil product called bunker fuel which is both very polluting and contributes meaningfully to GHG emissions. A recent initiative by the International Maritime Organization (IMO) not only reduced GHG emissions but also reduced sulfur, which is known to contribute to cloud formation. Scientists estimate that the effort to reduce GHG emissions contributed to a net increase in global warming once the cooling effect of cloud cover was taken into account.[4]

POLLUTION

The byproducts of human enterprise may have a polluting effect on the air, ground, and water that we depend on for life. Air pollution, primarily driven by industrial emissions, vehicle exhaust, and the burning of fossil fuels—colloquially referred to as smog—is a severe public health challenge in many emerging economies (e.g., China, India, Mexico). In these urban centers, the concentration of toxic pollutants and fine particulate matter ($PM_{2.5}$) often far exceeds safe thresholds.

Burning biomass, like wood and leaves, can also create harmful air pollution that affects more than just the immediate area where the burning takes place. For example, palm-oil farmers in Southeast Asia sometimes use "slash and burn" techniques to clear land for replanting, releasing so much smoke and particulate matter into the air in 2010–2015 that the "haze" conditions in nearby Singapore led authorities to restrict much outdoor activity.[5]

The economic and social impacts of air pollution are vast in the forms of loss of labor productivity and incidence of respiratory and cardiovascular diseases. Some studies estimate that exposure to outdoor air pollution contributes to 4.2 million premature deaths worldwide every year.[6] This does not include fatalities from less frequent but more alarming releases of airborne toxic chemicals such as the 1984 Union Carbide incident in Bhopal, India, which killed an estimated 3,800 people immediately and up to 10,000 in total during the first few days.[7]

Pollution is not limited to the air we breathe. Ground and water pollution can be deadly for ecosystems and people in the surrounding area. Examples may be related to improper disposal of industrial waste—see the Hinkley groundwater contamination case in California which inspired the movie *Erin Brockovich*[8]—or use of chemicals before their negative effects are fully understood. DDT, or dichloro-diphenyl-trichloroethane, was a popular synthetic insecticide in the United States between the 1940s and the early 1970s. Seeping into the groundwater, this chemical made its way into river fish, which are an important food source for bald eagles. Consumption of elevated levels of DDT was found to cause bald eagles to lay eggs with shells that were too thin to survive and the population of bald eagles plummeted.[9]

GARBAGE

Garbage, in all its forms, is slightly different from pollution in that many countries have formal systems for the collection and disposal of garbage. Large public companies, like Veolia and WMI, provide these services to hundreds of millions of people around the world and have rich market capitalizations as a result.[10] But the modern world creates hundreds of millions of tons of waste each year, with many potentially negative consequences. Two industries receiving particular attention in the 2020s include plastics and apparel.

The modern world generates over 450 million metric tons of plastic each year.[11] Plastics are derived from fossil fuels; there are many different types of plastic which vary in the degree to which they biodegrade over time—some in years or decades, others are expected to persist for centuries. Plastic pollution affects marine and terrestrial ecosystems alike; well-publicized examples include the "Great Pacific Garbage Patch" and countless images of marine species caught with plastic in their stomachs or killed by plastic wrapped around their necks.[12] We now know that microplastics—fragments less than 5 millimeters in size[13]—are found all around the world and in the human bloodstream, with as yet unknown consequences.

Apparel waste is another increasingly important issue. For most of human history clothing was made by hand from natural materials. Like so many other industries, apparel manufacturing has evolved with the advent of steam and electricity, specialized machinery, and especially synthetic fabrics. These were combined in the 2000s to great effect in the development of "fast fashion," exemplified by H&M and Inditex (better known to many by its brands, including Zara), whereby inexpensive clothing is produced rapidly by mass-market retailers in response to the latest trends. The 2020s brought "ultra-fast fashion" in the form of Chinese brands like Shein and Temu. In all cases, the firms offer consumers an almost irresistible combination of rapidly changing styles available at super-cheap prices, leading to increased consumption.

As opposed to more durable (or expensive) clothing for which mending is an attractive option, cheap clothes are more likely to be discarded. When clothes are donated or recycled in developed countries like Canada and the United States, that often means items are shipped to places like Accra, Ghana, where as much as 40% end up in mountains of textile waste or clogging up the beach.[14] Although secondhand is more affordable than new clothing, the volume of cheap clothing verges on overwhelming.

The above examples are transparently negative views on these two industries, but a word of balance is appropriate here. Plastics have revolutionized many industries, making items more accessible and affordable to millions and improving many lives as a result. Where we used to use paper bags for our groceries, made from trees, cheap plastic bags seemed like a better choice. Today, the push is to bring reusable bags for your purchases, but cloth bags require energy to produce and distribute too. Which type of bag appears to be more environmentally friendly depends on the calculus you use, something we will explore again later in the book. Advocates for the apparel industry might point out the positive social and economic effects of more comfortable and affordable clothing for consumers at the base of the economic pyramid. Recycling would seem to be a solution to both problems. However, recycling rates for plastics and apparel are at most 10–15% globally, with considerable variation by country[15]—which doesn't mean that we shouldn't recycle, but that it's not (yet) a meaningful solution. Like much in the field of sustainability, multiple perspectives must be considered when evaluating the impact of these industries.

LAND HEALTH

Deforestation remains rampant around the world, with an annual loss of approximately 10 million hectares of forest and jungle. This widespread tree loss is mainly driven by the expansion of agriculture, logging for timber, and urban development. One impact of deforestation concerns carbon sequestration. Trees naturally absorb carbon dioxide, so cutting down trees leads to an increase in atmospheric GHGs, accelerating climate change. Additionally, deforestation causes soil erosion and loss of habitat for the species that live there. Of course, the initial wave of deforestation occurred hundreds of years ago when mankind cut down trees for building and fuel across much of Europe and North America; this is not a new phenomenon. What is new this time, however, is that GHG concentration is rising at a time when we have fewer trees to help sequester the extra carbon dioxide.

The popular press often writes about cutting down trees in the Amazon, for example, but pays less attention to soil health. Intensive farming practices and expanding use of chemical fertilizers can reduce soil quality, both for crop yield and for carbon sequestration. As some have pointed out, as a planet we produce more than enough food to feed the more than seven billion humans living today; we don't have a food production issue but rather a food distribution issue. That modern agricultural practices have dramatically increased crop yields is indisputable. The issue that may require more attention is the long-term effect of these practices. The United Nations Food and Agriculture Organization estimates that 25% of arable land may already be degraded,[16] with unknown consequences for future food security as the global population continues to expand.

BIODIVERSITY LOSS

Global biodiversity is in sharp decline; the Worldwide Fund for Nature estimates that populations of mammals, birds, fish, amphibians, and reptiles declined by an average of 73% between 1970 and 2020.[17] The loss extends to myriad plant and insect species as well. Some of this may seem a bit abstract—after all, the dodo and passenger pigeon went extinct more than 100 years ago without any meaningful impact on human progress. But once again, we should remember the complex system that exists in the natural world.

Aside from being, perhaps, the "right thing to do" to protect other living things, it can be hard to assign a monetary value to species reduction or disappearance. A case in point concerns pollinators, especially bees. A lack of bees to pollinate almond trees in California, for example, would almost certainly reduce agricultural yields and increase costs for environmental remediation efforts. As we will revisit later in the book, assigning a value to bees because of their link to crop values may be easier than valuing whales or white rhinos—but the fact that biodiversity is *difficult* to value doesn't mean that biodiversity is *without* value.

WATER: FRESH AND OCEANS

Fresh water constitutes a small fraction of the total water available on Earth, and only a fraction of that is accessible for human use. Access to clean fresh water is a critical issue for billions of people. Pressure comes from ever-growing populations and practices that take rivers and aquifers for granted. For example, we grow water-hungry crops, like those almonds in central California (Central Valley), under the assumption that mountain snowmelt and local aquifers will always provide enough water for everyone. When fresh water is available, in many places it is poisoned by agricultural runoff, as well as discharge from companies and overburdened sanitation systems. Climate change alters precipitation patterns, adding further pressure to an already stressed resource.

Water issues are not limited to fresh water; climate change has a profound effect on ocean ecosystems. Ocean waters are already a critical carbon sink, and increased levels of carbon dioxide in the atmosphere cause them to absorb increasing amounts of carbon dioxide. This leads to acidification of the waters that harms shell-forming marine organisms. Ocean water temperatures are also rising, contributing to the bleaching of coral reefs that are home to 25% of marine life.[18] Collectively, these changes not only impact biodiversity but also lead to economic losses in the fishing and tourism sectors.

There is yet another change that should be of concern, particularly to island nations and those living in low-lying cities like Ho Chi Minh and Miami. The warming ocean waters lead to thermal expansion, further exacerbating sea-level rise.[19] Natural systems are intertwined, and changes in one part of the system may have impacts on other parts.

SUMMARY

Environmental challenges explored in this chapter—from climate change to other human-influenced degradation of the air, land, and water around us—are formidable and interconnected issues. Climate change serves as an overarching threat, reinforcing and magnifying the consequences of deforestation, biodiversity loss, and water scarcity, for example. Each problem, significant on its own, also carries significant weight that further contributes to systemic instabilities with natural and economic ramifications.

The combined effect of multiple environmental stressors means that changes in one area may have cascading consequences that are difficult to predict—and to counteract. Therefore, when taking steps to address any of these environmental issues, we should take care to consider potential linkages to other aspects of the system. As we shall see in Chapter 2, this extends beyond environmental issues to the impacts on people and society more broadly.

CHAPTER 2

Social Issues

In the mid-2020s, societies around the world face a diverse set of social challenges. At their most fundamental, there are issues related to basic human rights like food, water, and shelter, and to inequal access to education, financial services, and health care. Higher up the hierarchy are social issues associated to labor practices; diversity, equity, and inclusion (DEI) that encompasses gender, race, and other variables; and business practices that impact employees, customers, and entire supply chains. Many of these social issues are important enough to be incorporated into the UN Sustainable Development Goals (Figure 2.1), including poverty, hunger, health, education, gender equality, water and sanitation, and reduced inequalities.

Social issues do not exist in a vacuum but rather are highly sensitive to local context. For example, DEI is a politically charged topic in the United States, such that even within a single country there is considerable debate and disagreement about what it means and what should be done about it. Should we expect Afghanistan, Belgium, and China to share similar views on DEI? Differences in historical context, including religion and cultural practices, make it exceptionally unlikely for that to be the case.

As a book on sustainable investing, this chapter presents a high-level overview of some of the most common issues (Figure 2.2), not to advocate for a particular point of view but rather to ensure the reader appreciates social issues as they relate to companies and investors. Many companies exist to address gaps in social infrastructure, not as charity but as a for-profit enterprise. Of course, charitable organizations do a lot of important work around the world to plug gaps in social infrastructure, e.g., providing access to food, water, and shelter in areas of great need. But companies also see these gaps as opportunities to develop a business that can deliver profits while simultaneously making a positive difference in the world. Future chapters will refer to social factors as both challenges and opportunities.

Many social issues are also tightly coupled with environmental issues covered in Chapter 1. For example, labor practices in areas under extreme heat stress must evolve to protect employees from potentially dangerous work conditions in industries such as agriculture and construction. In another example, pollution disproportionately harms low-income and

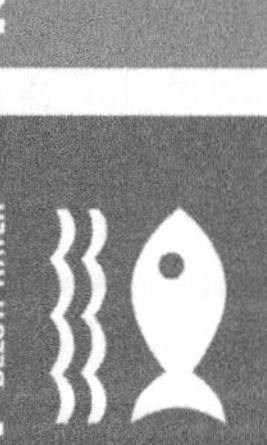
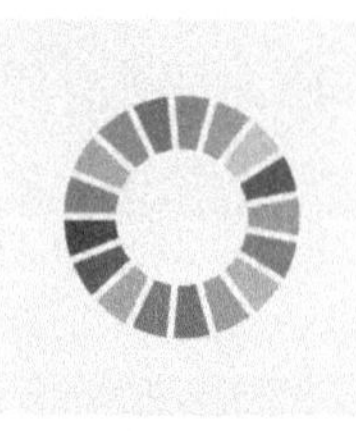
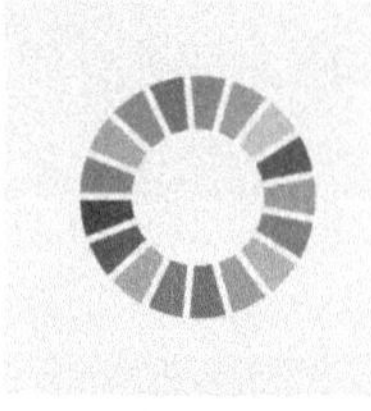

FIGURE 2.1 United Nations Sustainable Development Goals.

Source: UNITED NATIONS / https://upload.wikimedia.org/wikipedia/commons/a/a7/Sustainable_Development_Goals.svg / Public Domain / Wikimedia Commons.

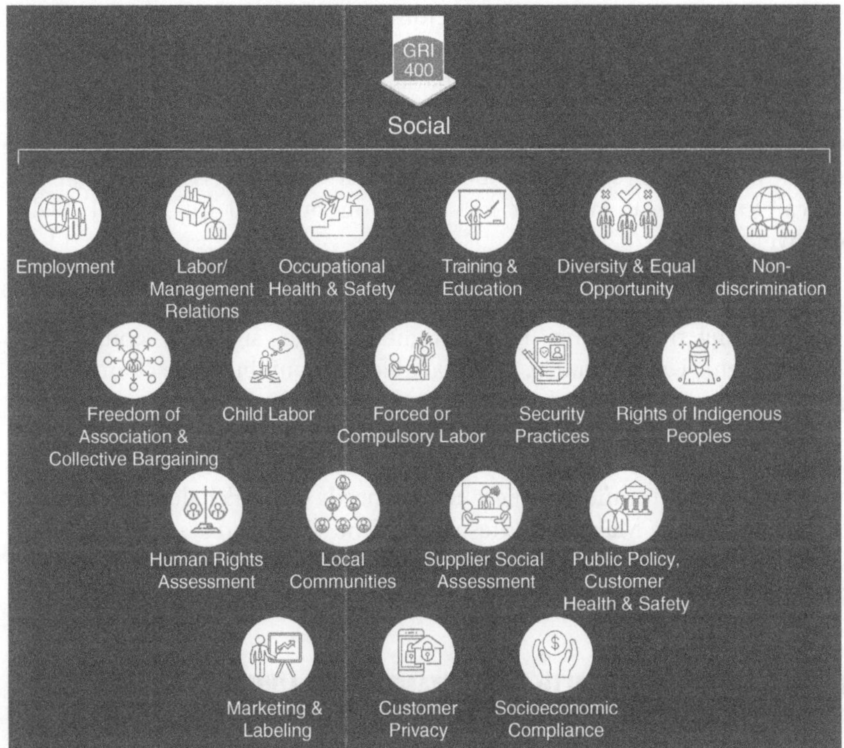

FIGURE 2.2 Global Reporting Initiative (GRI) Standards for social issues. *Source:* Global Reporting Initiative / https://www.globalreporting.org/media/ nmmnwfsm/gri-policymakers-guide.pdf / last accessed Aug 19, 2025, p.11.

minority communities, since industrial facilities, waste dumps, and hazardous infrastructure are often sited near neighborhoods populated by economically disadvantaged groups. At the intersection of environmental and social issues lies the concept of "climate justice," and this chapter concludes with a review of this important topic.

BASIC HUMAN RIGHTS: FOOD, WATER, SHELTER

"All human beings are born free and equal in dignity and rights" states Article 1 of the 1948 Universal Declaration of Human Rights (UDHR). The UDHR goes further in Article 25.1 to state that "[e]veryone has the right to a standard of living adequate for the health and well-being of himself and of his family" including food, shelter, clothing, and necessary social services. Food should be safe, consistent with cultural preferences and nutritious enough to support healthy and stable life. Shelter provides security, some measure of protection from the elements, and privacy. The right to water and sanitation, not included in the original UDHR, was acknowledged as a human right in 2010 by the United Nations General Assembly.[1] Water is critical for survival, not just for hydration but also for overall health and hygiene.

In the developed world, it is easy to take these rights for granted. However, billions of people still lack reliable access to food, water, and shelter. Declaring these to be "human rights" obliges signatory countries to uphold them. Unfortunately, the available accountability mechanisms are not sufficient to ensure that governments meet these obligations. Corporations, too, must respect these rights within the context of their own scope of operations. In fact, some companies have successfully developed business models to address these unmet needs (e.g., Échale a Tu Casa in Mexico, or India's Mahindra Lifespaces).[2] The scope and systemic nature of these issues suggest that solutions require close collaboration across governments, companies, international aid agencies, and other actors.

ACCESS: EDUCATION, HEALTH CARE, STANDARD OF LIVING

Above and beyond the basic rights to food, water, and shelter discussed in the preceding section, the UDHR sets forth additional economic and social rights including education, health care, and an adequate standard of living. Similar to other universal rights, commitments made by UN member states have not proven adequate to the task. In many low-income and developing countries, large populations lack access to these essential services.

Access to education, for example, is inconsistently available. While some progress is being made in primary education, enrollment in higher education depends on geography, attitudes toward gender, and economic conditions. Girls and women are especially affected, a troublesome situation given the important role that women play in society generally, and economic development more specifically. Development agencies and the private sector have developed new models, such as community-based schooling and the integration of technology (e.g., Kenya's Eneza Education, or the Khan Academy in the United States),[3] but more work remains to be done.

Health care access faces similar challenges, not only in the developing world but also across rural parts of more developed countries. One important area of concern is the linkage between health care and other socioeconomic variables such as education and income. Disadvantaged communities often suffer in multiple aspects of development, and it may not be possible to solve one problem (e.g., health care) without addressing some of the other issues at the same time. Collaborative efforts involving states, local communities, private enterprise, and international organizations, like the World Health Organization (WHO), provide benefits to many; companies have also identified opportunities to profitably provide health care services to marginalized groups, often leveraging technology to manage accessibility as well as cost (e.g., Indonesia-based Halodoc).[4]

Embedded in the category of standard of living is access to financial services. Economic development relies on banking and other financial services, yet traditionally individuals at the base of the pyramid struggle to access financing. This may be because they lack existing accounts and documentation, or simply because they live in remote, rural areas without physical access to such services. Providing access to the "unbanked" or "underbanked" is referred to as financial inclusion; this goal is being pursued by a wide range of entities. For example, the G20's Global Partnership for Financial Inclusion[5] works with governments to promote inclusive financial services. Companies like M-Pesa in Kenya or Nu in Latin America[6] use technology, like mobile payments, to provide products and services that are essential for the economic livelihoods of these marginalized groups.

BUSINESS PRACTICES: EMPLOYEES, CUSTOMERS, SUPPLY CHAINS

Employers are responsible for their relationships with their employees. There is increasing pressure to address potentially unjust, unsafe, or illegal practices including:

- no child labor or forced labor;
- workplace safety;
- fair compensation/paying a living wage;
- equal treatment of employees regardless of background (DEI).

Whether or not these are universal standards, in many (most?) cases there are economic justifications for addressing these issues such as reducing turnover or absenteeism, improving productivity, and, in some cases, avoiding fines and legal action. Firms that develop a reputation for being an attractive place to work may have an advantage in recruiting and retaining talent. In an influential academic paper from 2011,[7] Professor Alex Edmans looked at the stock price performance for US companies that appeared in the annual Forbes "America's Best Companies to Work For" list. The author found that employee satisfaction is correlated with stock returns, i.e., companies ranked in the Forbes list outperformed, when controlling for market, value, size, and momentum factors (so-called Carhart 4-factor alpha), by 3.5% per year from 1984 to 2009. In 2021, another paper[8] revisited this topic using new techniques and found that companies with the best employee satisfaction exhibited excess returns of 2–2.7% per year. Significantly, while the outperformance was consistently positive across most of their sample, the performance was strongest during periods of market crisis.

Finally, in 2023 Professor Edmans and his co-authors broadened his original inquiry to international markets, looking at the relationship between workplace conditions and labor market flexibility, e.g., the freedom with which employers can hire and fire employees. They found that ". . . the link between employee satisfaction and stock returns is significantly increasing in a country's labor market flexibility."[9] When firms have more freedom to choose their own labor practices, employees are more satisfied with increasing benefits, leading to improvements in hiring, retaining, and motivating employees.

Although not limited to employee matters, DEI is an area of increasing focus for employers and government regulations. The three words are similar; however, they have slightly different meanings. Collectively, DEI is defined as "a set of values and related policies and practices focused on establishing a group culture of equitable and inclusive treatment and on attracting and retaining a diverse group of participants, including people who have historically been excluded or discriminated against."[10] From this definition we can see how the three terms are interrelated yet distinct:

- Diversity reflects differences in gender and race, and variables such as sexual orientation (LGBTQ+), educational background, and even the different ways that people think (cognitive diversity).
- Equity exists when people have similar opportunities, regardless of background.
- Inclusion encompasses the other two terms, but with specific emphasis on historically marginalized groups such as Indigenous populations.

What effect do DEI policies have on a company? Consultants and academics alike have analyzed the relationship between DEI and various measures of organizational performance. Proponents of diversity would like to believe that more diverse firms are more innovative, creative, and have better financial performance. Along these lines, well-publicized reports[11] from consulting firm McKinsey & Co. propose a positive relationship between diversity and improved financial performance. However, these reports do not hold up well against academic scrutiny.[12] A more recent report[13] on diversity in the asset management industry summarizes the research well: while cognitive diversity can boost creativity and decision-making, its link to financial performance is mixed, with skills-based diversity showing the strongest positive effect. It stresses that effective leadership, inclusion, and psychological safety are essential to realizing the benefits of diversity without which there may be coordination issues, reduced team cohesion, and misunderstandings between team members with differing perspectives.

Social issues for employers extend beyond relationships with their employees, to customers and supply chains as well. For example, when interacting with customers, deceptive marketing practices and other unethical behavior can pose a risk to company reputation and brand equity. Similar reputational risks exist if company suppliers (and to a lesser extent, customers) themselves engage in illegal or undesirable behavior such as poor labor conditions or unethical sourcing. Issues with treatment of customers or supplier behavior can cause significant economic damage through a loss of trust, manifesting in loss of sales and profits.

CLIMATE JUSTICE[14]

While environmental degradation affects every corner of the globe, its impacts are not distributed equally. Vulnerable communities—often those least responsible for creating the crisis—bear the brunt of climate change, biodiversity loss, and pollution. Consider the following:

- Small island nations, like Tuvalu and the Maldives, face grave risks due to rising sea levels.
- Sub-Saharan Africa experiences prolonged droughts and food shortages.
- Urban poor in cities, like Rio de Janeiro or Lagos, live in informal settlements prone to flooding and heatwaves, lacking access to cooling systems or safe drinking water.

In all these examples, people and nations face considerable risks despite their negligible contributions to greenhouse gas emissions. Addressing this inequality is at the heart of "climate justice": countering the burdens that disproportionately fall on marginalized groups through more equitable policies and practices. Policies that prioritize equity—such as universal access to clean energy and affordable housing—reduce emissions while improving the quality of life for those who need the most help.

Some of the burdens that arise from climate change are the associated health impacts that affect the poor and vulnerable far more than the wealthy and secure, e.g., heat stress, disease, and malnutrition. Consider how these impacts may relate to women, children, and older people. Heat stress may increase the risk of pregnancy complications, and children are more likely to suffer from asthma when exposed to air pollution. Older people, with more naturally occurring health issues, are susceptible to illness or worse due to any of these conditions.

If the vulnerable are more exposed to the negative effects of climate change, whose responsibility is it to look after these people and to advocate for climate justice? Governments play an important role in promoting climate justice through regressive policies and direct programmatic support. Charities are active in many regions, providing much-needed assistance to vulnerable populations. Business and investors, however, have an equally important role to play. The base of the economic pyramid is not limited to charity; it's a market segment. With an appropriate business model, companies can profitably provide much-needed services to these markets, creating value for business owners while addressing inequalities for underserved populations.

SUMMARY

Social issues are complex, interlinked with each other as well as a variety of environmental factors. These issues are context-sensitive, varying significantly by geography, economic segment, gender, and other variables. Collectively, how a company relates to social issues like these can be a matter of strategic importance for customer acquisition and retention, employee motivation, and investor trust. For this reason, many companies actively promote their social-minded activity, but a degree of caution is warranted. One issue concerns measurement. Metrics, like carbon emissions, are more readily quantifiable than community relations or labor practices, making it difficult for external stakeholders to evaluate social performance. Another issue is that individuals and organizations may have strong beliefs or preferences, such that appealing to one subgroup may unintentionally alienate another—like the "ESG backlash" taking place in the United States in the mid-2020s.

Nonetheless, like the list of environmental issues in Chapter 1, the list of social problems is quite large. Any country or company that aspires to be a top performer across all social dimensions will take some comfort in knowing that its efforts are well directed, and if effective, will make a meaningful difference to the lives of the target population. Firms with the leadership, vision, and resources to tackle these challenges likely benefit from strong governance practices, as we will see in the following chapter.

CHAPTER 3

Governance Issues

Corporate governance is a set of rules, practices, and procedures that describe and guide supervision and control, principally through the Board of Directors and its various committees. Together, they provide oversight to ensure that management is balancing the competing interests of diverse stakeholders—not just shareholders but also employees, customers, suppliers, and the broader communities in which a company operates.

The building blocks of "good governance" typically include clear accountability, transparency, and engagement with shareholders. Accountability requires the Board of Directors to be responsible to stakeholders for the decisions and actions of the company. Clear rules should be in place to ensure boards make decisions that are best for the firm and its stakeholders using the best available information. Additional roles, such as committees for important matters like audit and compensation, should be clearly communicated to others as necessary. Transparency requires a commitment to provide accurate financial reports and other corporate records to shareholders in a timely fashion. Rules and processes, e.g., disclosure policies or risk management processes, should be shared with stakeholders to build trust and credibility. Companies should have a regular meeting with shareholders, typically annually and announced with sufficient notice so that all who wish to attend may do so.

While these are best practices, each company establishes its own governance protocols within the boundaries of regulations that vary by jurisdiction. In the United States, for example, the primary sources of federal-level rules are the Securities Act of 1933 and the Securities Exchange Act of 1934. These regulations require companies to satisfy certain requirements for transparency, accountability, and engagement with shareholders. The need for such regulation is revealed by periodic corporate governance failures such as Enron (December 2001),[1] Wirecard (June 2020),[2] and others. These cases, which resulted in significant loss of jobs and financial capital, were characterized by major shortcomings in corporate governance, including supervision of management by the Board of Directors. Scandals such as these occurred despite regulations in place to prevent them, serving as a catalyst for further regulatory reform. Notable examples in the United States include:

- The Watergate incident in the early 1970s that led to the Foreign Corrupt Practices Act (FCPA, 1977).[3]
- Financial scandals at Enron and WorldCom which drove the enactment of the Sarbanes-Oxley Act (SOX, 2002).[4]
- The Global Financial Crisis of 2007–2008 which instigated the Dodd-Frank Wall Street Reform and Consumer Protection Act (Dodd-Frank, 2010).[5]

The sheer volume of scandals (see Table 3.1) suggests that strong internal controls are another important aspect of effective governance. Without proper controls, organizations may be more susceptible to ethical failures, such as financial crime, leading to financial and reputational damage that can result in serious economic impairment or even bankruptcy. The case of Barings Bank is a good example. In 1995, after several years hiding increasing losses, derivatives trader Nick Leeson fled Singapore after incurring hidden losses of £827 million. As these losses were twice the bank's capital, Barings declared bankruptcy that same year.[6]

TABLE 3.1 Financial Scandals

Year	Company	What Happened
1995	Barings Bank (UK)	Rogue trader Nick Leeson caused £827 million in losses through unauthorized trades.
2001	Enron (US)	Massive accounting fraud using off-balance-sheet entities that ultimately led to the company's bankruptcy.
2002	WorldCom (US)	Inflated assets by nearly US$11 billion by misclassifying expenses as capital investments. The fraud led to bankruptcy and major investor losses.
2003	Parmalat (Italy)	Collapsed after it was revealed the company had fabricated €14 billion in assets through fake bank accounts and fraudulent accounting.
2008	Madoff Securities (US)	Bernie Madoff ran a US$65 billion Ponzi scheme and was sentenced to 150 years in prison.
2008	Siemens AG (Germany)	Paid US$1.6 billion in fines for operating a global bribery network to win contracts, one of the largest corporate corruption cases in history.
2009	Satyam (India)	India's biggest corporate fraud: founder admitted to inflating profits and cash balances by over US$1.4 billion.

Year	Company	What Happened
2011	Olympus (Japan)	Hid US$1.7 billion in investment losses over more than a decade using fraudulent acquisitions and accounting tricks.
2015	Volkswagen (Germany)	Installed software in diesel cars to cheat emissions tests, leading to billions of euros in fines and lawsuits worldwide.
2015	1MDB (Malaysia)	A Malaysian state fund was looted of over US$4.5 billion through embezzlement and bribery, implicating global banks and officials.
2016	Wells Fargo (USA)	Employees opened millions of fake accounts to meet sales targets, exposing toxic incentive structures.
2016	Odebrecht (Brazil)	Brazilian construction giants paid bribes across Latin America to win contracts; executives and politicians were implicated.
2017	Equifax (US)	Poor cybersecurity led to the breach of personal data of 147 million people; criticized for delayed disclosure.
2018	Hyflux (Singapore)	Singapore water and energy firm collapsed under US$2.7 billion in debt due to mismanagement and overleveraging.
2018	Nissan-Renault (Japan)	CEO Carlos Ghosn was arrested for underreporting compensation and misuse of company assets.
2020	Wirecard (Germany)	German payment firm collapsed after €1.9 billion found missing, exposing massive accounting fraud and failures in audit and regulatory oversight.
2020	Luckin Coffee (China)	Chinese coffee chain fabricated US$300 million in sales to inflate performance; stock collapsed after exposure.
2022	FTX (Bahamas/ Global)	Crypto exchange misused US$8 billion in customer funds; filed for bankruptcy; founder Sam Bankman-Fried convicted of fraud.
2023	PwC Australia	Breached confidentiality by using leaked tax policy information to help clients avoid future regulation.
2023	British American Tobacco (UK)	Fined over US$635 million for violating US sanctions, selling tobacco to North Korea; also accused of bribery in Africa and tax avoidance across multiple countries.

Source: Selected from https://en.wikipedia.org/wiki/List_of_corporate_collapses_and_scandals and https://digitaldefynd.com/IQ/biggest-business-scandals/.

The importance of strong corporate governance may be clear, but why is governance combined with environmental and social issues in ESG? Environmental issues have been important to companies, investors, and governments for many years—think of the first Earth Day held in 1970. The first "official" mention of ESG as a framework is commonly said to be the 2004 report *Who Cares Wins* published by the United Nations Global Compact and 20 participating financial institutions.[7] The Chartered Financial Analyst (CFA) Institute published its first corporate governance manual[8] the following year, adding to the spotlight on governance as a critical issue. If ESG is intended to represent important issues that aren't included in financial disclosures, then clearly governance issues are also important.

Still, there are important differences between governance and the other issues. For example, while there are specialized financing instruments and investment strategies for environmental and social issues, no equivalent exists for governance issues. It could be argued that strong corporate governance enables strong environmental and/or social performance. However, some well-governed companies are not top sustainability performers (e.g., Nestlé shows strong governance but faces ongoing criticism for poor environmental practices[9]; the opposite may also be true, e.g., Tesla leads in environmental innovation but is frequently criticized for weak corporate governance[10]. Regardless, governance is an important issue that has the potential to impact employees, shareholders, and ultimately communities. The remainder of this chapter introduces some of the important attributes of governance of interest to regulators and shareholders alike.

DUAL-CLASS SHARES[11]

Most companies issue one "class" of stock when they go public; every share therefore confers the exact same benefits to the shareholder, including the right to vote—usually "one share, one vote"—and economic ownership. In contrast, a dual-class share structure allows companies to issue more than one class of stock with varying voting rights and economic ownership:

- Superior shares (also known as founders' shares) have extra voting rights; may have special dividend rights.
- Regular shares with limited or no voting rights; may have limited dividend rights.

The origins of dual-class listings date back at least to the initial public offering (IPO) of the US automobile company Dodge Brothers Inc., in 1925. Following this IPO, investor backlash pressured the New York Stock Exchange

(NYSE) to restrict such listings until succumbing to corporate pressure in the 1980s (Ford Motor Company was granted an exception in 1956). As of the mid-2020s, exchanges in the United States, Canada, Hong Kong, and Singapore are among those that permit dual-class shares; many others do not.

The motivation for dual-class shares is to enable company founders to maintain decision-making control, even when their ownership has been diluted below 50%. Especially in the technology sector, founders argue that dual-class structures support innovation by insulating company owners and management from short-term market fluctuations.

A typical dual-class configuration utilizes Class A shares for the regular shareholders and Class B shares for superior shares. Meta Platforms, formerly known as Facebook, is a good example. When the firm went public in 2012, it issued Class A and Class B shares. The Class A shares were made available to public investors and have one vote per share. Class B shares, with 10 votes per share, were distributed predominantly to founder Mark Zuckerberg and key insiders. Because his Class B holdings confer roughly 60% of the votes, this configuration means that Zuckerberg controls the company even though his economic ownership of Meta Platforms is well below 50%. Occasionally, firms will issue a third class of shares, Class C, without voting rights.

However, critics argue that minority shareholders are unfairly disadvantaged by dual-class structures; without the threat of losing a vote to act as a check on their power, founders are free to run their companies however they see fit. In one of the most egregious examples, when Snap Inc. went public in 2017, it only listed the nonvoting Class C shares. This caused institutional investors some concern[12] and they subsequently pressured the providers of major indices to exclude stocks without voting rights from important indices like the S&P 500. Because index inclusion generates demand for the shares, investors hoped that the threat of missing out on that demand would act as a deterrent to future founders eager to insulate themselves from external shareholders.[13]

Institutional investors continue to press for changes to dual-class listings to provide more rights for minority shareholders. One proposed solution is to allow such listings when founders agree to incorporate a sunset provision, a future date at which point the firm would restructure its shares to a single class.

BOARD OF DIRECTORS

The Board of Directors serves as the primary governance body of the firm. It is guided by fiduciary duty to act in the best interests of the firm and its shareholders, providing oversight of the chief executive officer (CEO) and top management, and maintaining strong internal controls. Directors are nominated by the company and elected by shareholders to serve a term of predetermined length before potentially standing for reelection. Typically, the Board of Directors includes audit and compensation committees to oversee these important functions.

Given the importance of the Board, its relative strength in key areas is subject to external scrutiny:

- **Independent directors.** Some CEOs prefer to surround themselves with family members people they know well, or former employees. Directors with strong ties to the CEO are less likely to provide effective oversight than a truly independent director. Best practice is for a majority of directors to be truly independent.
- **Committee chairs.** The chair of a committee holds considerable influence. For this reason, best practice is for the chairs of the audit committee (which approves the firm's financial statements) and compensation committee (which determines compensation for the CEO) to be completely independent.
- **Board diversity.** Traditionally, a group of "old White men" (at least in many Western countries), in the past few decades there has been a noticeable push from shareholders for more diversity on boards. Diversity, it is believed, is associated with improvements in decision-making, creative thinking, and risk management. In the West, diversity means gender, race, and sometimes age; diversity research suggests that less visible attributes, such as cognitive diversity, may be more valuable.[14]
- **Chairman/CEO duality.** When the CEO also serves as Chairman of the Board, he is responsible (as Chairman) for oversight of himself (as CEO). This is considered less than ideal for somewhat obvious reasons. However, if performance is strong enough for long enough, investors may decide to look the other way. Warren Buffett at Berkshire Hathaway is a good example and has survived shareholder votes calling for him to relinquish one of the two roles.

When shareholders are dissatisfied with the performance of the company they may vote against management's (re-)nomination of directors. Firms have created ways to structure the terms of the Board of Directors to make it difficult for shareholders to make changes to the board; these so-called "entrenched boards" will be discussed in the later section on "Anti-Takeover Provisions."

EXECUTIVE COMPENSATION

An important dimension of corporate governance concerns top management compensation—especially for the CEO. Executive compensation is frequently a complicated mix of annual and long-term incentives, including a mix of salary, cash bonus, and company stock and/or stock options. Companies may make these sums available immediately or—especially for stock-based compensation—may defer the payments over time to promote long-term commitment to the firm.

Over the past six decades, CEO compensation relative to that of the median employee has reached spectacular heights—the CEO-to-worker pay ratio skyrocketed from 20.8 in 1965 to 290.3 in 2023.[15] Is all this financial largesse achieving the desired results, i.e., does increased (and especially options-based deferred compensation) lead to better corporate financial performance? When it comes to CEO pay there are three important aspects to consider: the structure of pay, the level of pay, and the process through which CEO pay is set. Deferred compensation, especially through stock options, creates improved alignment of incentives between the CEO and shareholders; if the company performs well, the CEO should be well remunerated through the appreciation of *previous* grants (wealth effect instead of income effect). However, academic findings on the relationship between the amount of CEO pay and firm performance are mixed—although there are certainly examples of what in hindsight appears to be excessive CEO compensation. Regardless, the process of setting compensation should be left in the hands of informed, independent directors on a board compensation committee (an advisory "say on pay" doesn't hurt).[16]

A recent addition to the landscape of executive compensation is the use of ESG-based key performance indicators (KPIs). Under this scenario, CEO compensation is based on the degree to which the firm (and by extension the CEO) achieves a target level of performance on a sustainability-related metric, e.g., percentage of female employees at the Vice President level or higher. A recent paper[17] analyzed S&P 500 firms and their use of ESG targets in their executive compensation plans during the 2023 proxy season. Compared to 2004, when only 12% of firms included such targets, in 2023, 63% of S&P 500 firms included ESG KPIs in their executive compensation, typically in their annual rather than long-term incentive plans. The median weighting of ESG measures was 10% of the annual incentive. Because annual incentives are a small percentage of total executive compensation, the median effect of successful ESG performance on CEO annual compensation would be a median of only 2.0%.

Furthermore, companies were far more likely to exceed all their ESG targets than they were their financial targets (see Table 3.2). Among the

TABLE 3.2 Performance in Financial and Environmental, Social, and Governance (ESG) Targets

Exceed/Miss	Target Type	Rate of Exceed/Miss (%, number)	
Exceed All Targets	Financial	44.3	212/479
	ESG	76.1	188/247
Miss All Targets	Financial	22.8	107/479
	ESG	2.4	6/247

Source: Badawi, A.B. and Bartlett, R (2024). ESG Overperformance? Assessing the Use of ESG Targets in Executive Compensation Plans.[18]

potential explanations for these results, the authors believe the evidence ". . . suggests that managers, especially in poorly governed firms, may exploit less transparent ESG metrics to set easily achievable targets to enhance compensation or appease investors."[19]

ANTI-TAKEOVER PROVISIONS

Anti-takeover provisions are legal techniques used by corporations to protect themselves from hostile takeover attempts by making it more difficult or financially burdensome for another company to gain control. By implementing these strategies, companies seek to protect incumbent management and, ostensibly, its long-term corporate strategy. When mergers grew in popularity in the United States in the 1980s, companies began using anti-takeover provisions to maintain their independence. The criticism is that these provisions also have the effect of "entrenching" management by limiting shareholders' ability to influence or provide a check on corporate decision-making.

Poison Pill

One of the most well-known strategies, the poison pill, activates when another entity amasses a significant ownership stake in the target company, usually between 15–20%. When this threshold is reached, the company issues new shares to existing shareholders at a discounted price—the hostile shareholder is specifically excluded. As a result, the ownership percentage of the acquirer is significantly diluted, making any takeover attempt more expensive than it would have been otherwise.

Netflix provides an example of this in practice. In January 2012, the firm had 55,418,632 shares of common stock outstanding, each with one vote. Later that year, Netflix adopted a poison pill in response to news that corporate raider Carl Icahn had acquired nearly 10% of the company, qualifying his firm as an "Acquiring Person" and the target of the resulting poison pill. To greatly simplify, the firm would issue a new class of stock that would dramatically dilute Icahn's holdings[20]:

- The company would issue 1,000,000 shares of Series A Participating Preferred Stock ("preferreds"), each with 1,000 votes.
- In aggregate, the Series A Participating Preferred Stock represented 1 *billion* votes, or 944,581,368 more than all the votes outstanding before this poison pill was enacted.
- Preferreds would be distributed to existing shareholders so that each would receive one "Right" for each common share of the company owned. Each Right entitled the holder to purchase one one-thousandth of a series A preferred share.
- In the crucial clause, ". . . if the Rights evidenced by this Rights Certificate are beneficially owned by an Acquiring Person, an Affiliate or Associate of an Acquiring Person . . . or any nominee of any of the foregoing, **such Rights shall become null and void** . . ."[21] [emphasis added].

Staggered Boards

Board members must be elected by shareholders, so if a potential acquiror controls enough shares, it can influence or even control the election. When a company staggers the Board, it divides the board members into multiple groups which are elected in different years. For example, a 15-member board might have five members stand for (re)election in year 1, another five members stand in year 2, and the final five in year 3. In this case, it is more difficult for a potential acquiror to gain control of a majority of board seats.

Voting Rights Plans

Adopting a voting rights plan adds clauses to a company's charter that adjust shareholder voting rights according to amount of stock a shareholder owns. For example, once a shareholder reaches a 20% ownership position, that shareholder may be restricted from voting on specific issues such as mergers, acquisitions, and changes in corporate control.

Triggered Option Vesting

The preceding provisions make it more difficult for potential acquirors to take control of a company. This final technique takes a different approach by making it more *expensive* for the acquiror. Many companies include stock options in their executive compensation plans, typically with deferred vesting over three or more years to incentivize executives to focus on long-term company performance and tie them to the company. Under a triggered option vesting provision, all unvested options immediately vest upon a change in control of the company. The resulting financial burden may act as a deterrent to potential acquirors.

WHISTLEBLOWER POLICY

As an important part of the system of checks and balances, many firms have policies that protect employees who wish to "blow the whistle" on suspected misconduct. By protecting them from retaliation, these policies promote a culture of ethical behavior and reporting of potential misconduct before it escalates. In jurisdictions like the United States, federal laws provide additional layers of protection, such as in the Dodd-Frank Act of 2010.[22]

Source: Generated with AI using
Microsoft Copilot.

Whistleblower policies encourage employees to speak up when they suspect something is going wrong, including criminal activities, corruption, bribery, mismanagement and waste, or anything that could pose a danger to employees, customers, or the public. Protections start with the reporting itself. Companies often provide multiple protected channels, such as a dedicated hotline, that can be used to confidentially make a whistleblower report, either on a named basis or anonymously. Once a report has been filed, the organization should provide strong protections against retaliation such as termination, harassment, exposure, or other discrimination.

Anonymity can be protected through two-way anonymous channels so that company management does not have direct contact with the whistleblower.

In one high-profile example from 2021, Francis Haugen, a former product manager at Facebook, provided testimony and internal company documents to journalists and regulators.[23] Among her inflammatory revelations:

- Facebook knew its platforms posed a mental health threat to users, especially teenagers.
- The company's algorithms amplified polarizing or extreme content.
- It was known internally that Instagram usage had a negative impact on teen girls' body image.

Once her identity was revealed, Ms. Haugen faced several challenges. Importantly, she had taken and released corporate documents as evidence to support her claims. Under US law she was protected when making disclosures to the government, but those protections don't automatically extend to releasing internal documents. In this case, she followed proper procedures by filing formal complaints with the Securities and Exchange Commission (SEC) and testifying to Congress before speaking with the media. As of mid-2025, Facebook had not pursued legal action against her.

SUMMARY

Good corporate governance provides a strong foundation for ethical and responsible corporate behavior. By promoting accountability, transparency, and shareholder engagement, effective governance policies and practices guide oversight of the firm and its management—but this is not always sufficient. Despite the regulations and supervision present in many jurisdictions around the world, occasional failures, like Enron and Wirecard, expose weaknesses that lead to new rounds of regulatory reform. This focus on corporate practice distinguishes governance from the environmental and social components of ESG, which focus on external aspects of the natural world (planet and people).

This chapter describes some of the most important components of corporate governance. At its foundation there is a principle of oversight through shareholder votes ("one share, one vote"). Unfortunately, this oversight can be eroded through dual-class share structures that protect founders' interests, potentially at the expense of shareholders. The Board of Directors, the primary governance body, is guided by fiduciary duty to protect the interests of shareholders through a series of committees. When the Chairman of the Board is also the CEO, however, this oversight may be weakened. Another tool for aligning the interests of management and shareholders is executive compensation. Theoretically, by providing sufficient long-term financial rewards, management should be motivated to maximize value of the firm as shareholders should also want. Evidence from corporate practice is mixed.

An underperforming company may become an acquisition target for another entity that believes it can help improve corporate performance. Management of the acquired firm may be replaced. If management puts its own interests first, it may adopt one of several potential anti-takeover provisions to make it more difficult (or expensive) to be acquired. Sometimes, corporate malfeasance is also an issue, as in cases of fraud like WorldCom or Parmalat. When employees suspect that something unethical, illegal, or dangerous is happening, whistleblower policies help encourage a culture of "see something, say something" by offering protection against retaliation.

*　　*　　*

The first three chapters have described some of the important environmental, social, and governance issues included under the umbrella of ESG. These issues are not new. These issues have the potential to create significant risks—and opportunities—for companies and investors alike. As we will see in Chapter 4, the United Nations and others have been building programs and capabilities to address these issues for years.

CHAPTER 4

Mobilizing for Action

The array of challenges described in the preceding chapters—environmental-, social-, and governance-related—deserve our collective attention. The impact of climate change could be the most catastrophic in the long run, and this is reflected in the attention and effort paid to climate change compared to all the other issues.

But the origins of environmental protection predate the widespread understanding of climate change. The works of George Perkins Marsh (*Man and Nature*, 1864) and John Muir[1] (*The Mountains of California*, 1894) contributed to the founding of the wildlife conservation movement. Rachel Carson's 1962 book *Silent Spring* brought widespread attention to the harmful effect of chemicals (dichloro-diphenyl-trichloroethane [DDT]) on the environment. The first Earth Day was held in April 1970. Finally, pent-up demand for government action led to the US National Environmental Policy Act (EPA) in December 1970. The Act created the Environmental Protection Agency (EPA), charged with implementing a wave of environmental legislation in the United States including the Clean Air Act (1970) and the Clean Water Act (1972); it also banned DDT in 1972. In the same year, a group of scientists sponsored by The Club of Rome published an influential book called *The Limits to Growth*. Based in part on computer modeling developed by Massachusetts Institute of Technology (MIT) scientist Jay Forrester,[2] the authors suggested that unless humankind slowed its utilization of Earth's resources and reduced environmental destruction, human populations and industrial activity would face an abrupt decrease.

Following this groundswell of interest in and support for environmental issues, beginning in the 1970s, many different initiatives, programs, and organizations were launched to promote awareness and change. In this chapter we consider two main areas of activity: initiatives led by the United Nations and collaborative efforts primarily designed for corporate engagement.

UNITED NATIONS INITIATIVES

The United Nations system plays a critical role in addressing complex global challenges, such as climate change and sustainable development, through various interconnected bodies and initiatives. This section explores the historical involvement and key contributions of some of the most important entities and frameworks. Despite having distinct mandates, they often work together to drive global action, grounded in science and guided by shared principles and objectives.

United Nations Environment Programme,[3] 1972

The United Nations Environment Programme (UNEP) is the principal UN body in the field of the environment, assisting governments globally, regionally, and nationally to address environmental challenges. Established in 1972, UNEP's work spans various critical areas including climate change, adaptation and resilience, and pollution. It provides global support for scientific research, as well as development finance in emerging economies.

One example of UNEP impact concerns the ozone layer, which absorbs much of the ultraviolet radiation which hits the planet, acting like sunscreen for the world. In the 1970s, scientists calculated that continued use of chlorofluorocarbons (CFCs), commonly used as refrigerants and in aerosol sprays, could destroy ozone in the atmosphere. By 1985, researchers discovered a hole in the ozone layer over the Antarctic that was expanding far more rapidly than expected. With support from UNEP, this led to the signing of the Montreal Protocol in 1987, which banned the use of CFCs.[4]

Intergovernmental Panel on Climate Change, 1988

Created in 1988 by the World Meteorological Organization (WMO) and UNEP, the purpose of the Intergovernmental Panel on Climate Change (IPCC) is to provide governments with scientific information needed to develop climate policies. The IPCC assesses thousands of scientific papers annually to provide comprehensive summaries of knowledge on climate change, its causes, potential impacts, and potential responses. Roughly every six years, it completes an assessment cycle and releases a series of reports aimed variously at policymakers, corporate leaders, and scientists. The IPCC completed its most recent six-year reporting cycle in 2021, publishing the last of the Sixth Assessment (AR6) reports in 2023. Its reports made clear the dire consequences of failing to limit warming to 1.5°C.[5]

United Nations Framework Convention on Climate Change, 1992

The United Nations Framework Convention on Climate Change (UNFCCC) was established in 1992 at the United Nations Conference on Environment and Development (the Rio "Earth Summit").[6] This framework treaty has led to subsequent agreements, like the 1997 Kyoto Protocol and the 2015 Paris

Agreement, which have built upon the UNFCCC, along with numerous decisions from the Conference of the Parties (COP, see later in this section).

The ultimate objective of the UNFCCC is to achieve stabilization of greenhouse gas (GHG) concentrations in the atmosphere at a level that protects ecosystems and economic development from danger of collapse due to human (anthropogenic) activity. Reporting is a key obligation under the UNFCCC; a set of commitments apply to all member countries (Parties):

- developing and periodically updating national inventories of emissions and removals;
- formulating, implementing, publishing, and regularly updating national programs for climate change mitigation and adaptation;
- promoting cooperation in the development and transfer of environmentally sound technologies.

The Conference of the Parties (COP), the governing body of the UNFCCC, is mandated to regularly review the implementation of the Convention and its related legal instruments. The term "COP" also refers to the annual meeting of the Parties for the Kyoto Protocol and the Paris Agreement. Significant milestones[7] in the COP process include:

- **COP1 (1995, Berlin).** Launched negotiations for the Kyoto Protocol. Parties agreed to national communications detailing emission limitation measures.
- **COP3 (1997, Kyoto).** Established the Kyoto Protocol; developed countries agreed to track and reduce emissions of six of the most prevalent (and damaging) GHGs. Developing countries were included without the same obligations. Laid the groundwork for carbon credits and trading.
- **COP11 (2005, Montreal).** Parties to the Kyoto Protocol agreed to its entry into force.
- **COP21 (2015, Paris).** Culminated in the adoption of the Paris Agreement. The agreement was signed by 196 countries, becoming the first legally binding international treaty on climate change since 1997.

Key elements of the Paris Agreement include:

- A goal to limit global warming to below 2°C, ideally 1.5°C.
- **Nationally determined contributions (NDCs).** Parties communicate their NDCs, which represent their commitments to reduce GHG emissions.[8] NDCs should also describe how social and economic consequences of response measures were considered.

- **Global stocktake.** A comprehensive process to assess collective progress toward the Paris Agreement goals.
- **Article 6[9].** Describes means for cooperation between countries to achieve the emission reduction targets in their NDCs. Options include direct exchange of mitigation outcomes (credits) between countries (Article 6.2) and participating in a trading platform overseen by the COP (Article 6.4).
- **Loss and damage mechanism.** Promotes approaches to address loss and damage associated with climate change impacts, particularly in vulnerable developing countries. Established a new finance goal from 2020 with a floor of US$100 billion per year.

United Nations Global Compact, 2000

In 2000, the United Nations launched the Global Compact (UNGC; https://unglobalcompact.org/what-is-gc) to encourage companies to act responsibly toward people and planet, and to bring them closer to the collaborative policy work that is the hallmark of the United Nations and its member states. Based on a set of 10 core principles, the UNGC describes itself as "the world's largest corporate sustainability initiative."

UNITED NATIONS GLOBAL COMPACT: INTERVIEW WITH GRIET CATTAERT, UNITED NATIONS GLOBAL COMPACT

In conversation with Matthew Dearth

Matthew
What is the Global Compact? Where did it originate, and what is its mission?

Griet
We are the largest corporate sustainability initiative in the world. The Global Compact started 25 years ago with a former Secretary-General of the UN who wanted to give a human face to business, to bring companies in to align with the values of the UN. Today, we have more than 20,000 companies that are committing to align their strategies and operations with ten principles in the areas of human rights, labour,

environment, and anti-corruption. Our headquarters is in New York, but we also have more than 60 country networks, and we have 5 regional hubs. We also work at national and regional levels to bring businesses closer together.

The Global Compact has 10 principles, including 2 on human rights and 4 on labor rights, that companies joining the initiative align with. There are 3 principles on the environment, and the last one, the tenth, is on anti-corruption. These principles are based on international standards and UN conventions. For companies that want to join our initiatives, they have to commit to these 10 principles and submit a CEO Statement of Continued Support which serves as a public declaration of UN Global Compact participants' ongoing commitment to the Ten Principles of the UN Global Compact at the highest level. Then they also have to submit every year a questionnaire where they explain what they're doing on the 10 principles. Last year, more than 11,000 companies used the questionnaire. We collaborate with companies that are committed, willing to take action, and eager to learn. But the way that we work is that all companies are welcome to join the initiative.

We want to help them learn, that's really one main aspect; also to learn from each other. There is a lot of peer learning and bringing companies together to discuss issues, so there is the connection aspect, learning and connecting. We also have events that we organize to bring the different stakeholders together, so we are also a multistakeholder initiative. As an initiative, we work with the governments, but we also have, for example, in the Board at the global level, we also have the unions represented. We have the civil society represented.

We also have a government representative, so it's really a multi-stakeholder initiative in a way.

The role of the UN Global Compact is to help companies understand how to implement sustainable practices. While we do set targets, principles, and international standards, we do not take a strong position in ongoing policy discussions. For example, with the Omnibus Proposal in the EU, we do not actively engage in advocacy but focus on guiding companies in aligning with global standards. If companies are following the UN guiding principles, for example, UN standards, you will be ready for all regulation that is coming.

(Continued)

(*Continued*)

Matthew
One of the things that I like about the Global Compact is that you have a broad set of issues that you want companies to internalize and then work on. Were they all part of the original 25 years ago or have the principles been evolving through time?

Griet
25 years ago we started with 9 principles; the tenth principle was added a couple of years later. Now, there is also a discussion on maybe we have to consider updating the principles. I'm convinced that they still make a lot of sense because they are really grounded in these international standards and they didn't change. We have 2 quite general human rights principles but of course, over the years and in 2011, we have the UN Guiding Principles on business and human rights that came out with a due diligence approach that changed a bit. And if you look at, for example, the OECD guidelines, they have been updated. The 10 principles haven't been updated since then.

We also have an initiative, the Forward Faster Initiative, and that's an initiative where we ask companies to set ambitious targets to really accelerate the achievement of the SDGs. We have identified five key issue areas where companies can make an impact across all SDGs. One of these is the living wage, which is an important social issue. Another is gender equality, which fosters greater trust within organizations. While gender equality is not explicitly referenced in the principles, it is a cross-cutting issue which remains a crucial topic that companies need to address. In the climate one we have two targets and one of the targets is on the just transition. That's also a newer topic that we also ask companies to work on sustainable finance. Then the last one is on water resilience.

These are five issue areas where we have set targets. We say, this is what you have to achieve. For example, in gender equality, we see it's about equal pay for work of equal value. They have to achieve that by 2030. The other one is on equal representation in leadership roles. These targets are not optional or left to companies to define on their own. We set clear expectations and ask companies to publicly commit to them and report on their progress. But the 10 principles are just a foundation.

I think where we want companies to work on is a principle-based approach. It's not about just looking at risks. It's more about how you develop your strategies, it should be principle-based. It's not just about setting a target here and just to do some due diligence and work on the most material risk. This means companies must respect human rights as a starting point. This differs from what we often see today where businesses primarily react to risks. Instead, we want companies to be rights-based in their approach, which presents both an opportunity and challenge.

Matthew
Right. But there's an inherent challenge in that different parts of the world may take issue with the statement that these are truly global principles. How does the Global Compact deal with that?

Griet
We have a navigator, specifically for human rights and labor rights, where we address key questions that come up frequently. This is something we often encounter, and the navigator provides guidance on what to do in such situations. In countries where we operate, especially in my work on labor rights, we often receive questions related to Principle Three, which covers freedom of association and collective bargaining. In many countries, this is considered a fundamental right and a core labor principle under the ILO. While it's assumed that all ILO member states must ratify this convention, that is not always the case, particularly for this specific principle. And the question in the navigator is about what to do if I operate in a country where the law there is not even respecting this principle.

What we always see is that companies have to live up to the international standards that say it's a human right. You always have to follow the international standard. And there are also ways to respect, for example, even if unions are not legally allowed, you can still work with workers representatives. There are still ways around to respect the spirit of the law and the principle of the right.

Matthew
That's consistent with what you described earlier. You're there to also provide the support for companies to see what to do. You can help

(*Continued*)

(*Continued*)

them understand how to abide by the principle, even in a country that may not fully comply with ILO standards in that example.

Griet

Yep, and of course, it's always about collaboration. I think multinationals operating in a country where rights are not respected also have the duty to put pressure and to work on issues. For example, we see that in many countries minimum wages are way too low to allow a decent standard of living. But we also see that if companies can afford paying more, you have to look into your wage levels and you also have to put pressure on governments, to open up minimum wage-level negotiations, to strengthen social dialogue, and to put pressure on social dialogue processes. It's also about that advocacy and that putting pressure on governments. Companies have a power to change things, and through our initiative, by bringing them together, they can make an impact.

It's also giving more bargaining power to talk to governments and to work as a coalition together.

Matthew

In a way the Compact sounds similar to the SDGs where it's easy to say, "life on land" and leave it at that. But actually, if you look inside you see that there are a whole bunch of very detailed items, and so the SDG acts as an umbrella goal. It also has its set of high-level principles that are big and broad enough that many of the social issues that we think of today are already covered.

Griet

Of course, and that is the struggle of it. For social, I think the challenge is that it's so broad and difficult to track and report on. The discussions we often have internally are about setting targets for social issues, but it's sometimes easier for environmental and climate targets than for social ones. Because, for example, with child labor, the target is obviously zero child labor, but then the question becomes, how do you track progress? And that's where it gets difficult, because social issues are often rights-based, making them harder to measure. I think that is always a challenge for us in the social team how can we track impact of companies on the social side because we believe they just have to respect the rights.

It's also why I see a lot of companies now having more and more social impact people working in the team. Before it was just the corporate sustainability officer, now a lot of multinationals have specific social dedicated teams. But it's a very broad topic. And the good thing with all the legislation is that you see that role is being elevated. For example, companies are putting a lot of investment into getting more and better understanding of their supply chains, but it's still a difficult topic to track.

Matthew

These are very, very big, complicated, messy issues. You brought up progress. How would you characterize progress? How do you look at that? How do you measure either quantitatively or qualitatively, where are some of the bright spots, and where are the things where we're not making the kind of progress that we want to?

Griet

I see in many companies that there is much more focus on social issues. There is really momentum, and there is also much more work being done on reporting and the standardization of frameworks, as well as quantifying and measuring these aspects to improve reporting. So, I really see momentum, and I've seen a lot of progress.

We have a lot of tools available for companies to assess where they are. We help companies to assess the gaps and to really direct them to take steps, and we recently launched one on non-discrimination. I think, especially in the supply chain, there are a lot of actions companies are taking, and it's also due to the legal pressure that they have to take responsibility. I think there is now with the due diligence, [and] companies are doing their double materiality assessment. They're looking into the most material risks.

And that's maybe another challenge that companies are prioritizing. Their first-tier suppliers are not always focusing on the highest risks and biggest impacts. Companies start by working with their key suppliers, which is okay, but they are not always looking at the biggest risks that exist further down the supply chain. What I see is that often they are also prioritizing a specific commodity, which is maybe even better than just the first-tier supplier.

(Continued)

(*Continued*)

Matthew
It sounds like you're counting on specific companies to be leaders and then bringing them together.

Griet
Yes, and in the Global Compact, we have a thought leadership space where we try to bring together companies that are really upfront on specific topics in Think Lab, where we work closely together. What we try to do as Global Compact is then to scale it and to make it available to all companies. We have learned from these pioneer companies doing the work on good governance, living wage, and due diligence. I think that is what we need today—we need much more good practice examples and how to learn from it. I think the business associations also do a lot on this, but they are always in a specific sector. I think companies join our initiative because they want to learn from other industries at a global, national, and regional level. The nice thing about the Global Compact is that we bring these companies together.

Matthew
How do you identify things that can help companies in any industry and get the word out so that it can scale?

Griet
I'm in the global office working on global content development, but we work closely with our regional hubs in the country offices to translate it. It's not just something that is being developed at a global level, but also about making it practical, translating it into the national languages. It's really important to make it closer to businesses, especially for SMEs, so it's more than just the big global companies speaking all the time.

Matthew
I feel like the next decade is trying to figure out how to push things down to SMEs and support them. What are some of the obstacles to making more progress on these principles?

Griet
I think, especially when speaking about social issues, it sometimes feels like a competing exercise. But we always emphasize that there are

strong linkages between them. For example, climate change will have the greatest impact on the most vulnerable populations, so it's crucial to tackle both together. However, many companies tend to focus first on environmental issues, particularly due to new regulations requiring SMEs to provide emissions data. As a result, they often start there, prioritizing data collection and reporting before addressing social aspects. They receive so many questionnaires and we have so many different reporting frameworks. We move towards more alignment but what I see now is even, you have the European standards, but you have then the GRI, the SASB. What we hear from smaller companies is that they're overwhelmed by data points that they have to collect. They don't have time even to take action. I think you have to emphasize that it's a means to an end for an impact, and it's not just about the reporting.

Matthew

Can you give us a sense for where you think the future is for the Global Compact and the companies that you're working with on these important principles? Where do you think we're headed?

Griet

I'm very positive about the future of the Global Compact. We are growing, we see a lot of companies joining us. I think what we can really do is to help companies on how to work together. I'm a strong believer in collaboration. I really don't think companies can do it all by themselves and yet they are under a lot of pressure, for example, the Secretary-General is really telling companies they have to step up.

Governments are not always taking the steps that are needed. I really believe that companies can play a very strong and important role, but it's not just them. We still need the governments to put regulations in place. I'm a strong believer in collaboration between companies, governments, and civil society organizations. As Global Compact, because we are a global initiative, we can bring the different voices together across different sectors. I really believe that that is the way to learn from each other.

However, big challenges are also coming our way; the climate is not going to get better soon. Looking at the world's political stability, we're going to face a lot of challenges [in] the coming years. But I really believe that business can move fast. Companies need to, and I think that's also where innovation comes in. There is so much that can happen, and in a positive way. Let's stay positive, it can also go in the right direction.

United Nations Environment Programme Finance Initiative, 2003

The United Nations Environment Program Finance Initiative (UNEP FI), launched in 2003, convenes the UN Principles for Responsible Banking (PRB), a global network of leading banks committed to supporting and accelerating a positive global transition for people and planet, in alignment with the UN Sustainable Development Goals (SDGs). UNEP FI has contributed to the technical development of sustainable taxonomies, including a common framework for Latin America and the Caribbean and contributions to national taxonomies in Brazil, Panama, and Costa Rica.

United Nations Principles for Responsible Investment, 2006

Launched in a partnership between UNEP FI and UN Global Compact in 2006, the UN Principles for Responsible Investment (PRI) maintains a voluntary framework which all investors can use to incorporate environmental, social, and governance (ESG) issues into their investment analysis and decision-making. Signatories to the PRI commit to follow six core Principles:

- Incorporate ESG issues into investment analysis and decision-making processes.
- Be active owners and incorporate ESG issues into ownership policies and practices.
- Seek appropriate disclosure on ESG issues by investee entities.
- Promote acceptance and implementation of the Principles within the investment industry.
- Work together to enhance effectiveness in implementing the Principles.
- Report on activities and progress toward implementing the Principles.

Adoption of the PRI has grown to over 4,000 participating institutions, but such growth is not without its issues. Because some investors value sustainability, a subset of signatories may join to signal that they care about sustainability without actually caring, in order to collect assets that generate fee income for the signatory.[10]

United Nations Sustainable Development Goals, 2015

The UN SDGs are a set of 17 interrelated objectives that, if achieved by the target date of 2030, would create a better and more sustainable future for all. The SDGs are an extension of the eight lesser-known Millennium Development Goals (MDGs),[11] launched in 2000 with a target of 2015. As the MDGs were set to expire, the United Nations convened a group to decide how best to continue and expand work toward the goals. The resulting SDGs include goals related to many of the environmental and social issues mentioned in Chapters 1 and 2, plus additional goals such as Sustainable Cities and Communities (11) and Peace, Justice, and Strong Institutions (16).

OTHER FORMS OF COLLABORATION: INDUSTRY-LED INITIATIVES

Corporate initiatives focused on sustainability promote cooperative approaches to sustainability that go beyond what any individual company can achieve on its own. Important examples include:

Glasgow Financial Alliance for Net Zero

The Glasgow Financial Alliance for Net Zero (GFANZ), which represents approximately 40% of global private financial assets, encourages investments in developing economies to support the transition to a sustainable financial system. One of its more specialized subgroups, the Net-Zero Banking Alliance (NZBA), encourages banks to align their financing activities with science-based targets and Paris-aligned transition pathways.

Sustainable Apparel Coalition

The Sustainable Apparel Coalition (SAC) brings together over 250 global stakeholders from the fashion industry to develop a suite of tools (the "Higg index") to measure and disclose the social and environmental performance of their value chains.

Roundtable on Sustainable Palm Oil[12]

The Roundtable on Sustainable Palm Oil (RSPO) sets environmental and social standards for constituents along the palm-oil supply chain.

Each of these efforts is susceptible to some degree of resistance or criticism. As we will discuss later in the book, and as mentioned above with respect to the UN PRI, firms may on occasion seek to join an industry effort because it makes them look good. When political winds change, such as has recently been the case in the United States (2025), firms that appear unshakably committed to an initiative suddenly (and often quietly) excuse themselves from the group. Such cases may call into question the efficacy and impact of these initiatives, but in a world that needs all our help, we need all the help we can get.

SUMMARY

Like discovering that your teenage child believes that Luke Combs was the first artist to record the song "Fast Car,"[13] in the world of sustainability it is important to understand the history and all the work happening behind the scenes. In this chapter, we see how sustainability, especially environmental conservation, is not "new news" at all. Rather, for over a century, people have been writing and agitating for a closer, more natural relationship with our physical world. The United Nations, in particular, has been an active partner in these efforts, combining science with policy in an attempt to address some of the most pressing environmental and social issues.

And yet, none of these efforts—individually or collectively—has been sufficient to halt the human-led damage to the planet, or the many and various forms of injustice facing so many millions of people every day. To make a material difference will require that firms alter their business practices; this will not come easily or cheaply. Part Two, which follows, considers the corporate perspective, from measurement and disclosure of corporate activities to financing the operational changes required to achieve the desired levels of sustainability.

Corporate Sustainability

The previous chapters have set the stage for the rest of the book. We know there are challenges facing us, and despite the best efforts of well-intentioned actors at the United Nations and other organizations, the pace of change is not keeping up with the scale of the problem. We need to do more.

Since companies are the primary way of organizing economic activity, they have an important role to play in addressing these issues. Note this is in no way meant to diminish the role that we as individuals can play, or that of governments and state-owned enterprises. We all need to do our part. But when discussing sustainable finance the roles are clearer: individuals and other asset owners provide capital to companies, either public or private, through a variety of different means. Government provides regulations to encourage companies to act in a certain way in order to meet a set of sustainability goals. These are the high-leverage roles, the ones where decisions have the ability to impact at scale. Of course, we as individuals should care about our carbon footprint; it's just that financing and investing brings more firepower to address the issues. And, of course, governments should improve the sustainability of government-managed organizations, from ministries to public schools and militaries. But our ability to influence those actions is limited *in our capacity as investors*.

Therefore, Part Two begins by considering why companies should care about more than making money. Assuming that companies should, in fact, care about sustainability, they will likely need to make changes. Understanding why this might be the case is the subject of Chapter 5.

In Chapter 6, we lay the information foundation for everything that follows with sustainability measurement and disclosure. If Chapter 5 makes the case that companies should improve their sustainability, we won't know exactly what needs to be done without measuring existing processes and practices. Among other things, this chapter summarizes the various standards and frameworks that companies use in their sustainability reporting.

Once the data are gathered and the firm has identified projects to improve the sustainability of their business practices, implementation will cost money! Chapter 7 looks at the specialized financing options available to firms wishing to raise capital for their sustainability-related investments, from green bonds to sustainability-linked instruments and others.

CHAPTER 5

The Relationship Between Companies, People, and Planet

Modern society is organized into different units, e.g., where we live (neighborhoods), how we practice our faith, and especially where we work. Oversimplifying, we will begin by making a distinction between the public and private sector,[1] after which the discussion turns to different theories about the relationship between companies, shareholders, and stakeholders. The important international context is covered, followed by a recap of the academic literature on the relationship between environmental, social, and governance (ESG) issues, and corporate financial performance.

PUBLIC SECTOR

The public sector includes all manner of government-run organizations, e.g., hospitals, schools, and the government itself. Public sector employees are paid by the government, which is usually funded by taxes raised in that jurisdiction. Accordingly, the public sector clearly has some degree of duty or obligation to its taxpayers. If something goes wrong with a government agency, however, it can be very challenging to remove a government official from office, especially before the next election. Instead, if we don't like the schools or other government services where we live, we might be more likely to move to another jurisdiction or school district than to try to change the services.

When it comes to issues like climate change, governments at different levels face some degree of accountability. For example, national governments which are signatories to the Paris Agreement are obligated to submit a nationally determined contribution (NDC). Entities like Climate Action Tracker evaluate the degree to which the NDCs are aligned with the Paris Agreement goal of below 2°C. Even so, for the many countries with NDCs that are not aligned with the Paris Agreement, there isn't a strong mechanism to hold them accountable for lack of ambition.

There are signs that the lack of government accountability may be changing. For example, in *KlimaSeniorinnen v. Switzerland*,[2] a group of older women claimed that the Swiss government breached their human rights by acting inadequately on climate change. The European Court of Human Rights ruled in their favor, ordering the authorities to strengthen their climate policies. A similar case occurred in Australia[3] in 2022 where the United Nations Human Rights Committee ruled that Australia violated the rights of Torres Strait Islanders (to culture, private life, family, and home) and ordered the government to provide compensation and consultation with islanders, as well as measures to protect the community. At the state level in the United States, the government of the state of Montana also lost a climate-related lawsuit where plaintiffs claimed the state's infringement of their constitutional right to a clean and healthful environment by allowing fossil fuel projects regardless of the implications on the climate.[4]

Since 2024, there have been several important rulings from international courts related to climate change. In May 2024, the International Tribunal for the Law of the Sea found that carbon dioxide (CO_2) produced by burning fossil fuels counts as marine pollution and that countries were legally required to mitigate the impacts. In 2025, an advisory opinion from the Inter-American Court of Human Rights said countries have a legal duty to address climate change. Finally, on July 23, 2025, the International Court of Justice, the United Nations' "highest court in the world," issued a groundbreaking advisory opinion which declared the human right to a sustainable environment to be essential for other human rights. As a result, countries are obligated to protect the climate and that polluting countries may be liable for reparations on a case-by-case basis.[5]

We should take care not to overstate the impact of these lawsuits, but neither should we ignore them. Research shows that investors care about climate litigation, with negative short-term impacts on stock prices around filings and decisions.[6] When private citizens care about an issue, they have tools that enable their voice to be heard. If projections for increasing frequency and severity of climate-related disasters come true, we might expect more of this kind of climate action.

PRIVATE SECTOR

In most developed countries, economic activity is dominated by companies, i.e., the private sector. The question of who owns these companies is particularly important. Many companies have chosen to issue shares to investors through an initial public offering, and their shares subsequently trade on one of the many stock exchanges around the world.[7] Other firms that have not listed their shares on a stock exchange remain "private companies."

The distinction between public and private companies is relevant to our conversation about sustainability because when things go wrong, we want to know whom to hold accountable. When companies do something bad, we might want to hold their owners accountable, if private, or their chief executive officer (CEO) and Board of Directors, accountable, if the company is public. There are other ways to express our displeasure with a company, e.g., if we have a problem with how a company treats its customers, we might direct our business to a competitor. If we own shares in that company, we can sell the shares and invest in a different company.[8] No matter whether a company is private or public, it is still appropriate to ask a fundamental question: why should a firm care about something other than making money?

BALANCING PROFIT AND . . . SOMETHING ELSE?

Owning a profitable company has been an important driver of wealth creation for hundreds, if not thousands, of years. In recent history, one of the voices most closely associated with "profit maximization" is Nobel prize-winning economist Milton Friedman. His famous 1970 article in *The New York Times Magazine*[9] proposed that the purpose of a company is to maximize profits for shareholders. In what became known as "shareholder value maximization" (SVM) theory, companies would seek to maximize profits and leave the provision of public goods and services to the government. Friedman also pointed out that, in the pursuit of profits, companies would also recognize when it was in their long-term best interest to care about the welfare of stakeholders, e.g., supporting healthy communities and managing important natural resources.

Following the publication of his article, however, many companies chose to maximize short-term returns to the detriment of long-term performance. Corporate raiders would buy companies and carve them up to maximize their gains without much consideration for the employees they fired and businesses they closed. Firms polluted without regard for the health consequences. CEO pay relative to the pay of the median worker increased nearly 14× in 58 years (Figure 5.1).[10] If SVM was the best way to run a business, why did it lead to such negative consequences? Could there be a better way to think of running a firm?

One of the well-known academic responses to this era of corporate excess was the concept of "stakeholder theory," given voice by R. Edward Freeman of the University of Virginia.[11] A stakeholder refers to anyone (individual or group) that affects or is affected by a business—creditors, employees, customers, suppliers, and communities are frequently included in this category. Other potential stakeholders for certain industries might include governments, regulators, and even the environment in an abstract way. Freeman's idea was not to say "forget about profits, all the other

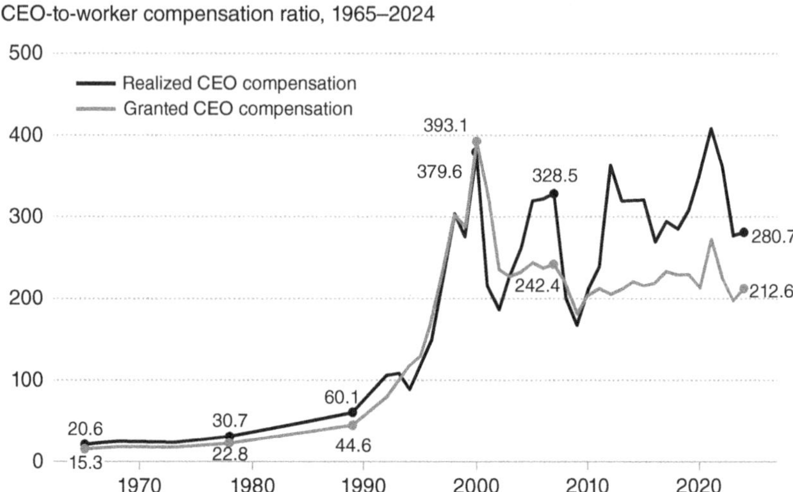

FIGURE 5.1   Ratio of CEO-to-median-worker compensation.
Source: Economic Policy Institute / https://www.epi.org/publication/ceo-pay-in-2023/ / last accessed Aug 19, 2025.

stakeholders matter more than shareholders." Instead, he said that companies should take the needs of stakeholders into consideration: He also linked the heart of the theory and practice to core values—such as those he earned and learned growing up on a Georgia farm—especially the truth that "one needed to be responsible for the effects of one's action on others."[12]

NEGATIVE EXTERNALITIES AND CORPORATE SOCIAL RESPONSIBILITY

"The effects of one's action on others" is a powerful concept. When the effect is negative, the field of economics refers to this concept as a "negative externality," i.e., where producing or consuming a good causes harm to others. These effects may be the result of companies making decisions that maximize their profits but bring harm to others, either deliberately or unintentionally. Examples of corporate—and individual—negative externalities include:

- Dumping poisonous waste into a river may cause health issues for humans and kill fish in the river.
- Burning coal to produce electricity releases greenhouse gases (GHGs) and other pollution like lead and mercury.
- Smoking a cigarette where the smoke may be inhaled by nonsmokers, i.e., secondhand smoke.

If those who generate the negative externalities do not choose voluntarily to stop their actions, then possible corrective actions include social pressure, lawsuits, and, ultimately, government action. This perspective appears to align with Friedman's SVM theory—the government is responsible for addressing negative externalities. In theory that sounds reasonable, but in practice most governments fall short. The relatively late and slow adoption of taxes on carbon pollution (GHG emissions) is but one example.[13] Freeman went in another direction altogether and emphasized the "responsibility" rather than just measuring the consequences. The use of this term links stakeholder theory to another concept that was gathering momentum in the 1980s, "corporate social responsibility" (CSR).[14]

The attention given to the "responsibility" of a company reflects in no small part a disillusionment with the effects of a shareholder-focused system. The first attributed use of the term "corporate social responsibility" predates Friedman's 1970 *New York Times Magazine* article; American economist Howard Bowen coined the term in 1953. Like Freeman after him, Bowen believed that corporations have profound effects on society and therefore should take society into account when making decisions. As early as the 1970s, the concept of a "social contract" was taking shape, stressing corporate obligations to the societies within which they operate. Finally, in 1991, Professor Archie Carroll from the University of Georgia combined earlier research on stakeholders and the responsibility of firms to society when he published the "Pyramid of Corporate Social Responsibility" (Figure 5.2).[15]

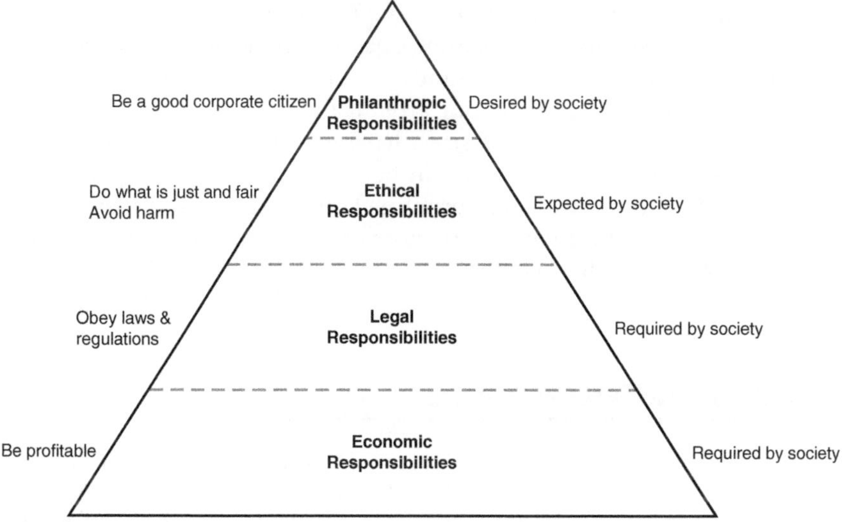

FIGURE 5.2 Pyramid of Corporate Social Responsibility.
Source: Carroll (1991) as cited in Agudelo et al. (2019).

The first two levels of the CSR pyramid are for firms to make money—otherwise they fail—and to obey laws and regulations. These responsibilities are labeled "requirements" on the right side of the pyramid. On the third level, ethical responsibilities, i.e., doing what is just and fair and avoiding harm, are "expected" by society. Ethical behaviors extend beyond the level of legal responsibilities to include actions which are not (yet) codified in the laws and regulations governing behavior. Finally, the top of the pyramid includes philanthropic activities which represent good corporate citizenship; this is labeled a "desired" level of responsibility. This framework contributed to the growing call for a change in corporate behavior, from a profit-maximizing approach to one where profitability coexists with responsibilities to other stakeholders.

The 1990s were fertile ground for both CSR research and practice. As more companies began to launch formal CSR programs, Professor Donna J. Wood (University of Northern Iowa) and others developed frameworks for assessing "corporate social performance," i.e., the outcomes and impacts of those CSR programs.[16] Also in the 1990s, John Elkington introduced the concept of the "triple bottom line," referring to people, planet, and profits. The idea was to challenge prevailing business practice and hold companies accountable for their broader impacts on society and the environment.

As we will see in Chapter 6, these ideas are deeply embedded within the new field of sustainability accounting, where companies are expected to *measure* their impacts on people and planet. What many people wanted, however, from Freeman to Carroll, Wood, and Elkington, was less about measurement and more about *real change*. From this perspective the results are at best mixed. Corporate social responsibility has become a common term, included on thousands of corporate websites—not just in the United States and Europe, but around the world. Companies across industries and countries, of all sizes, have established CSR budgets and committees; employees participate in beach cleanups and prepare meals for the needy and mentor underprivileged children . . . and these are all good things to do. But they fall far short of the reimagining of the corporate relationship with stakeholders, with people and planet, that was hoped for.

SHAREHOLDER WELFARE MAXIMIZATION

In 2022, Nobel laureate Oliver Hart (Harvard University) and Luigi Zingales (University of Chicago) published their theory of "shareholder welfare maximization" (SWM) combining aspects of SVM theory and stakeholder theory.[17] The authors start by observing that shareholders appeared to be voting for proposals that might not be maximizing profits (all examples from 2021):

- 81% of DuPont shareholders approved a proposal requiring the company to disclose how much plastic the company releases into the environment each year and to assess the effectiveness of DuPont's pollution policies.
- 64% of ExxonMobil shareholders approved a proposal requiring the company to describe "if, and how, ExxonMobil's lobbying activities (direct and through trade associations) align with the goal of limiting average global warming to well below 2°C (the Paris Climate Agreement's goal)."
- 52% of Duke Energy shareholders approved a proposal that requests disclosures on contributions to candidates, parties, committees, and social welfare (501(c)(4) in the United States) organizations.
- 95% of Wendy's shareholders approved a proposal requiring the company "to disclose concrete evidence on the effectiveness of its Supplier Code of Conduct in protecting the human rights of workers at its produce and meat suppliers, with respect to COVID-19 in particular.[18]

These voting results suggested to the authors that something more was at work behind them—that at least some shareholders may be interested in the welfare of others ("prosocial" investors). When investors have sufficient information on costs and benefits to stakeholders, prosocial shareholders may vote in favor of proposals that are better for the welfare of others than for the financials of the company. Their paper shows that as long as a majority of shareholders are at least somewhat prosocial, companies should maximize shareholder *welfare* instead of *value*.[19]

While this may sound like a good theory, is this how it works in reality? There are important conditions that need to be satisfied for the theory to work. First, there would need to be some changes to the mechanics of voting. When investors hold their economic interest in a company through an investment in a mutual fund or unit trust, the investment manager holds the right to vote for that investment. As we will explore further in Part Four on sustainable investing, these investment managers are typically bound by fiduciary responsibility to vote for profit maximization. While the voting examples cited above must certainly include votes by investment managers and not just individual shareholders, there is no guarantee that an investment manager will incorporate social welfare into its voting choices the same way as all its clients would.

Hart and Zingales offer three potential solutions. The first, "pass through voting," would allow individual investors to vote on the basis of their pro-rata share of stocks, that they own indirectly in passive mutual funds and exchange-traded funds (ETFs). For example, BlackRock launched its BlackRock Voting Choice in 2022, allowing clients with institutional separately managed accounts (SMAs) to participate in the proxy voting process more easily.[20] Mutual fund managers could also poll their investors and let them direct the fund's voting. A second potential solution is for investors to select from predetermined voting policies, such as those promoted by proxy advisory services like Institutional Shareholder Services (ISS).[21] This wouldn't exactly match every investor's individual preferences, but with enough thoughtfully constructed policies it could be a step in the right direction. Finally, the investment managers could include proxy voting policies in their fund strategies, e.g., "an S&P 500 dark green fund that votes in favor of all shareholder resolutions that promote a greener economy, as long as their cost of reducing CO_2 emission does not exceed \$200 per ton."[22]

Not all issues would (or should) be eligible for a vote. Hart and Zingales suggest that firms should be able to decide which social issues should be put to a shareholder vote, especially ". . . situations where there is a technological interaction between the social and business activities of a corporation."[23] For those relevant social issues to be voted upon, for SWM to work, shareholders must have timely access to all the information needed to evaluate the proposal in the context of their individual preferences. While it may be difficult to determine whether firms have completely and transparently disclosed all the relevant information the shareholders need, timely dissemination will be easier to evaluate. Current practice allows companies to provide supplementary materials (through proxy amendments) in the days leading up to a shareholder vote. This should be monitored to make sure shareholders receive the information they need with enough time before a vote to develop an informed opinion.

INTERNATIONAL CONTEXT

Should companies around the world all exhibit similar attitudes toward stakeholders? The above discussions of SVM, stakeholder theory, CSR, and SWM might suggest that there should be a single, universal model for how companies relate to stakeholders. The diversity of cultures around the world presents some challenges to that assumption. Among differences in culture and religion, another important variable to consider is the origin of the prevailing legal system. The "civil law" system, with roots in the United Kingdom (and previously in Roman Law), prioritizes the belief that free markets can self-regulate and solve problems.[24] As one of the major colonial powers of the 17th to 20th centuries, the United Kingdom exported its legal system to its colonies, e.g., the United States, Australia, and Hong Kong. At least superficially, civil law therefore seems more closely aligned with SVM as proposed by Milton Friedman.

But the United Kingdom was not the only colonial power. Continental European countries like France, Germany, the Netherlands, and Spain shared elements of a "common law" system. Under common law, the state plays a more active role in shaping relationships between stakeholders. Common law, therefore, seems more aligned with stakeholder theory and CSR.

An interesting paper by Liang and Renneboog, published in 2017,[25] investigated the impact of legal origin on the behavior of corporations. The authors analyzed over 23,000 companies in countries with different legal origins—English Common, French Civil, German Civil, Scandinavian Civil, and Socialist—and the relationship between legal origin and Morgan Stanley Capital International's (MSCI) Intangible Value Assessment (IVA).[26] The authors also considered other country-, industry-, and firm-level variables that could be related to CSR activity. Interestingly, legal origin of the country in which the firm is headquartered had the strongest relationship with the IVA ESG scores. Companies in common law countries have lower CSR scores along most of the environmental and social dimensions, while the opposite is true for companies in civil law countries.

Without trying to assign blame or praise to any one country or its companies, the importance of this finding is to underscore that ESG issues may vary considerably across markets. Investors and regulators should not assume that what holds true for companies in Canada will also be true in Austria, for example. It does *not* mean, however, that there shouldn't be a common set of information for companies to measure and disclose, describing their relationship to people and planet. Comprehensive measurement and disclosure establish a strong foundation for rigorous study and comparison of corporate activity; this is the primary topic of Chapter 6, which follows.

ENVIRONMENTAL, SOCIAL, AND GOVERNANCE ISSUES, AND CORPORATE FINANCIAL PERFORMANCE[27]

Notwithstanding the compelling nature of the theories described above, finance researchers always like to see the data, and this area of study is no exception. One of the questions explored in the finance literature is to what extent there is a relationship between ESG and corporate financial performance. A recent study assesses 81 papers from top finance journals based on which of the inputs to a discounted cash flow (DCF) valuation are tested by each paper:

$$Value = f\left(Profitability,\ Tax,\ Reinvestment,\ g, r_E, r_D, \frac{D}{D+E}\right) \qquad Value = \sum_{t=1}^{\infty} \frac{E(CF_t)}{(1+r)^t}$$

On balance, from a cash flow statement perspective, there is evidence of a positive relationship between ESG and revenue growth, as well as the reinvestment rate. Viewing the research through the balance sheet lens, the relationship is positive for the leverage ratio (closer to optimal leverage) and negative for the cost of debt (more ESG means lower cost of debt), which is good for the firm. Even though not every driver of valuation enjoys a positive relationship with ESG/CSR, the presence of positive relationships—and a lack of negative relationships—offers some support for sustainability as a potential driver of financial performance.

SUMMARY

This chapter explores the relationship between types of organizations in the public and private sectors and sustainability issues. The public sector bears primary responsibility for addressing the complex system of unpriced environmental and social externalities. Inconsistent action to reduce GHGs means that governments should be held accountable and required to do more; recent lawsuits suggest that citizens are starting to act on this accountability.

In the private sector, the dominant theory since the 1970s (SVM) has encouraged companies to put profit above everything else. Backlash against environmental damage and corporate excess has led many toward a more stakeholder-focused approach, from stakeholder theory and CSR to the triple bottom line and SWM. None of the theories work very well in practice—yet. Work is ongoing, and there is much more to be done.

This work on corporate responsibility will need to respect local context, for different countries operate from different perspectives driven by (among other things) the legal origin of the country. Even in countries with a strong stakeholder orientation, like many in Europe, government and corporate ambition must go beyond current practice if we are to address climate change and the other Sustainable Development Goals. It is encouraging, therefore, that the state of academic research on the relationship between ESG and corporate financial performance is at least nonnegative, and in some parts positive.

CHAPTER 6

Sustainability Measurement and Reporting

INTRODUCTION

Companies need to do more to improve their relationship with people and planet, this much should be clear from Chapters 1–5. But if you were to ask "how much more?" or "what, specifically, should companies do differently?" first you would need to know what they are doing *today*—the company's current sustainability footprint. Gathering this information is no small task. It requires determining what should be measured, how it should be measured, and how it should be reported and disclosed to stakeholders.

ORIGINS

Long before companies were asked to measure sustainability data, they were accustomed to measuring and reporting *financial* data through the practice of accounting. Over the past few thousand years, accounting has evolved from clay tablets to double-entry accounting in the late 15th century, and finally to modern accounting systems with standardized financial statements. The "certified public accountant" (CPA) designation dates to the 19th century. It was a profession that was in great demand following the introduction of income tax in the United States, and even more so after the adoption of Generally Accepted Accounting Principles (GAAP) in the wake of the Great Depression in the 1930s.

Sustainability measurement, it so happens, has its origins in an environmental disaster. On March 24, 1989, the oil tanker Exxon Valdez ran aground off the coast of Alaska, spilling 11 million US gallons (over 41 million liters) of oil and devastating the pristine coastal environment. The powerful negative public reaction to this event prompted two nonprofit organizations (Ceres and The Tellus Institute) to partner with the United Nations Environment Programme (UNEP) in the 1997 founding of the Global Reporting Initiative (GRI). Up to this point, only a limited number of companies disclosed any meaningful information about their environmental footprint. The objective of GRI, however, was to create a framework that all companies could use to measure and disclose their environmental, social, and economic impacts. The 2000 release of its first set of guidelines started an irreversible movement toward increased transparency through standardized measures and publication of sustainability reports.

One of the critical areas of measurement concerns greenhouse gas (GHG) emissions. Grounded in the 1997 Kyoto Protocol which stipulated the measurement of six critical greenhouse gasses, the GHG Protocol established a clear methodology for tracking emissions according to "scope". Scope 1 emissions are directly emitted by the party in question, e.g., burning fossil fuels to generate electricity or steam. In Scope 2 emissions, the party in question purchases services (electricity, steam, etc.) from another firm which generates emissions in the provision of those services. Finally, Scope 3 emissions occur in the party's value chain, either upstream or downstream, from one of 17 activities such as employee commuting or distribution of finished products. Standardized methodologies for scope make it possible to compare emissions across entities of all sizes, sectors, and geographies.

SUSTAINABILITY AND ACCOUNTING: INTERVIEW WITH FANG EU-LIN, PwC SINGAPORE

In conversation with James Cheo

James
What's the role of an accountant when it comes to sustainability?

Eu-Lin
Accountants do debits and credits, they make sure that financial information, particularly financial statements, are done to a very high quality based on the International Financial Reporting Standards (IFRS). There is a lot of alignment with international standards, and in Singapore, we follow the SMR [Senior Managers' Regime]—which is based on the IFRS, so there is a lot of alignment with international standards. The standards have been built out over decades; you then produce a set of financial statements.

I love reading financial statements. Personally, I don't like doing financial statements. Sometimes, I might not even like auditing it because I spent a large part of my life auditing them. But it is very useful. Because all of these metrics go into credit ratings and financial decisions with market implications.

Accountants audit the financial statements based on the auditing standards. Accountants and auditors provide credibility and trust in the process of creating financial statements. Auditors are deeply involved in the process of ensuring financial statements are of high quality and that satisfy regulation and internal accounting standards.

Now, on sustainability in accounting, accountants have been involved in sustainability for a long time. Accounting appeared quite overtly in the GHG [greenhouse gas] Protocol in 1999. I was very pleasantly surprised to see the authors of the GHG Protocol, I thought it was a bunch of engineers, biologist[s], but half of them were accountants from Coopers and Lybrand, Price Waterhouse, KPMG, Ernst and Young. Accountants are there because they can measure.

However, [an] accountants' framework is a double entry, and the GHG Protocol doesn't have a double entry system. In the GHG Protocol, there is Scope 1, 2, and 3, and there are overlaps. I am fine with overlaps; just don't have under measurement of GHG.

There is a role for accountants in sustainability. Accountants are great at measuring, have strong instincts, and, at this point in time, accountants provide high trust in the reporting. There might be a disorderly transition of skill sets when it comes to sustainability accounting, in which the standards for sustainability accelerated—for example, the European CSRD [Corporate Sustainability Reporting Directive] in the last few years—while the skill of accountants, from the preparation to the auditing might not catch up as fast.

James
How do you measure sustainability? What are the components that you're looking at?

Eu-Lin
Sustainability assurance encompasses three interconnected but different domains—environmental, social, and governance, or ESG. Within these three domains, there are topics ranging from climate change to diversity and inclusion to board effectiveness reviews.

The topics differ in their measurement and analytical perspective. For E [environmental], it is GHG emissions and GHG intensity.

(Continued)

(*Continued*)

The environmental impact of a company can be objectively measured—Scope 1, 2, and 3. We have to go back to first principles, which is the GHG Protocol. Once a material sustainability issue, like GHG, water, or waste, is identified the ISSB [International Sustainability Standards Board] will give a set of metrics for disclosure, either from an impact or financial perspective. That's when the accountant comes in to devise those disclosures or to audit them.

And the same goes for S [social] and G [governance]. There are aspects which are measurable, and parts which are less measurable. For example, the TCFD [Task Force on Climate-related Financial Disclosures] has many qualitative discussions and less about quantification, just like the GRI [Global Reporting Initiative], CSRD, or the ISSB. For financial statements, there's a lot of qualitative discourse about governance and managing risk. The preparation of qualitative disclosure is easy to prepare but difficult to audit since there are no hard numbers.

MATERIALITY

GRI's reporting guidelines approached issues from the perspective of the company's impact on people and planet, what today we call *impact materiality*. But what exactly does "materiality" mean? According to the Cambridge Business English Dictionary, materiality is defined as "a measure of how important a piece of information is when making a decision."[1] From the perspective of the GRI founders who were concerned with the impact of companies on the world, this perspective makes sense. But it is not the only perspective one can have. Rather than focusing on the impact that companies have on people and planet, another point of view prioritizes issues of financial risk to investors. This approach is more like traditional financial accounting, leading to a *financial materiality* perspective.

While some issues may be important to both perspectives, what is considered "material" may be quite different. For example, the point of view taken is very important for the fossil fuel companies like ExxonMobil. If you are concerned about greenhouse gas (GHG) emissions, then one of the most material *environmental impacts* that ExxonMobil has on the world is that customers burn its oil and gas products, releasing carbon dioxide (CO_2) and other gases into the atmosphere (Scope 3 emissions) which contributes to climate change. However, if you are an investor concerned with ExxonMobil's future financial prospects, you might be more concerned with understanding the company's *financial risks*. From this perspective, you would consider potential negative financial impacts if growth in renewable energy reduces demand for oil and gas, or if more countries adopt ever-increasing carbon taxes, or perhaps even outright bans on fossil fuel extraction that leaves some proven deposits as "stranded assets."

A robust system of measurement and reporting requirements must take the interests of all stakeholders into account, not just climate activists (impact materiality) or shareholders (financial materiality). One proposal is to create a system that simultaneously captures both types of materiality, or what is called *double materiality*. We will come back to this shortly.

MEASUREMENT AND DISCLOSURE[2]

Since the introduction of the first measurement and reporting framework in 1997, multiple organizations have introduced their own frameworks ("what to report") and standards ("how to report") with slightly different focuses and approaches. Among the long list of available solutions[3] for corporate measurement and reporting the following are some of the most widely utilized:

- **Global Reporting Initiative (GRI).**[4] As introduced above, the GRI (1997) was the first, and is the most widely adopted, framework and standard for sustainability reporting. Its framework emphasizes an organization's impact on the economy, environment, and society. The standards are intended to cover the issues of companies across all industries and address the concerns of a wide range of stakeholders, including investors, consumers, employees, and civil society. The initial GRI standard, launched in 2000, established a set of baseline information and detailed metrics for companies to track and disclose to their stakeholders.
- **GHG Protocol.**[5] The GHG Protocol was launched in 1998 to develop internationally accepted GHG accounting and reporting standards. The World Resources Institute and the World Business Council for Sustainable Development led the initiative which published its first set of corporate standards in 2001. Since then, it has evolved as the standard-bearer for accurate measurement and reporting of GHGs, with guidance for several industries and topics such as Scope 3 emissions.

- **Carbon Disclosure Project (CDP).**[6] Established in 2000, the CDP (formerly the Carbon Disclosure Project) runs a global disclosure system for investors and companies on environmental issues, including climate change, water, and forests. The CDP sends questionnaires to companies to collect data on their environmental performance, compiling this data into a database that is available to the public and to subscribers.
- **Climate Disclosure Standards Board (CDSB).**[7] Founded at the World Economic Forum in 2007 by the CDP, CERES (one of the founders of GRI), and the World Resources Institute, the CDSB framework helps standardize climate change-related disclosures within mainstream corporate reporting, including environmental information (particularly related to climate change), natural capital, and their business impacts.
- **International Integrated Reporting Council (IIRC).**[8] Formed in 2010, the IIRC emphasizes integrated reporting, seeking to improve the quality of information available to providers of financial capital. The IIRC aims to enhance accountability for a broad range of capitals (financial, manufactured, intellectual, human, social and relationship, and natural), and encourages the understanding of the interdependencies of these various forms of capital. The IIRC framework requires reevaluation of a company's business model and is principle-based.
- **Sustainability Accounting Standards Board (SASB).**[9] Founded in 2011, SASB takes a more investor-centric approach, focusing on financially material sustainability issues. SASB provides industry-specific standards for about 77 sectors and subsectors. SASB defines "material" issues as those that are reasonably likely to have a significant impact on a company's financial performance or condition. SASB merged with the International Integrated Reporting Council (IIRC) in 2021 to form the Value Reporting Framework.
- **Science Based Targets Initiative (SBTi).**[10] Established in 2015 as a collaboration between the CDP, the United Nations Global Compact, the World Resources Institute, and the Worldwide Fund for Nature, SBTi helps companies set ambitious GHG reduction targets in line with climate science and the goals of the Paris Agreement.
- **Task Force on Climate-related Financial Disclosures (TCFD).**[11] Created in 2015 by the Financial Stability Board (FSB), the TCFD provides a framework for reporting on climate-related risks and opportunities. The TCFD focuses on four core elements: governance, strategy, risk management, and metrics and targets. The TCFD recommendations have gained significant support in the financial sector. The TCFD is organized in a "top-down" manner, starting with the broad sections and then moving into the specifics.

- **Task Force on Nature-related Financial Disclosures (TNFD).**[12] The TNFD was formally launched in June 2021 by a coalition of organizations including Global Canopy, the United Nations Development Programme, the United Nations Environment Programme Finance Initiative, and the Worldwide Fund for Nature. Released in 2023, its inaugural framework helps organizations integrate nature-related issues into their decision-making and disclosure practices.

This proliferation of frameworks and standards eventually reached a point where companies and investors began to complain. For companies, they sometimes needed to report the same information in slightly different formats to comply with different standards, or sometimes needed to measure the same concept (e.g., carbon emissions) in a different way. The net effect was a perceived combination of resource inefficiency (duplication of effort) and lack of clarity on which standards were most important to which stakeholders. Investors complained that inconsistency across standards made it difficult to efficiently analyze sustainability data in the course of their investment decisions. The general consensus was that something should be done to address these pain points, but each standard-setting organization was committed to its own approach—until the consolidation started in 2020.

SUSTAINABILITY ASSURANCE: INTERVIEW WITH FANG EU-LIN, PwC SINGAPORE

In conversation with James Cheo

James
Sustainability assurance shares some similarities with financial auditing. The main objective is the same—to determine whether disclosures are free of material misstatements that could affect investor decisions. To do that, let's talk about assurance levels and materiality.

Eu-Lin
Sustainability assurance and financial auditing concepts are the same.

On sustainability assurance, there are a few levels—limited (lower), reasonable (high), and absolute (highest).

For limited assurance, according to the IAASB [International Auditing and Assurance Standards Board], a conclusion of a limited assurance engagement conveys if anything has come to the assurance practitioner's attention to believe the information is materially

(Continued)

(*Continued*)

misstated based on evidence obtained. For example, a typical limited assurance conclusion includes "nothing has come to our attention that causes us to believe the statement is not, in all material respects, fairly stated." Limited assurance usually occurs when [the] data and governance structure are still evolving.

For reasonable assurance, in contrast with limited assurance, a reasonable assurance engagement conclusion is framed on a positive basis. For example, a reasonable assurance conclusion usually includes, "in our opinion, the information is properly prepared, in all material respects, based on the standard." To get from limited to reasonable assurance, there must be key controls. For example, effective controls—internal controls, IT systems, etc.—around GHG emissions, which are tested regularly to operate effectively.

Absolute assurance can provide full confidence in a company's sustainable practices, but this is in practice unreachable.

James
How about the materiality?

Eu-Lin
Impact materiality focuses on the broader impacts of a company's actions on people and the planet, including impacts throughout its value chain. Financial materiality, on the other hand, assesses how sustainability issues impact the company's financials. By conducting robust materiality assessments, companies can identify the most relevant sustainability issues to include in their reporting, ensuring transparency and informed decision-making.

While traditional materiality assessment focuses solely on a company's impact and outlook, double materiality requires reporting on broader impacts, such as climate and society. This approach recognizes the interconnectedness of internal and external impacts, emphasizing the company's broader sustainability footprint.

The concept of materiality is crucial in both financial and sustainability reporting. The main objective of an assurance engagement is to reach a conclusion of no material misstatement in a financial or sustainability report.

The concept of double materiality is gaining prominence in corporate sustainability reporting, particularly with the new European Commission standards. Under the EU [Corporate] Sustainability Reporting Directive (CSRD), companies are required to perform a double materiality assessment, considering both impact materiality and financial materiality.

While the EU is incorporating double materiality into its standards, there is ongoing debate about its adoption in other regions. The International Sustainability Standards Board is facing pressure to include double materiality in global reporting frameworks.

STANDARDS CONSOLIDATION

In response to pushback from companies and investors, the major sustainability standards organizations have taken important steps toward consolidation (Figure 6.1). The first move, in November 2020, was a merger of IIRC and SASB to form the Value Reporting Foundation (VRF), effective June 2021. The VRF in turn supported the creation of the IFRS Sustainability Standards Board (ISSB), announced in November 2021 at COP26 in Glasgow, United Kingdom, and operational in August 2022. The ISSB operates under the aegis of the IFRS Foundation, responsible for the IFRS widely used for financial reporting; the IFRS Foundation was perceived as an organization with the credibility required to develop and oversee global sustainability reporting standards and as a logical home for what became ISSB.[13] The VRF allowed itself to be consolidated into the new ISSB, along with CDSB and (a year later) the TCFD. In 2023, the ISSB released its first set of standards, ISSB 1 and 2. Later that year, the TCFD disbanded, leaving its principles integrated into the ISSB standards.

An important detail in this chart is that the GRI "complements" the ISSB; it has not been consolidated. The other standards rolled up into the ISSB—IIRC, SASB, CDSB, TCFD—emphasize *financial* materiality rather than *impact* materiality. Because the GRI is the most widely used standard, and because the ISSB is still relatively new, companies and investors still have some work to do when preparing sustainability reports and making investment decisions, but at least the "alphabet soup" of standards has been improved.

ENVIRONMENTAL, SOCIAL, AND GOVERNANCE DATA AND DISCLOSURE: EMILY WOODLAND AND HEIDI YIP, BLACKROCK

In conversation with James Cheo

James
On ESG [environmental, social, and governance] data and disclosure, where are we today and what can be improved?

(Continued)

(*Continued*)

BlackRock

It's really about data. The quality of data is always underpinned by disclosure. It allows investors to evaluate how companies consider issues that are material to their business models and track progress against the goals that they have stated, and especially where companies have issued targets that they are working toward, to hold them accountable to that. On climate-related risks and opportunities, disclosures help investors understand how the companies are addressing and tackling those risks and taking advantage of opportunities where they might be already aligned with the low-carbon transition.

We've been advocating for a very long time with our companies for disclosures aligned to TCFD [Task Force on Climate-related Financial Disclosures] reporting and International Sustainability Standards Board (ISSB), which features what is material for investment returns. We have come a long way in terms of companies reporting in alignment, particularly with TCFD standards. There are still some jurisdictions that are more comprehensively doing this than others. And what we're really welcoming now is the establishment of the ISSB disclosure standards. The two main challenges are: (a) the data is just not there, or (b) it's fragmented in a way that makes comparison across sectors or across regions quite hard to make. A common ground framework, like ISSB, is something that we're very supportive of, and we find the direction of travel very encouraging.

BlackRock encourages its portfolio companies to provide these financially material disclosures because it's beneficial to our clients to understand better what companies are doing. We also recognize that it's important to lead by example in our own disclosures and in enhancing transparency. We have been putting out more information in our regular reports, PRI [Principles of Responsible Investment] reports, TCFD statements, as well as on our website.

What our investment stewardship team does is actively engage with companies to encourage them to make these disclosures in line with the reporting framework developed by ISSB. Our alternative investment teams also work with their portfolio companies and clients to collect and share ESG metrics that might be important for them. Various digital platforms have been set up to collect that information.

The progress on ESG data and disclosure is quite bifurcated on the public and private market sides. BlackRock's approach and stance is to push for more data to be made available to our portfolio managers and clients, to enable better understanding of the risk and performance of assets within the portfolio. We are constantly working with both industry and our investee companies to encourage higher-quality solutions.

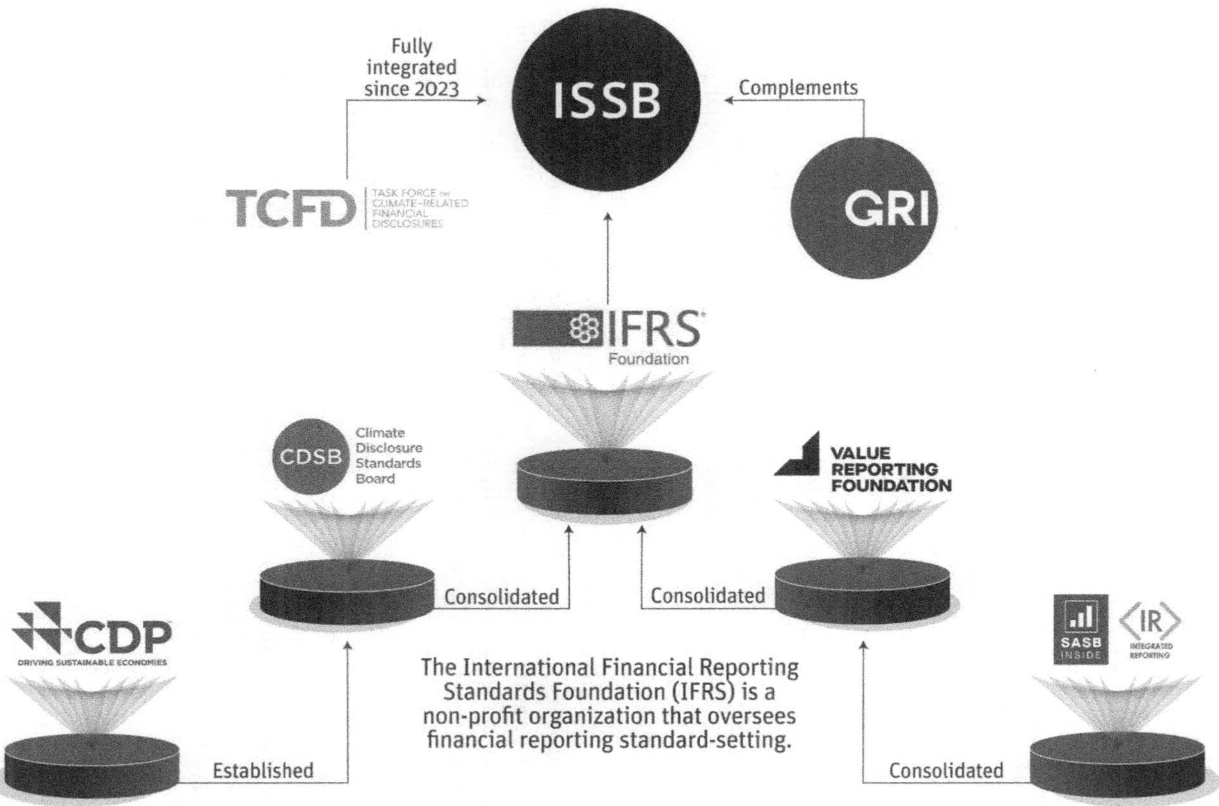

FIGURE 6.1 Consolidation of major sustainability standards organizations.

Source: RepRisk, https://www.reprisk.com/regulatory-hub/frameworks-and-regulations/regulatory-briefing-issb.

SUSTAINABILITY REPORTS

Following some much-needed consolidation of reporting frameworks, all companies should disclose roughly the same information, right? Not exactly. Companies may disclose their sustainability information in different ways; as we will see in Chapter 7, there are no regulations on how to present the data, only on what information needs to be disclosed. Most large, publicly listed firms around the world publish stand-alone "sustainability reports," but within this group there are many possibilities—even for direct competitors in the same industry.

Here are two examples from Singapore's real estate industry, City Developments Limited (CDL) and UOL Group (UOL). Both are large public companies with market caps of SGD5.46 billion and SGD5.88 billion, respectively.[14] Looking first at their 2024 annual reports, their financial tables of contents are relatively similar (Figure 6.2). Their income statements are slightly different but follow the same basic structure (Figure 6.3). This clear comparability (though not equivalence), enabled by agreed-upon financial accounting standards and decades of practice and precedent, makes it relatively easy for stakeholders to compare the financial performance of the two firms.

When it comes to sustainability reports, however, the differences are stark. Starting with the "Contents" for each firm's 2024 Sustainability Report, we can see that CDL's runs over 200 pages; UOL's is less than half that long (Figure 6.4). UOL has very clear sections on Environment, Social, and Governance—in that order. CDL makes reference to "EESG," adding "economic" as a fourth element, and reorders the issues to begin with governance and economic performance.

If an investor was interested in comparing the GHG emissions of each firm, it's not immediately apparent where to look. CDL includes the information in multiple places, first in 3.2 Decarbonization to Net-Zero (p. 73) (Figure 6.5), and then twice in the Annexes: "Key Performance Summary" (p. 174) and "Breakdown of Environmental Performance" in 2024 (p. 182) (Figure 6.6). To find similar information in UOL's report, the investor is clearly encouraged to visit "GHG Emissions" (p. 26) (Figure 6.7).

The relative complexity of CDL's report is in part a function of the amount of detail provided. For example, CDL provides a breakdown of the top five materials used (metric tons) and the embodied carbon footprint (p. 77), as well as a rich narrative description of its EESG ambitions and initiatives through the report. But this is a matter of *choice*. CDL chooses to write such a detailed report, and UOL chooses to provide less detail. Both firms satisfy local regulatory disclosure requirements—the subject of Chapter 8.

City Development Limited (CDL)[a]   UOL Group (UOL)[b]

FIGURE 6.2 Comparison of 2024 annual report financial tables of contents of City Developments Limited (CDL) and UOL Group (UOL).

[a]*Source:* Annual Report 2024, p. 80.   Available at https://ir.cdl.com.sg/annual-reports-agm/annual-reports
[b]*Source:* 2024 Annual Report, p. 99.   Available at https://www.uol.com.sg/investors-and-media/annual-reports/

City Development Limited (CDL)[a]

CONSOLIDATED STATEMENT OF PROFIT OR LOSS

Year ended 31 December 2024

	Note	Group 2024 $'000	Group 2023 $'000
Revenue	31	**3,271,197**	4,941,121
Cost of sales		**(1,809,260)**	(3,292,550)
Gross profit		**1,461,937**	1,648,571
Other income	32	**272,015**	158,237
Administrative expenses		**(574,748)**	(581,452)
Other operating expenses		**(473,537)**	(406,828)
Profit from operating activities		**685,667**	818,528
Finance income		**186,637**	97,970
Finance costs		**(559,070)**	(491,578)
Net finance costs	32	**(372,433)**	(393,608)
Share of after-tax profit of associates		**14,150**	3,415
Share of after-tax profit of joint ventures		**46,641**	44,233
Profit before tax		**374,025**	472,568
Tax expense	33	**(162,061)**	(123,762)
Profit for the year	32	**211,964**	348,806
Profit attributable to owners of the Company:			
– Ordinary shareholders		**190,849**	305,059
– Preference shareholders		**10,467**	12,254
		201,316	317,313
Non-controlling interests		**10,648**	31,493
Profit for the year		**211,964**	348,806
Earnings per share			
– Basic	34	**21.3 cents**	33.6 cents
– Diluted	34	**21.3 cents**	33.3 cents

The accompanying notes form an integral part of these financial statements.

UOL Group (UOL)[b]

Consolidated Income Statement

For the Financial Year Ended 31 December 2024

	Note	The Group 2024 $'000	The Group 2023 $'000
Revenue	4	**2,794,764**	2,681,701
Cost of sales		**(1,680,135)**	(1,625,839)
Gross profit		**1,114,629**	1,055,862
Other income			
– Finance income	4	**53,933**	37,271
– Miscellaneous income	4	**19,666**	16,499
Expenses			
– Marketing and distribution		**(126,339)**	(115,125)
– Administrative		**(163,012)**	(158,566)
– Finance	7	**(204,069)**	(200,396)
– Other operating			
• Impairment loss on financial assets		**(2,171)**	(5,363)
• Others		**(154,415)**	(145,020)
Share of profit/(loss) of associated companies		**1,614**	(10,942)
Share of (loss)/profit of joint venture companies		**(6,059)**	898
		533,777	475,118
Other gains	8	**38,912**	452,653
Fair value gains on investment properties	20	**45,396**	20,201
Profit before income tax		**618,065**	947,972
Income tax expense	9(a)	**(94,969)**	(85,499)
Net profit		**523,116**	862,473
Net profit attributable to:			
Equity holders of the Company		**358,185**	707,708
Non-controlling interests		**164,931**	154,765
		523,116	862,473
Earnings per share attributable to equity holders of the Company (expressed in cents per share)	10		
– Basic		**42.39**	83.76
– Diluted		**42.39**	83.76

The accompanying notes form an integral part of these financial statements.

FIGURE 6.3   Comparison of 2024 annual report income statements of City Developments Limited (CDL) and UOL Group (UOL).

[a]*Source:* Annual Report 2024, p. 92. Available at https://ir.cdl.com.sg/annual-reports-agm/annual-reports

[b]*Source:* 2024 Annual Report, p. 109. Available at https://www.uol.com.sg/investors-and-media/annual-reports/

City Development Limited (CDL)[a]

UOL Group (UOL)[b]

FIGURE 6.4 Comparison of "Contents" of 2024 annual sustainability reports of City Developments Limited (CDL) and UOL Group (UOL).

[a]*Source:* Sustainability Report 2024, (p. 2). Available at https://www.uol.com.sg/sustainability/all-reports/
[b]*Source:* https://www.uol.com.sg/wp-content/uploads/uol-reports/files/UOL_Group_Sustainability_Report_FY2024.pdf (p. 3).

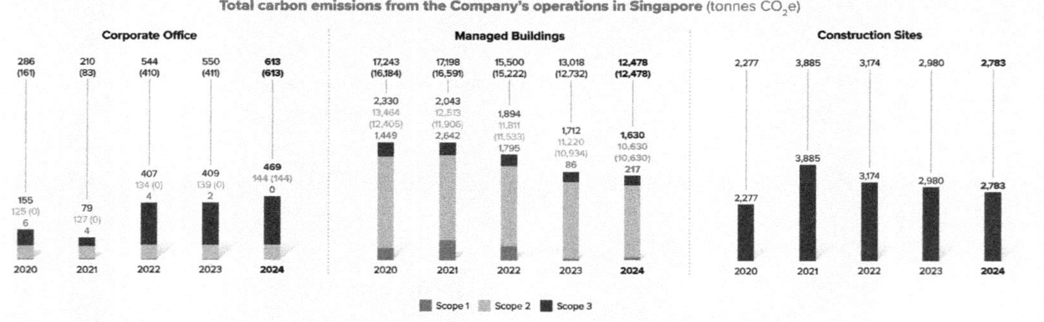

CARBON REDUCTION STRATEGY AND PERFORMANCE

Total carbon emissions from the Company's operations in Singapore (tonnes CO_2e)

Corporate Office

	2020	2021	2022	2023	2024
Total	286 (161)	210 (83)	544 (410)	550 (411)	**613 (613)**
	155 125 (0) 6	79 127 (0) 4	407 134 (0) 4	409 139 (0) 2	469 144 (144) 0

Managed Buildings

	2020	2021	2022	2023	2024
Total	17,243 (16,184)	17,198 (16,591)	15,500 (15,222)	13,018 (12,732)	**12,478 (12,478)**
	2,330 13,464 (12,405) 1,449	2,043 12,513 (11,906) 2,642	1,894 11,811 (11,533) 1,795	1,712 11,220 (10,934) 86	**1,630** 10,630 (10,630) 217

Construction Sites

	2020	2021	2022	2023	2024
	2,277	3,885	3,174	2,980	**2,783**

Scope 1   Scope 2   Scope 3

- **Scope 1** includes direct emissions from fuel used in power generators, petrol for company vehicles, loss of refrigerant in air-conditioning systems, loss of insulating and arc quenching media in switchgear systems and discharge of fire suppression agents.
- **Scope 2** includes indirect emissions from purchased electricity consumed by the operational activities of the Company at both our corporate office and managed buildings.
- **Scope 3** includes emissions arising from property development operational activities (e.g., fuel used in power generators and heavy vehicles, purchased electricity, electricity upstream emissions and transmission losses, and water usage), and other indirect emissions (e.g. electricity upstream emissions, distribution and transmission losses, local and international courier services, employee commute, business air travel (excluding the influence of radiative forcing) and hotel accommodations, water usage at corporate office and managed buildings).

Notes (applicable throughout this chapter):
- The Company's operations in Singapore refers to Corporate Office, Managed Buildings and Construction Sites. They exclude hotel properties.
- In line with our International Sustainability Standards Board (ISSB) alignment efforts, we are progressively expanding our data coverage, including wholly owned or managed overseas operations. For details specific to CDL Group's overseas assets, please refer to the Key Performance Summary.
- Figures stated in charts may not add up due to rounding of decimals.
- In accordance with GHG Protocol, Scope 2 emissions are calculated using both location-based and market-based methods. The figures shown in brackets represent calculations using a market-based method and include the reduction in emissions from the purchase of RECs.
  - **Corporate Office:** The Company's Corporate Office in Singapore occupied approximately 5,025m² across four floors in Republic Plaza. The measurement applies to all environmental performance reported in this chapter.
  - **Managed Buildings:** In 2024, the Company managed four office buildings, two retail buildings and two industrial buildings in Singapore, with an average monthly net lettable area of 104,880m², 43,641m² and 23,190m² respectively. The measurement applies to GHG calculations, with all other environmental performances reported using the net lettable area.
  - **Construction Sites:** In 2024, the Company measured and monitored the environmental impact and performance of nine active construction sites in Singapore with a GFA of 110,740m² built for that year. The measurement applies to all environmental performance reported in this chapter.

CITY DEVELOPMENTS LIMITED
INTEGRATED SUSTAINABILITY REPORT 2025 (18ᵗʰ Edition)

74

FIGURE 6.5   Greenhouse gas (GHG) emissions information in section "Carbon Reduction Strategy and Performance" (p. 73) of 2024 annual report of City Developments Limited (CDL).
Source: https://cdlsustainability.com/pdf/CDL_ISR_2025.pdf (p. 73).

The figure reproduces a page (p. 182) from an external report:

BREAKDOWN OF ENVIRONMENTAL PERFORMANCE IN 2024

GHG Emissions Performance from CDL's Construction Sites

Project size	Number of projects	Site bid price ($mil)	Manhours worked (hr)	GHG emissions (tCO$_2$e)	GHG intensity (kgCO$_2$e/$mil/year)	GHG intensity (kgCO$_2$e/hr/year)
GFA <80,000m²	9	5,589	10,701,912	2,783	497.98	0.26

GHG Emissions Performance from CDL's Managed Buildings

Type of building	Number of buildings	Floor area (m²)	Scope 1	Scope 2 Location-based	Scope 2 Market-based	Scope 3	Total Location-based	Total Market-based	GHG intensity (kgCO$_2$e/m²/year) Location-based	GHG intensity (kgCO$_2$e/m²/year) Market-based
Office	4	104,880	0	6,068	6,068	918	6,986	6,986	66.61	66.61
Retail	2	43,641	217	4,520	4,520	703	5,440	5,440	124.66	124.66
Industrial	2	23,190	0	43	43	9	51	51	2.21	2.21
Total	8	171,711	217	10,630	10,630	1,630	12,478	12,478	72.67	72.67

Energy and Water Performance from CDL's Managed Buildings

Type of building	Number of buildings	Floor area (m²)	Energy Consumption (kWh)	Energy intensity (kWh/m²/year)	Potable water Consumption (m³)	Water intensity (m³/m²/year)	NEWater Consumption (m³)	Water intensity (m³/m²/year)
Office	4	104,880	14,729,207	140.44	87,913	0.84	46661	0.42
Retail	2	43,641	11,022,233	252.57	98,560	2.26	0	0.00
Industrial	2	23,190	103691	4.47	4,186	0.18	0	0.00
Total	12	171,711	25,855,132	150.57	190,659	1.11	46,661	0.27

CITY DEVELOPMENTS LIMITED
INTEGRATED SUSTAINABILITY REPORT 2025 (18ᵗʰ Edition)

182

FIGURE 6.6 Greenhouse gas (GHG) emissions information in Annex: "Breakdown of Environmental Performance in 2023" (p. 182) of 2024 annual report of City Developments Limited (CDL).
Source: https://cdlsustainability.com/pdf/CDL_ISR_2025.pdf (p. 182)

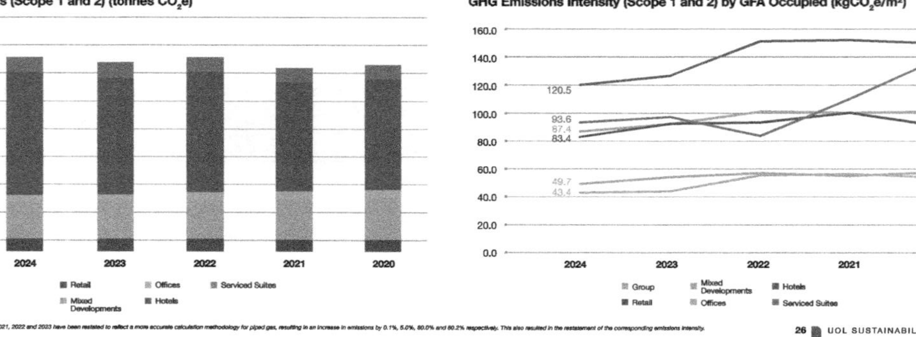

FIGURE 6.7   Greenhouse gas (GHG) emissions information in section "GHG Emissions" (p. 26) of 2024 annual sustainability report of UOL Group (UOL).
Source: Sustainability Report 2024, p26. Available at https://www.uol.com.sg/sustainability/all-reports/

SUSTAINABILITY REPORTING: INTERVIEW WITH MICHAEL TANG, SGX

In conversation with James Cheo

James
Can you breakdown the sustainability reporting framework?

Michael
There are a few components of sustainability reporting. First, there are ESG [environmental, social, and governance] factors that the company is looking at. The ESG factors should be derived after a series of stakeholder engagement[s] by the company to determine which ESG factors are most relevant or appropriate for its business. From environmental factors like greenhouse gas emissions, energy usage, water usage, and waste management, to social factors like labor practices and human rights, to governance issues. For now, while we encourage companies to report a set of core ESG metrics that is commonly reported, there is no prescription to say that all companies must report this fixed set of ESG metrics. The report should also contain an elaboration by the company of what's most material for them.

The second component will be the companies' performance against the chosen ESG metrics and what they're doing in terms of the policies, practices, and performance related to these ESG factors. If the company decided that waste management is one of the key factors that they [are] tracking as a company, then how is the company performing, in terms of your waste discharge, how is the company dealing with the waste, etc., and, ultimately, what sort of policies are implemented to manage waste?

The third component is targets that the company has set for each of these ESG factors; targets or KPIs [key performance indicators] on energy usage for this year, and the next five years, for example.

The fourth component is a set of reporting standards or framework to guide your reporting. There are many sustainability reporting standards. In Asia, the most well-used set of standards is the Global Reporting Initiative (GRI), but for specific industries, companies may decide that they want to add on more industry-specific frameworks. For example, in the palm-oil industry the Roundtable on Sustainable Palm Oil has additional requirements. For the choice of frameworks or standards, the company can use them with an explanation of why they've chosen to use these frameworks.

(Continued)

> *(Continued)*
>
> Finally, what's required from companies is a statement from the Board, on how the Board has overseen the sustainability issues and what is the management's role in dealing with these issues. This is to put the responsibility for sustainability on the Board of Directors, who will then be able to set the appropriate governance structure frameworks, KPIs, and incentives to achieve these targets.

SUMMARY

Since 1997, organizations have been pushing for companies to measure and disclose more information about their sustainability performance. From the formation of GRI to the recent launch of ISSB, the industry draws ever closer to a single accepted framework and set of standards for reporting. With experience, the industry has incorporated the concept of materiality from financial accounting as a means of focusing on the most important issues from the long and growing list of sustainability measures. And as we will explore in Part Four, measurement and disclosure of material sustainability information is a critical input to many investment processes.

Yet, increasing focus and clarity does not mean that all firms will report the same information and in the same way. Companies retain considerable flexibility in how they organize their sustainability reports and even some flexibility in what data they report; this is not altogether different from financial reporting, so we should not be too surprised. But we should be clear that if more consistent measurement and disclosure is a priority, government and regulatory action will be required. This will be discussed in Chapter 8.

Financing Sustainability: Green, Social, and Sustainability Bonds and Other Instruments

Measurement and disclosure of sustainability performance, described in Chapter 6, is a critical first step. After all, as the popular expression goes, "treasure what you measure." But measurement is only the first step; the act of measurement itself doesn't make a firm more sustainable. Once a company fully develops its measurement capabilities and identifies a sustainability-related risk or opportunity to address, the firm will likely need to make some kind of investment. For example, it may need to upgrade its equipment, change operational processes, hire and/or train new employees. All of these changes require capital.

Corporate investment is an ever-present issue in business. Before the concept of "ESG" (environmental, social, and governance issues), before Milton Friedman's shareholder value maximization theory, companies that wanted to grow or change their practices needed money to invest. Adding sustainability concerns to the list of possible investments just makes the list longer. However, because the world needs companies to improve their relationships with people and planet, the finance industry has created new instruments that firms can use for sustainability-related investments. This chapter begins with a recap of corporate financing, followed by a review of financing instruments that have been built specifically for sustainability investments.

CORPORATE FINANCING

Imagine you own a business in Vietnam that makes performance T-shirts as part of the supply chain for a global brand. Your facilities receive the raw fabric from another supplier and, through a combination of specialized machinery and well-trained labor, transform that fabric into a finished T-shirt. It's a low-margin business (the brands ultimately have control over most of the decisions) but you are profitable enough to provide decent jobs and wages. One day your customer (the brand) tells you that it needs you to reduce your greenhouse gas emissions by 20% in the next three years or it will move its business to one of your competitors who can. To meet this demand will require an investment of hundreds of thousands of dollars in new, energy-efficient equipment. Will you make the investment? How will you decide?

This decision is part of the world of corporate finance, specifically capital budgeting and financing. Many textbooks have been written on the topic, and a detailed analysis is beyond the scope of this text. However, the following discussion of financing instruments is more meaningful with a solid foundation in corporate finance. To that end consider the typical steps in the budgeting and financing process.

Identify Project Financials

The first step is to understand the costs and benefits of the project under consideration. Typically, this is measured through a series of cash flows, both expenses and revenues, over time. In the T-shirt manufacturing example above, the firm might spend $100 in year 1 to meet its emissions reduction targets; as a result, its customer might increase its business by $25 per year, leading to a breakeven after four years.

Assess the Attractiveness of the Project

Using cash flow projections, the firm can calculate the *net present value* (NPV) of this investment. If the NPV is positive, the firm should decide to make the investment.

Obtain Financing for the Project

Once the firm decides to pursue a project, it needs to arrange financing. Typically, companies choose between a range of different financing options:

- Internal financing using funds generated by the ongoing business of the firm, e.g., retained earnings. When a firm has strong cash flows this may be the preferred means of financing because it doesn't incur incremental expenses or changes to the ownership of the firm.
- External financing through debt instruments, i.e., borrowing money with a promise to repay with interest over an agreed-upon time frame. The most common forms of short-term debt—bank loans, lines of credit, commercial paper—differ slightly in structure and purpose.

Long-term debt, e.g., bonds and term loans, can be either public or private and vary widely in duration and structure. In all cases, excessive use of debt can leave a company struggling to meet its repayment obligations ("credit risk").

■ Equity financing involves raising capital by selling an ownership stake in the firm. No repayment or interest payments are required, but buying an ownership interest is riskier for investors and therefore more expensive for the firm.

A final important concept at the center of corporate finance decisions is the relationship between the project NPV, the cost of capital, and the so-called "hurdle rate." When calculating the NPV of a project it is important to account for the cost of obtaining funds for the project. All else being equal, a firm would prefer to minimize its financing costs. Larger, more stable firms will enjoy lower costs of capital than smaller, less stable firms; in the same way the cost of capital will be lower in developed markets than emerging markets.[1] A robust NPV calculation will incorporate the expected cost of capital under different financing scenarios.

Remember that NPV is a measure of the absolute profitability of a project over some time period. While this is certainly a useful figure, many companies need to evaluate projects of different sizes and time horizons; absolute profitability is often complemented by a measure of return on investment called "internal rate of return" or IRR. While there are many worthy criticisms of IRR, it remains a widespread and useful tool for corporate decision-making, especially since IRR is easy to compare to a company's minimum acceptable rate of return, or the hurdle rate. To see how these concepts fit together, consider a company choosing between four different projects with a discount rate of 8% and a minimum IRR (hurdle rate) of 10% (Table 7.1):

TABLE 7.1　Comparison of Corporate Finance Concepts

	Project A	Project B	Project C	Project D
Initial investment ($)	1,000	1,000	1,000	400
Y1 ($)	200	400	500	200
Y2 ($)	300	400	500	200
Y3 ($)	400	400	300	150
Net present value (NPV) @ 8%	−128.86	32.47	121.63	48.65
Internal rate of return (IRR) @ 10%	–	9.7	18.9	25.4

Source: Generated using Claude.[2]

Project A has a negative NPV, so clearly the firm will ignore this project, but the other three projects have positive NPVs. In theory, the firm should pursue all positive-NPV projects. However, most companies have a finite investment budget so choosing between Projects B, C, and D may involve trade-offs. Project B is profitable but doesn't meet the hurdle rate requirement. Projects C and D are both profitable and clear the hurdle rate, but Project C creates more absolute value for the firm so it may be chosen first. If the investment budget is smaller, however, Project D becomes an attractive option as well.

SUSTAINABLE FINANCE FRAMEWORK

When a company adds a sustainability dimension to its projects, there are several important implications for the corporate financing process if it raises external capital. First, the project must be sustainable "enough" satisfy both company management and the providers of external capital. Second, the process by which projects are proposed and selected should be disclosed to third parties of interest (e.g., banks, investors). Third, companies should be clear about what happens with the financing received—were the funds used for the sustainability project or something else? And finally, the company should engage a third party to provide assurance that the firm did everything it said it would do. None of these are essential components of self-funding, or indeed of external financing *without* a sustainability component; these issues are most important when the financing is going to be used for sustainability-related projects.

The extra dimension of sustainability presents a new list of things that could go wrong, e.g., the firm says it wants the money to install solar panels but buys a corporate chalet in the Swiss Alps instead. To minimize the risk of financial mishap or malfeasance, the International Capital Market Association (ICMA) maintains a list of principles firms should follow when engaging in a sustainable financing transaction. The principles are voluntary but represent best practices to promote integrity in this growing and important market. The core principles mirror the implications described above:

1. use of proceeds;
2. process for project evaluation and selection;
3. management of proceeds;
4. reporting.

Additionally, there are two further recommendations to promote greater transparency:

(i) [sustainable finance] frameworks;
(ii) external reviews.[3]

By now, the reader should have a basic grasp of core principles 1–4; the sustainable finance framework, however, is a new concept that merits some explanation. The framework serves as a one-stop shop for investors wishing to learn about the firm's approach to sustainable financing transactions.[4] It should clearly summarize the firm's sustainability strategy, the types of projects that the firm might consider for financing, and how the firm aligns with the four core principles. By including external assurance of the framework—point (ii) above—the principles improve investor confidence in the integrity of sustainability-related financing transactions.

SUSTAINABILITY-RELATED BONDS

One of the most prevalent types of sustainability financing instruments is a bond. This should come as no surprise, since bonds are among the most common forms of financing overall for companies, as well as countries (both are known as "issuers"). Like a loan, bonds represent a promise to repay the capital at the end of the term, plus any stipulated interest payments along the way. Large issuers will often have multiple bonds outstanding across different sizes, durations, and currencies at any point in time. The interest rate paid is related both to the interest rate environment at the time of issue, plus an adjustment for the credit risk of the issuer.

Companies issue bonds to meet a variety of financing needs—called "use of proceeds"—ranging from the specific (e.g., to pay for an acquisition) to the more general ("general corporate purposes"). Within the context of sustainable financing, however, the instruments themselves have different structures and may be applied to different investments.

Use-of-Proceeds Bonds: Green, Social, and Sustainability

The origin story of sustainability-related use-of-proceeds bonds predates the 2008 Global Financial Crisis. In 2006, the International Finance Facility for Immunization (IFFIM) raised US\$1 billion in what became the first social bond; proceeds were used to fund an immunization program for children in the poorest countries. The first use-of-proceeds bond specifically for environmental purposes was issued by the European Investment Bank (EIB) in 2007. The "Climate Awareness Bond" raised €600 million in a five-year note to support investments in renewable energy and energy efficiency.

Over the following five years, the so-called "green bond" space started gathering momentum. Other multinational development banks, like the World Bank and the African Development Bank, issued their own bonds with use of proceeds designated for "green" projects. Nikko Asset Management launched the first green bond fund in 2010, and the first corporates, such as Bank of America Merrill Lynch, issued green bonds in 2013.

With this increase in activity, market participants recognized the need to start building principles for what qualified to be called a green bond. In 2014, a group of investment banks worked together with ICMA to launch the first set of green bond principles: proceeds should be used for projects that meet certain "green" criteria; a disclosed process for project identification and selection; transparent management of proceeds; and annual reporting on the use of funds. Importantly, the work of the group led to the creation of activity-level standards for "climate bond" certification, building the foundation for technical screening criteria and taxonomies that emerged in 2020.

As of the mid-2020s, there are many different "flavors" of use-of-proceeds bonds. The most common is still green bonds, but there are also social bonds and sustainability bonds (which address both green and social projects). Collectively, they are referred to as "GSS" bonds. According to Climate Bonds Initiative (CBI), as of year-end 2024, cumulative issuance of GSS bonds exceeds US$6.9 trillion, of which US$5.6 trillion is considered "aligned" with the CBI guidelines (Table 7.2). This activity is based on over 54,000 aligned issuances since 2007.

The market grew rapidly during and after the COVID-19 pandemic, albeit unevenly (Figure 7.1). The clear leader before 2020, green bond issuance enjoyed a step-change of sorts, increasing from under US$200 billion per year to roughly US$600 billion per year by 2021. The largest changes were in the issuance of social and sustainability bonds. Social bonds were widely used during 2020 and 2021 to help provide a safety net of benefits during those difficult years; from *de minimis* levels of issuance pre-2020, annual social bond issuance reached approximately US$300 billion in 2020 and has stayed above or near US$200 billion per year through 2024. Sustainability bonds also grew in popularity during this time and have remained at or near US$200 billion annual issuance through 2024.

With all this issuance, there are some sensible questions to consider. How do green bonds compare with traditional (also known as "vanilla")

TABLE 7.2   Aligned Green, Social, and Sustainability Bonds Scorecard, 2024

	Green	Social	Sustainability
Total size of market (cumulative)	US$3.5 trillion	US$1.1 trillion	US$998 billion
# of countries	98	53	75
# of currencies	60	48	44

Source: Modified from with Climate Bonds Initiative, https://www.climatebonds.net/files/documents/publications/Climate-Bonds-Initiative_Global-State-of-the-Market-Report_May-2025_2025-06-18-123430_mejk.pdf / last accessed Aug 20, 2025.

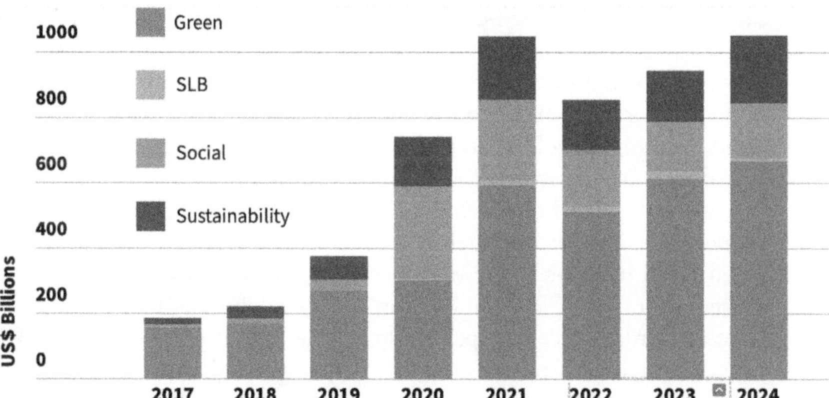

FIGURE 7.1　Aligned green, social, and sustainability bond issuance increased to US$1.05 trillion in 2024 (SLB = sustainability-linked bond).
Source: Climate Bonds Initiative / https://www.climatebonds.net/files/documents/publications/Climate-Bonds-Initiative_Global-State-of-the-Market-Report_May-2025_2025-06-18-123430_mejk.pdf / last accessed Aug 20, 2025.

nongreen bonds?[5] Why would companies choose to issue a sustainability bond instead of a vanilla bond? Why do investors buy green bonds? And do green bonds really make a difference? Researchers from academia and industry have considered these questions from multiple perspectives:

- **Risk.** Credit risk for a bond is typically assessed at the issuer level, i.e., whatever entity is obligated to make interest payments. Green and nongreen bonds are both issued by the "company" and should therefore have the same risk. Interestingly, research has identified an underlying relationship between ESG issues and credit risk with the potential to affect green and non-green corporate borrowing. A 2019 paper by Henisz and McGlinch[6] summarizes and extends this research, presenting recent examples of how ESG and credit risk can be linked.
- **Expense.** It costs money for a firm to issue a bond. In addition to the costs typically associated with issuing a nongreen bond, issuers of green bonds incur extra expenses to monitor and report on use of proceeds.
- **Pricing.** If green and vanilla bonds have the same credit risk, then *ceteris paribus* the prices of equivalent[7] green and vanilla bonds should be the same. In fact, for a period of time, many companies were able to issue green bonds at a slightly lower interest rate, a saving in interest expense over the life of the bond. This premium (good for the company)—referred to as a "greenium" for green bonds—has become less common over time, in part because the greenium may have been associated with a temporary supply–demand imbalance. As more

capital flowed into green-oriented fixed income mutual funds, the fresh capital was competing for a finite number of green bonds. Once the supply of green bonds caught up to demand, the greenium disappeared.[8]

- **Impact.** There is more than one way to measure the impact of a green bond. At a high level, one recent study found that the *first* green bond issued by a company is associated with subsequent reduction in absolute emissions and improvements in sustainability risk.[9] There remains a question about how much of those effects are attributable to the green bond itself; in other words, would the company have achieved those results even without issuing the green bond? To address this concern, a more recent paper analyzed the "novelty" of projects associated with US corporate and municipal green bonds. The authors found that ". . . the vast majority of green bond proceeds is used for refinancing ordinary debt, continuing ongoing projects, or initiating projects without green aspects that are novel for the issuer. Only 2% of corporate and municipal green bond proceeds initiate projects with clearly novel green features."[10] The degree to which GSS bonds are susceptible to greenwashing is explored further in Chapter 8.

Sustainability-Linked Bonds

A more recent financing innovation is called a "sustainability-linked" bond (SLB). In an SLB structure the proceeds are fungible, in contrast with the use-of-proceeds requirement found in green, social, and sustainability bonds. The defining feature of an SLB is the relationship between key performance indicators (KPIs), sustainability performance targets (SPTs), and the interest rate paid to investors:

- The company selects some sustainability-related KPIs, hopefully ones that are material to the firm.
- After selecting the KPIs, the firm sets targets (SPTs) for each of the KPIs and a future date when performance will be measured.
- Finally, the company decides in advance how it will adjust the interest rate paid to investors depending on whether it meets or misses the SPTs.

Conceptually, the interest rate change could be a step-up or step-down (or both), as represented in Figure 7.2.

According to Bloomberg, the first sustainability-linked bond was issued by Beijing Infrastructure Investment Corporation Limited in 2018. Since then, the market has grown quickly but remains small: through December 2024, 1,048 SLBs have been issued totaling US$331.9 billion. Of this amount, only 136 bonds are aligned with the Paris Agreement; 413 SLBs

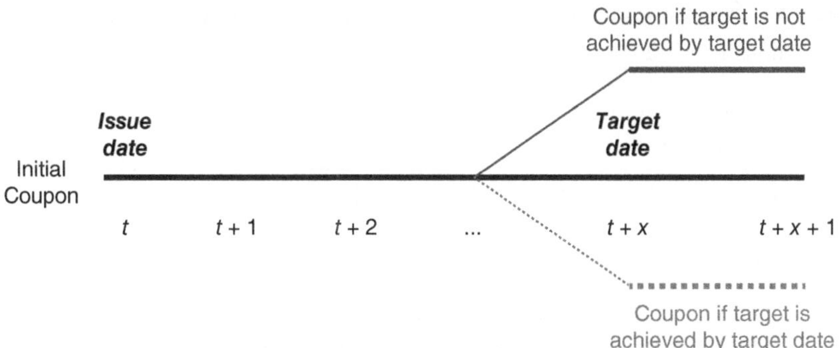

FIGURE 7.2　Interest rate: step-up or step-down.
Source: Kölbel, J. F et al, (2022) / with permission of Elsevier.

don't have any emissions-related targets at all.[11] SLBs are a new and relatively niche instrument—remember, total green bond issuance is in excess of *US$5 trillion.*

An interesting example of SLBs is a bond issued in 2021 by Thai Union, one of the world's largest seafood companies. The THB5 billion seven-year senior, unsecured SLB carries an interest rate of 2.47% per annum. The original size was THB4 billion, but due to high demand (2.23x oversubscribed) the firm increased the offering to THB 5 billion. The firm used the following combination of KPIs/SPTs[12]:

- Remaining in the Dow Jones Sustainability Index (DJSI) Emerging Markets and ranking in the top 10 companies for the DJSI Food Products Industry Index.
- Reducing Thai Union's Scope 1 and Scope 2 carbon emissions from manufacturing operations by 4% annually (carbon intensity) from a 2019 baseline.
- Increasing the monitoring and surveillance of Thai Union's wild-caught tuna supply chains, whether electronically and/or through the use of human observers at sea, from 71% in 2021 to 100% by 2025.

It takes some digging to find the SPTs, especially since the public documentation is only available in Thai as of this writing. Following the source link for Table 7.3, the first document in the table says "fact sheet" in English. The configuration of interest rate adjustments is unusual in that Thai Union used both a step-up *and* a step-down adjustment depending on whether the company misses or meets its SPTs.

TABLE 7.3　Configuration of Interest Rate Adjustments for Thai Union Key Performance Indicators (KPIs)/Sustainability Performance Targets (SPTs)

Key Performance Indicator (KPI)/Sustainability Performance Target (SPT)	If Missed	If Met
Dow Jones Sustainability Index (DJSI) membership	+4bps	−4bps
Carbon emissions intensity	+4bps	−4bps
100% supervised tuna	+2bps	−2bps

Source: The Securities and Exchange Commission / https://market.sec.or.th/public/ipos/IPOSDE01.aspx?TransID=344650&SD=1907256419072564?lang=en / last accessed Aug 20, 2025.

In addition, the incentives/penalties are calculated for each individual SPT, meaning that the firm could have a net step-up or step-down of as little as two basis points. Even if, like the authors, your Thai is "a little rusty," the structure is readily apparent from a table on page 3 of the fact sheet (Figure 7.3).

Compared with use-of-proceeds bonds, sustainability-linked bonds offer several attractive features for issuers, the most salient of which is the fungibility of proceeds. Under an SLB structure, the firm is not required to dedicate the proceeds to projects that are aligned with sustainability goals. Issuers can use the proceeds from the SLB to buy a corporate jet or anything else they want to do, because the sustainability attributes are tied to the KPIs

ลักษณะพิเศษและความเสี่ยงสำคัญของหุ้นกู้

-　ลักษณะอัตราดอกเบี้ย: ผู้ลงทุนมีโอกาสได้รับดอกเบี้ยลดลงเมื่อผู้ออกหุ้นกู้ประสบความสำเร็จในการดำเนินงานตาม SPT 1 และ/หรือ SPT 2 และ/หรือ SPT 3 และมีโอกาสได้รับดอกเบี้ยเพิ่มขึ้นเมื่อผู้ออกหุ้นกู้ไม่ประสบความสำเร็จในการดำเนินงานตาม SPT 1 และ/หรือ SPT 2 และ/หรือ SPT 3 โดยจำนวนอัตราที่จะถูกปรับขึ้นหรือลงดังกล่าวข้างต้น สำหรับตัวชี้วัดและเป้าหมายความยั่งยืนแต่ละด้าน มีดังนี้

กรณี	การคำนวณ	การเพิ่มขึ้น / ลดลงของอัตราดอกเบี้ย
SPT ทั้งหมด สำเร็จ	-0.02% - 0.04% -0.04%	-0.10%
SPT 2 และ **SPT 3** สำเร็จ	+0.02% - 0.04% -0.04%	-0.06%
SPT 1 และ **SPT 2** หรือ **SPT 1**และ **SPT 3** สำเร็จ	-0.02% - 0.04% +0.04%	-0.02%
SPT 2 สำเร็จ หรือ **SPT 3** สำเร็จ	+0.02% - 0.04% +0.04%	+0.02%
SPT 1 สำเร็จ	-0.02% + 0.04% +0.04%	+0.06%
SPT ทั้งหมด ไม่สำเร็จ	+0.02% + 0.04% +0.04%	+0.10%

FIGURE 7.3　Effects of incentives and penalties on sustainability performance targets (SPTs).
Source: Thai Union fact sheet, p. 3.

and SPTs. Importantly, the issuer controls the selection of its KPIs and targets and sets its own step-up or step-down to be used as a penalty or incentive (or as in the case of Thai Union, both). Unfortunately, as we will see in the next chapter, this flexibility can be misused to give the appearance of caring about sustainability with questionable real-world benefits for people or planet.[13]

Transition and Adaptation Bonds

Much of the attention paid to sustainable finance centers around emissions *mitigation* through investments that are demonstrably green such as renewable energy.[14] For many industries and countries, however, the issues take on a different character: *transition* and *adaptation*.

Transition Finance   Transition finance is designed to help high-emission sectors reduce their emissions over time, while recognizing that these industries (e.g., aviation, cement, steel) may not have net zero-aligned technology solutions available today. Examples include sustainable aviation fuel and low-clinker cement—both lead to lower emissions but are not net zero-aligned.

One of the major challenges to transition finance is determining what exactly qualifies as transition. Conceptually, we might think of automobile transportation as an example. Along the continuum from internal combustion engines ("brown") to fully electric vehicles ("green") is the plug-in hybrid vehicle—not completely green, but a lot better than petrol-burning cars. Even plug-in hybrids have some level of GHGs, however, leading us to question what level of emissions is eligible for transition financing?

This question has no globally accepted answer yet; as we will see in Chapter 8 the answer varies by jurisdiction.[15] In the meantime, some bonds have already been issued as "transition bonds,"[16] including:

- Hong Kong utility company Castle Peak's US$500 million transition bond (2017).
- European Bank for Reconstruction and Development's €216.6 million transition bond (2021).
- Mitsubishi Heavy Industries (MHI) Group's JPY10 billion five-year transition bond (2022).
- Japan's JPY1.6 trillion sovereign Climate Transition Bond (2024).

Until clear, transparent criteria for transition finance are available, this market may struggle to further scale.

Adaptation Finance   Adaptation finance refers to funding that helps countries, states, and municipalities adapt to the impacts of climate change. This stands in stark contrast to green bonds' focus on *mitigation*, i.e., emission reduction. Adaptation projects[17] can take many forms, including:

- strengthening early warning systems;
- making new infrastructure resilient;
- improving dryland agriculture crop production;
- protecting mangroves;
- making water resources management more resilient.

If many of these seem like "normal" government projects, that's part of the challenge: how to define adaptation finance so that it is clearly differentiated from other types of financing and for projects with clear adaptation benefits. The need is great, especially in developing countries with less robust infrastructure. A 2024 United Nations Environment Programme (UNEP) report indicated an *annual* financing gap of approximately US\$187–359 *billion*.[18] And while much of the onus falls on governments, the private sector has a clear stake in adaptation. Unlike public funding, however, which can be systematically reported, private investment in adaptation often lacks centralized accounting, complicating efforts to gauge the full extent of adaptation finance available to developing countries.

The potential benefits from adaptation are significant and extend well beyond the direct project impact. Following a concept called "triple dividend of resilience" (TDR), in 2019, a report by the Global Council on Adaptation and World Resources Institute (WRI) described how adaptation investments yield three distinct potential dividends (Table 7.4).

A more recent report[19] by the WRI built a dataset of 320 adaptation investments by multilateral development banks (MDBs) from 2014 to 2024. They evaluated these investments using the TDR approach and found attractive IRRs—median in excess of 25%—and a roughly 10:1 return on investments over a 10-year period. Table 7.5, an excerpt from the report appendix, gives a good sense for what's possible with data from two water-related adaptation investments, one from China and the other from Brazil.

Conservation Finance

The fundamental premise underlying conservation finance is that natural ecosystems provide valuable services (e.g., healthy soil, abundant water, biodiversity) that justify economic investment. To this end, conservation finance

TABLE 7.4 The Triple Dividend in Action

Dividend	Example
Avoided losses	Early warning systems (EWS) save lives and assets worth at least 10 times their cost. Just 24 hours warning of a coming storm or heat wave can cut the ensuing damage by 30%.
Economic benefits	Drip irrigation technologies developed for water scarcity are now used widely because they lead to higher crop productivity than traditional irrigation systems.
Social and environmental benefits	Mangrove forests provide over US$80 billion per year in avoided losses from coastal flooding and protect over 18 million people. They contribute US$40–50 billion yearly in nonmarket benefits in fisheries, forestry, and recreation.

Source: Adapted from / https://gca.org/wp-content/uploads/2019/09/GlobalCommis sion_Report_FINAL.pdf.

includes financial mechanisms that generate funding for environmental protection, restoration, and sustainable management of natural resources. Among these mechanisms, blue bonds and debt-for-nature swaps represent two of the most significant developments in conservation finance, offering creative solutions to bridge the gap between environmental necessity and economic reality.

Blue Bonds Blue bonds provide funding for projects that benefit marine and coastal ecosystems, similar to green bonds but with a marine focus. Typically, the structure involves a government, development bank, or corporation issuing debt securities to investors with the commitment that all proceeds will fund qualifying blue projects. These projects must demonstrate clear benefits for marine ecosystems, such as reducing marine pollution, protecting coastal habitats, or supporting sustainable fisheries. The purpose of the bond is directly linked to the United Nations Sustainable Development Goal (SDG) frameworks, particularly SDG6 (clean water and sanitation) and SDG14 (life below water).[21]

The blue bond market has reached US$7.2 billion as of July 2024. Several notable blue bond issuances have established important precedents in this nascent market. The Republic of Seychelles issued the world's first sovereign blue bond in 2018, raising US$15 million to support marine protected areas and sustainable fisheries. Subsequently, larger issuances from

TABLE 7.5   Climate Adaptation Investment Cases

Subsector	Project Title	Discount Rate (%)	Number of Quantified Dividends	Dividend	Benefit	Value (Millions)	NPV (Millions)	BCR	EIRA (%)
Water Resources and Flood Management	Shanxi Urban-Rural Water Source Protection and Environmental Demonstration Project	Not provided	3	Avoided Losses	Reduced flood-related damage from better management	$94.16	$67.89	Not provided	17.9
				Induced Economic Benefits	Improved transportation	$27.10			
				Social and Environmental Benefits	Improved water supply and wastewater treatment	$2.28			
				Social and Environmental Benefits	Improved surface water quality				

Subsector	Project Title	Discount Rate (%)	Number of Quantified Dividends	Dividend	Benefit	Value (Millions)	NPV (Millions)	BCR	EIRA (%)
Water Supply and Sanitation	Paraiba improving water resources management and services provision project	10	1	Avoided Losses	Benefits of increased resilience water to scarcity	Not provided	$282.10	1.88	19.9
				Induced Economic Benefits	Improved water resources availability, management, and allocations	Not provided			
				Induced Economic Benefits	Avoided off-peak pumping costs	Not provided			
				Induced Economic Benefits	Energy savings, pollution reduction and *reduction in losses*	Not provided			
				Social and Environmental Benefits	GHG emissions reductions of −27,846 tCO2-eq per year	$4.00			

Source: Adapted from / https://www.wri.org/research/climate-adaptation-investment-case, Figure A-3.[20]

countries around the world have followed, including bonds from Barbados, Belize, Ecuador, and Indonesia. Development finance institutions, impact investors, and commercial banks have emerged as key purchasers of blue bonds, attracted by the combination of financial returns and measurable environmental impact (Table 7.6).

Debt-for-Nature Swaps Many biodiversity-rich countries face significant debt burdens that constrain their ability to invest in environmental protection. Debt-for-nature swaps represent a fundamentally different approach to conservation finance, involving the restructuring or forgiveness of sovereign debt in exchange for local environmental commitments.

The basic structure of a debt-for-nature swap involves three parties: the debtor country, the creditor (which may be another government, commercial bank, or multilateral institution), and often an intermediary conservation organization. The creditor agrees to cancel or reduce the debt obligation in exchange for the debtor country's commitment to invest a (significant) portion of the interest expense savings in environmental conservation activities within its borders.

These swaps can take different forms. Bilateral swaps occur directly between creditor and debtor governments, with the creditor nation canceling debt in exchange for conservation commitments. Commercial swaps involve conservation organizations purchasing discounted debt from commercial creditors on secondary markets, then negotiating with debtor countries to cancel the debt in exchange for conservation investments.

The conservation commitments resulting from debt-for-nature swaps vary considerably but typically include establishing or expanding protected areas, strengthening environmental institutions, supporting sustainable development in local communities, and implementing forest or marine conservation programs. These commitments are usually structured with specific performance indicators and monitoring mechanisms to ensure compliance.

Several high-profile debt-for-nature swaps have demonstrated the potential scale and impact of this mechanism. Ecuador's recent agreement with international creditors restructured over US\$1.6 billion in debt in exchange for marine conservation commitments around the Galápagos Islands. Belize completed a significant swap that restructured US\$553 million in commercial debt, enabling expanded marine protection covering 30% of the country's ocean territory. At a much smaller scale, in

TABLE 7.6 List of Blue Bond Issuances

#	Release	Issuer	Amount (USD M)	Currency	Redemption	Sources
1	Aug-18	World Bank (IBRD)	95	SEK	7 years	(Rosane 2018; World Bank 2018d, 2018e)
2	Oct-18	Government of Seychelles	15	USD	10 years	(World Bank 2018a, 2018b, 2018c)
3	Jan-19	Nordic Investment Bank	220	SEK	5 years	(NIB 2019b, 2019c, 2021; NIB and SEB 2019)
4	Apr-19	World Bank (IBRD)	10	USD	3 years	(Morgan Stanley 2019; World Bank 2019c)
5	May-19	World Bank (IBRD)	180	EUR	20 years	(Rosane 2018; World Bank 2018d, 2019b)
6	Nov-19	World Bank (IBRD)	29	USD	5 years	(World Bank 2019a)
7	Jan-20	Mowi ASA	220	EUR	5 years	(Mowi 2020a, 2020b, 2020c, 2022)
8	Oct-20	Nordic Investment Bank	150	SEK	5 years	(NIB 2020; NIB et al. 2020)
9	Nov-20	Grieg Seafood–Jun 2020	100	USD	5 years	(CICERO 2020; Grieg Seafood 2020a, 2020b, 2020c, 2020d, 2022)
		Grieg Seafood–Nov 2020	50		5 years	
10	Nov-20	Bank of China–CNH tranche	443	CNH, USD	2 years	(BOC 2020a, 2020b, 2020c; Davis 2020; Ernst & Young 2020, 2022)
		Bank of China–USD tranche	500		3 years	
11	May-21	World Bank (IBRD)	10	USD, COP	5 years	(World Bank 2021a, 2021b, 2021c, 2021d)
12	Jul-21	Seaspan Corp	750	USD	8 years	(Seaspan 2021a, 2021b; Sustainalytics 2021)
13	Sep-21	Asian Development Bank–AUD	151	AUD, NZD	15 years	(Asian Development Bank 2021a, 2021b, 2022a)
		Asian Development Bank–NZD	151		10 years	

(Continued)

TABLE 7.6 (*Continued*)

#	Release	Issuer	Amount (USD M)	Currency	Redemption	Sources
14	Nov-21	IDB Invest	37	AUD	10 years	(IDB 2020, 2021a, 2021b)
15	Nov-21	Government of Belize	365	USD	20 years	(Credit Suisse 2021; TNC 2021a, 2021b)
16	May-22	TMBThanachart Bank	50	USD	5 years	(IFC 2022e; TMBThanachart 2022a, 2022b, 2022c)
17	Jun-22	The Commonwealth of the Bahamas	385	USD	7–14 years	(Government of The Bahamas 2022; IDB 2022a; West 2022)
18	Jun-22	BDO Unibank Philippines	100	USD	7 years	(BDO 2022a, 2022b; IFC 2022b)
19	Oct-22	Government of Barbardos	147	USD	15 years	(Government of Barbados 2022a, 2022b; TNC 2022)
20	Oct-22	IDB Invest	25	AUD	15 years	(IDB 2020, 2022d)
21	Nov-22	People's Government of Hainan Province	167	CNH	2 years	(Credit Agricole 2022; HKSAR Government 2022; Linklaters 2022)
22	Nov-22	Maruha Nichiro Corporation	36	JPY	5 years	(Maruha Nichiro Corporation 2022a, 2022b, 2022c)
23	Nov-22	IDB Invest	34	AUD	20 years	(IDB 2020, 2022c)
24	Nov-22	Banco Internacional	79	USD	4 years	(Banco Internacional 2022; IFC 2022a, 2022d)
25	Nov-22	BRK Ambiental	380	BRL	20 years	(BRK Ambiental 2022a, 2022b; Environmental Finance 2022; Sustainalytics 2022b)
26	Dec-22	CABEI–AUD	21	AUD, JPY	5 years	(CABEI 2022a, 2022b; Sustainalytics 2022a)
		CABEI–JPY	72		5 years	

Source: Bosmans, P et al, 2023 / MDPI / CC BY 4.0.[22]

January 2025, Indonesia completed a US$35 million swap with the United States and nongovernmental funders to protect two high-priority coral reefs:

". . . in place of existing debt commitments, Indonesia will redirect the US$35 million to establish a conservation fund that will issue grants to civil society organizations and support projects designed to restore and maintain the country's reefs. This effort will also benefit the Indigenous Peoples and local communities that rely on healthy coral reef ecosystems for sustenance and livelihoods."[23]

Both blue bonds and debt-for-nature swaps provide mechanisms for mobilizing capital at scales that match environmental challenges, create sustainable funding streams for long-term conservation activities, and establish clear performance frameworks that link financial flows to environmental outcomes. Additionally, these instruments can strengthen local institutions and capacity for environmental management.

However, these mechanisms also face important limitations. Blue bonds require sophisticated capital market infrastructure and regulatory frameworks that may not exist in all jurisdictions. The relatively small size of many blue bond issuances can limit their impact, while the costs of issuance may be prohibitive for smaller projects. Debt-for-nature swaps face challenges related to debt sustainability, ensuring additionality of conservation commitments, and maintaining long-term political commitment to environmental obligations.

LOANS

To this point in the chapter the financing options have been mostly external and public, i.e., bonds issued to the market. As mentioned in the earlier section on "Obtaining Financing for the Project," bank loans and term loans are very common sources of external financing for normal purposes; the same is true for sustainability-related investments. For example, just as ICMA publishes the green *bond* and sustainability-linked *bond* standards, it publishes similar standards for *loans* (green loans, sustainability-linked loans [SLLs]). Also, just like other sustainability-related instruments, SLLs are more expensive to issue than vanilla bank loans.[24]

Since they are often private agreements between the lender (typically, a bank) and borrower (company), the lender and borrower must agree to disclose the ESG-related components of a loan issuance. Unfortunately, the average individual investor will find it difficult to obtain data on bank loans. Two 2025 studies of this market found that (i) issuers that choose *not* to disclose the KPIs and SPTs appear to be greenwashing, with their ESG ratings deteriorating after the SLL issuance; and (ii) the *bank(s)* enjoy a reputational benefit from issuing green loans through a short-term reduction in their credit-default swap rates (a measure of perceived riskiness).[25]

SPECIAL TOPIC: FINANCED EMISSIONS

The banking sector itself does not account for a lot of emissions; its Scope 1 emissions are negligible, and its Scope 2 emissions are mostly due to office environments. Where banks shoulder more responsibility is with respect to the financing they provide to high-emission industries, a Scope 3 category referred to as *financed emissions*. For example, when an electric utility in Indonesia wants to build (another) coal-fired power plant (CFPP), it will usually ask one or more of the local banks to arrange the financing. The bank becomes complicit in the emissions generated by the CFPP because it was the bank financing that enabled the utility to construct the plant.

To properly understand this issue, a worldwide consortium of financial institutions formed PCAF, the Partnership for Carbon Accounting Financials. PCAF developed a methodology used by over 600 institutions to quantify the greenhouse gas (GHG) emissions related to lending and investment activities, enabling them to measure and disclose their contribution to climate change. Armed with this information the banks can be proactive. In the months leading up to COP 26 in Glasgow, United Kingdom, in 2021, the Glasgow Financial Alliance for Net Zero—GFANZ—was launched to much fanfare. The goals for GFANZ were admirable, all leading up to a grand mobilization of capital for the developing and emerging markets of the world. As of this writing, many of the largest members have withdrawn from GFANZ coincident with the shifting political tides in the United States.

Notwithstanding changes in the global discourse, some banks continue doing the hard work. For example, Singapore-based UOB has developed sector-level decarbonization pathways, clearly disclosing the trajectory for the firm's lending to high-emitting industries.[26]

OTHER FINANCING MECHANISMS

Traditional financing mechanisms often struggle to address the unique challenges of sustainability projects, especially those which involve high upfront costs, long payback periods, and uncertain returns.

Blended Finance[27]

Blended finance combines public and private capital to reduce investment risks and attract private sector investors to sustainability projects (Figure 7.4). Rather than a new type of instrument, blended finance is a structuring approach that enables investors with different objectives to participate together in the same transaction. Especially relevant in emerging markets, bringing different investors together addresses the two main obstacles to many deals, either (i) high risk (perceived or real), or (ii) poor risk-adjusted returns relative to alternatives.

For *risk reduction*, a typical structure might involve a development bank providing a first-loss guarantee alongside private financing, reducing the overall risk profile of the investment. In the case of *poor risk-adjusted returns*, if development funding accepts a below-market ("concessional" in Figure 7.4) rate of return, the investment may be able to afford market-rate payouts to private investors.

The blended finance market[28] is small but growing, with over US$250 billion in cumulative blended structures from roughly 6,800 developed market

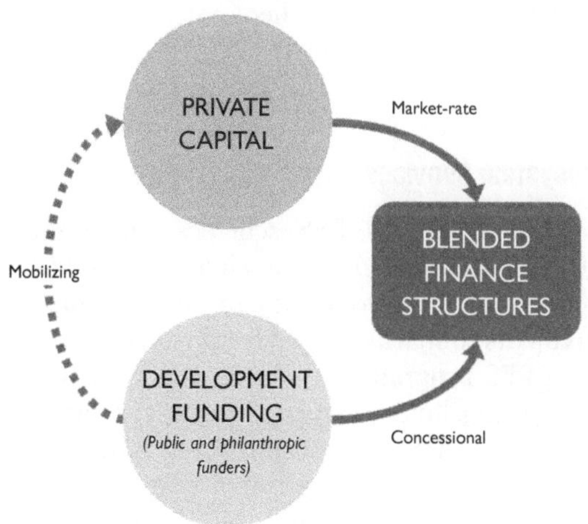

FIGURE 7.4   Blended finance.
Source: Convergence Blending Global Finance / https://www.convergence.finance/ blended-finance/ last accessed Aug 20, 2025.

transactions. With a median deal size of US$64 million, there is plenty of room for larger and more such structures to address the significant funding gap for mitigation, transition, and adaptation finance.

Carbon Contracts for Difference

Carbon Contracts for Difference (CCfD) function as risk-sharing mechanisms between governments or large corporations and clean technology developers, providing price certainty for emission reduction outcomes over long time horizons. The buyer (typically a government or large corporation) agrees to pay the seller (a clean technology project developer) a predetermined "strike price" for each metric ton of CO_2 reduced or avoided. If the carbon price is below (above) the strike price, the buyer (seller) compensates the seller (buyer) for the difference. For example, if a CCfD sets a strike price of US$50 per metric ton of CO_2 and the market price is only US$30, the buyer pays the seller US$20 per metric ton for the agreed-upon volume. This mechanism provides revenue certainty for expensive clean technology projects while protecting buyers from excessive costs if carbon prices rise dramatically.

CCfDs are attracting attention for industrial decarbonization projects such as green hydrogen production and steel manufacturing, both of which require substantial capital investments and face uncertain returns. By providing price certainty, CCfDs enable project developers to secure financing at lower costs and reduce the overall risk profile of sustainable investments. The German government has pioneered the use of CCfDs through its "Klimaschutzverträge" program,[29] where early results suggest that CCfDs can reduce project financing costs by 20–30% compared to traditional funding approaches.

Payment for Ecosystem Services

Payment for ecosystem services (PES) schemes compensate landowners and communities for maintaining or enhancing natural systems that provide environmental benefits. PES programs can take various forms, from direct government payments to market-based trading systems. For example, Costa Rica's pioneering PES program pays landowners for forest conservation.[30] Results-based financing links payments to measurable environmental outcomes, such as verified carbon sequestration or biodiversity improvements. This performance-based structure ensures that payments are only made when verifiable environmental benefits are achieved.

GREEN BONDS: INTERVIEW WITH MITCH REZNICK, CFA, FEDERATED HERMES

In conversation with James Cheo

James
What makes a green bond green?

Mitch
What distinguishes a green bond from a mainstream bond is that the proceeds are dedicated to finance a project that has an environmental benefit, and at the same time has an intention of creating value. A green bond delivers financial returns and creates environmental benefit. The obligation of a green bond, from a credit risk point of view is no different than the mainstream bond of a company. Let's say a senior unsecured obligation ranks *pari-passu* from a credit risk point of view with other mainstream bonds.

James
What are green bonds? And how do they relate to, and differ from, social, sustainability, and sustainability-linked bonds?

Mitch
It's important to distinguish between use-of-proceeds bonds and sustainability-linked bonds. Use-of-proceeds bonds, as the name suggests, fund projects with dedicated environmental and/or social benefits. Sustainability-linked bonds do not finance particular projects but rather finance the general functioning of an issuer that has explicit sustainability targets that are linked to the financing conditions of the bond.

Now, sustainability-linked bonds are not specifically project linked and the sustainability-linked bond has an incentive built in which is to say that if the company hits certain sustainability targets, then the bond carries on as a mainstream, but there's disincentive if they miss these objectives. Then there's some sort of pecuniary effect—most often that's a coupon mechanism where there's a coupon step-up, so missed the target, and there's an increase in cost of capital. The point is, what distinguishes these are not project-based and they have an element of steering the entire, the whole corporate entity in the direction of sustainability, or as a way of making a statement to the market that

(Continued)

(*Continued*)

this company has a desire to move in a sustainable direction. So, it's a way of signaling to the market what the corporate is doing as a whole.

One final comment I'll say to this, is that the use-of-proceeds bonds should also be linked to a corporate ambition. For some, you're moving in some positive direction toward sustainability and impact as well.

James

What are greeniums? Should a company raise bonds with a green label on it [to] be cheaper for them, or should the investor pay more and does it exist?

Mitch

The greenium is a benefit to the issuer because a greenium lowers the cost of capital to issue the green bond, and there are a couple of drivers behind that. First, it's a benefit to the company from a financial point of view. You could argue it's a detriment to the bond buyer. The greenium, when it exists, it exists in different sizes and different parts of the credit risk spectrum. For example, we're talking about two to three basis points for very highly rated entities like governments, supranationals, and highly rated banks. The greenium will get a bit wider as you get into the lower credit risk, say BBB area, because credit spreads are much wider, from a percentage basis if it's say 1% of 100 basis points, is more than 1% of 10 basis points.

So, the greenium has existed and collapsed [in] different points in the market. And part of that is that supply and demand of the green bond market evolves and also the general bond market itself has evolved. The green bond market has its own structural idiosyncrasies and structural tailwinds, but it's also a bond market and it's subject to the forces of the bond market in general; when rates are rising, there's very poor issuance, the cost of capital goes up, like in 2022, when there was a big decline in bond issuance. However, I would argue that the green bond market outperformed in supply in 2022, when the whole issuance market was slowing down as a result of the rise in interest rates.

James

What are the forces driving the greenium?

Mitch

There are specific green bond funds out there; they are required to buy green bonds. So, that will be a technical strength that will create a forced buyer for the green bonds. And if they're strong, the bond pricing will squeeze in, you'll have a greenium that will benefit the issuer. Another reason for the greenium, when it exists, is that there's a social and environmental impact benefit for the issuer; so the buyer of that is paying for, is willing to finance and subsidize impact on the amount of a handful of basis points. The third thing is that, from a volatility point of view, green bonds are less volatile. From a risk-adjusted point of view, they can be better valued, they outperform when markets really sell off because you have a sticky buyer base, because of the technical forced buyer component. So, those are three important drivers. Again, the greenium comes and goes but I don't see it as being overly material, and I don't see it as subsidized credit risk at this point, or a misprice of credit risk.

James

What are the regulations and standards around green bonds?

Mitch

There's lots of guidance around green bond issuance because of this desire to mitigate risks of greenwashing. There are two market standards that are very important. The International Capital Market Association (ICMA) is the foundational standard provider for green bonds. It's the standard provider that I used when I created our own green bond scorecard. And it's detailed, fully developed, and it evolves.

Then there's the Climate Bonds Initiative (CBI), which is often used; they'll assess and score and then, of course, you have the rating agencies, so there's no shortage of sort of assessors, but ICMA is the foundational [one] in my view. It covers governance, the structure of the green bond, and making sure that the use of proceeds are project eligible. Projects eligible, that ICMA have identified as appropriate projects for green bonds, can range from climate mitigation to water biodiversity, and there are whole taxonomies around which projects are eligible.

There is a language around transparency, making sure that the proceeds are verified, reported, and tracked, to make sure that the dollars are being used for the actual project, from origination to use of proceeds. There's also regulation that's forming; the European Union

(Continued)

(*Continued*)

has launched some green bond regulation to mitigate against greenwashing. However, be mindful of overregulation. There's always going to be an element of greenwashing. And I'm okay with that. I'd rather have a US$3 trillion imperfect market than US$100 billion perfect market; there's always an element of greenwashing and wastage in any bond market. I've been in the high-yield bond market for 20 years. The role of the analyst, and why this is necessarily a qualitative process, is to determine to what extent there's veracity and strength to the security you are buying across both financial and sustainability elements. So, I don't want regulation to kill the market in pursuit of perfection. I want it to guide the market and we will determine strength, which is always a continuum. It's not binary.

James
What is your view on transition bonds?

Mitch
I do understand why transition financing is controversial but let me explain why transition financing is a good thing. First, it involves a brown company issuing a bond in support of a transition of the company itself, which we absolutely want. We want capex and subsidies to move away from fossil fuels and toward renewables. How is that going to happen if we don't allow some of these companies to issue green bonds to benefit from the green bond market? This is where the corporate governance comes in for the green bond market; if those green bonds are attached to corporate governance policies to make companies move away from fossil fuels toward green then I'm very comfortable.

By the way, green bonds issued by cyclical companies help me as an asset manager because sustainability funds and green bond funds have a bias toward being underweight cyclicals. If I can buy a green bond that is in a cyclical industry, it allows me to create a more diversified portfolio and outperform through the cycle with less volatility and less tracking error. If I run that bond through the green bond framework, and it passes, then I'm comfortable with transition bonds.

James
You mentioned the credit rating agencies. When they issue ratings on conventional bonds the ratings are quite similar across different agencies. How does that look for green bonds?

Mitch
Rating agencies have been in business for 120 years. And credit analysis probably goes back 1,000 years. So, there's substantial correlation between the ratings. With the green bonds, the assessment services are all relatively new, but they have different nomenclature for conveying the same thing, which is, they are all guided by the ICMA principles, and even the banks are guided by the ICMA principles when they create these bonds. Rating agencies are creating interpretations based on a set of universal principles. And there's some convergence there.

The part that that I worry about is, companies pay for the rating, and if the rating is going to be very poor, they don't get the ratings. So, it seems like you need a certain assessment to get into the market, but you never see anyone fail or very rarely. That's particularly true in the sustainability-linked markets. Where I do have concerns [is] about conflicts of interest—the verification services might be guiding a company [on] how to issue and then they rate it at the same time. Nevertheless, I'm more concerned about the ESG rating market than the green bond assessment market, because at least in the green bond assessment market, you have a framework that we can lean to, whereas the ESG rating market is just the wild, wild west.

James
So, as a green bond investor, is there an element of engagement to the companies that you invest the bonds in and how do you track if they miss certain targets or how they use the proceeds?

Mitch
So, engagement is not an offset. It's not like you buy a coal company and then you engage with them. Engagement is about corporate behavior toward sustainability. It's a constructive dialogue over time. We have a dedicated fixed-income engagement team on engagement. We have a dedicated team and [we are] analyzing sustainability trajectories. So, if we see companies missing targets or milestones, we want to understand why. And it could be something exogenous like, for example, a war in Ukraine drives up the cost of energy or makes energy less available; we can understand that if the sustainability governance is still on track, that's verified by engagement.

So, engagement is not writing a letter. It's not one-directional, it is bidirectional. If companies are failing from an engagement point of view, that they're not genuine, then we will downgrade our

(Continued)

(*Continued*)

sustainability assessments and that could trigger action; potentially, we could get out of the name. So, the green bond isn't a guarantee of delivery, but it's a leading indicator because you're making yourself vulnerable by establishing these goals and you've got these dedicated proceeds. And ultimately, that's the overall objective for us.

James
What do you think the trajectory is for the green bond market and how [do] you think [it] will play out in the years ahead?

Mitch
[The] green bond market is close to US$3 trillion in issuance, there's lots of refinancings in there. It's hard to tell, but we're in kind of a US$2 trillion-plus market. If you look at green bond issuance more recently, it's hovering in 10% of issuance of the market and varies by region. My expectation would be that the green bond market today is about 2–3% of the global bond market, including government bonds, but in the corporate credit market, it's about 6%.

Where's it going to trend over time? In the coming years, we're going to see a steady level of maturity at 10% of issuance, to 15% at times. Green bonds are going to be a permanent part of the market. It's a substantial market, and it transcends all types of issuers.

Dedicated mandates will continue [to] exist. You could argue that the green bond market over time should actually fall, once the world delivers net zero. I hope we'll see more diversification. Sustainability doesn't exist in silos; climate is, is inexorably linked to biodiversity loss, which is inexorably linked to social stress. Therefore, we'll see diversification of green bonds toward water use and a shift away from climate; climate will always be the biggest piece but we'll see a shift toward biodiversity.

Asia has typically been the second-largest region for issuance. China's the big driver of green bonds. It depends on how active China is going to be in the green bond market.

When I first started looking at the green bond market, the average credit rating was double A minus, now we're into the single A's and that makes sense. I'd like to see those value offerings and triple B and double B into the market creates more well-rounded market, we've seen a what's called a quality evolution over the past few years, and I think that will continue as well.

Blended finance is absolutely the future. There are limits to what capital markets can do, in terms of impact. This is where innovative structures—whether it's repackaged green or blue bonds, debt-for-nature swaps, or debt-for-climate swaps—come into play. That's probably speaks to my next point, which is that I think the private markets have a really important place in the sustainability and use-of-proceeds market as well.

James
What are the hindrances to the future trajectory of green bonds? Do you think it's based on the goodness of the company that wants to make the impact or it's regulation to make certain things mandatory, such as a higher carbon tax?

Mitch
Regulation is helping because the one thing that's uniform in regulation across the world is disclosure. And as disclosure becomes mainstream in the next couple of years, all large companies will have to disclose on environmental. Greenwashing is always a concern. The green bond market has to prove that the returns are satisfactory so that investors don't feel like they're giving up and over time, longer term. I think regulation, potentially, is a hindrance if it becomes too onerous. Then it could kill off the market. Some companies don't have dedicated projects that require enough capital to issue a green bond and for them a sustainability-linked bond is a great outcome. So, you need high-capex intensive projects, where a use-of-proceeds bond actually makes sense. For smaller companies, it can be challenging; you're a smaller company and US$25–50 million bond is going to be tough to issue.

James
Any final words?

Mitch
Let's not be afraid to buy green bonds of companies that are really carbon intensive. There's an investment benefit. As a portfolio manager, it gives me access to cyclicality which is sometimes lacking in sustainability strategies, which are largely underweight [in] energy, if not zero exposure to energy. These are real challenges that sustainability investment managers face. And the final component I would say is that the good governance element, this is a real thing. So, if you're buying sustainability, you're automatically buying into a company with a good governance bias to the portfolio. And there's a decent possibility of a downside protection component to that.

SUMMARY

Given the long list of sustainability issues and growing societal pressure to take action, companies should expect to add sustainability-related projects to their list of investments. Some firms may be able to finance those investments through working capital or other means, but for those which cannot—or those wishing to be seen pursuing sustainability projects—there are new, alternative financing instruments available for just this purpose:

- Use-of-proceeds bonds (green, social, sustainability) stipulate that the proceeds go to projects which meet the applicable project criteria.
- Proceeds from SLBs and SLLs are fungible, but interest rates are subject to change depending on whether the issuer meets targets on one or more sustainability-related KPIs.
- Transition and adaptation finance are important but scaling slowly due to a lack of standardized criteria.
- Conservation finance is important, especially for developing countries rich in natural capital but less secure financially.
- Other financing solutions, including blended finance, CCfDs, and PESs, are in various stages of development. Blended finance is the furthest along but none have reached a tipping point yet.

With so many options on the table, companies may still protest that they cannot pay for their decarbonization plans, for example, but the time may be approaching when financing ceases to be the bottleneck. Reaching this milestone will have important implications for companies and investors alike.

Three

Regulations and Companies

In Part Two we explored the relationship between companies and sustainability issues, from base principles (why should firms care about more than profits?) to disclosures (what do we need to know about firms and their relationship with stakeholders?) and investments (how can firms pay for sustainability improvements?). Stakeholders want firms to care about more than profits, and, as a result, firms are expected to follow established frameworks and standards to measure and disclose their sustainability performance. When important gaps are identified—from reducing emissions to improving employee welfare—companies can finance the necessary investments using specialized instruments and structuring mechanisms. Collectively, these are positive developments.

Without regulatory pressure, these developments are dependent on company management voluntarily deciding to care, to measure, and to improve. Unfortunately, too few management teams are interested in making the kind of changes that are required to address the sustainability issues discussed in Part One. There are two primary channels through which pressure may be applied: government regulation and investor behavior. The investor channel receives thorough treatment in Part Four. For now, Part Three examines government regulation along several different dimensions:

- **Corporate Disclosure Requirements** (Chapter 8): Making sure that companies track and report sustainability data so that management and stakeholders share an accurate view of corporate behavior.
- **Greenwashing and How to Prevent It** (Chapter 9): Faced with undesirable corporate behavior, regulators define what qualifies as green,

what is expected in corporate marketing, and the enforcement mechanisms to ensure these laws and statutes are followed.

- **Putting a Price on Pollution** (Chapter 10): Where the market fails to account for a negative externality, governments step in to put a price on pollution.

When it comes to sustainability regulation, every jurisdiction faces its own challenges. Because it is further along than many others, these chapters will make frequent reference to the European Union's approach to sustainability regulation. Other countries will also be explored, either larger economies making a significant contribution to greenhouse gas emissions, or other countries taking bold or innovative action. Readers missing their country of interest can use the concepts discussed here (e.g., taxonomy) to conduct their own research and compare with the material below.[1]

CHAPTER 8

Corporate Disclosure Requirements

Chapter 6 described the evolution of sustainability reporting frameworks and standards. As of mid-2025, between the Global Reporting Initiative (GRI) and the International Sustainability Standards Board (ISSB) 1 and 2, companies have a more manageable list of metrics to track and disclose—yet disclosure is still inconsistent across firms when compliance is on a voluntary basis. Where governments take an interest in the quantity and quality of sustainability disclosures, regulations may require firms headquartered in the jurisdiction to measure and report key data.[1] The governmental body taking most proactive measures in this regard is the European Union (EU); the first section presents a comprehensive overview of its five key pieces of legislation. The second section discusses actions taken by other important global players, from the United States and China, to India, the United Kingdom, Australia, and Singapore.

DISCLOSURE REGULATION: EUROPEAN UNION[2]

The EU has embarked on an ambitious journey toward a creating a more sustainable economy and achieving climate neutrality by 2050, underpinned by its European Green Deal. To drive this transition and ensure transparency and accountability, the EU has introduced a series of interconnected legislative and standard-setting initiatives:

- European Financial Reporting Advisory Group (EFRAG)—provides technical advice
- Corporate Sustainability Reporting Directive (CSRD)—who needs to report and what (framework)
- European Sustainability Reporting Standards (ESRS)—standards to be followed when reporting
- Corporate Sustainability Due Diligence Directive (CSDDD)—what firms are expected to measure within their supply chains

Together, these initiatives form a complex but coordinated regulatory environment aimed at steering businesses toward more sustainable practices.

European Financial Reporting Advisory Group[3]

EFRAG is a private association established in 2001, serving the European public interest in both financial and sustainability reporting. Its mission is to develop and promote European views in the field of corporate reporting, both its traditional purview of financial reporting (e.g., coordinating with the International Financial Reporting Standards [IFRS] on global standards development) and more recently on sustainability reporting.

EFRAG's primary role with respect to sustainability reporting is to provide technical advice to the European Commission with respect to the ESRS or draft amendments to existing ESRS. The organization works on sector-agnostic standards, sector-specific standards, and standards tailored for listed and voluntary small- and medium-sized enterprises (SMEs).

Corporate Sustainability Reporting Directive[4]

The CSRD is designed to enhance corporate transparency on environmental, social, and governance (ESG) issues. Recognizing the need to track progress toward the 2050 climate-neutrality goal embedded in the EU's Green Deal, the European Commission introduced the CSRD in 2021 to bring more transparency and accountability to companies' sustainability efforts.

The CSRD is a replacement for the Non-Financial Reporting Directive (NFRD), issued in 2014 and in force as of 2018. The NFRD was the EU's first attempt at standardizing reporting of ESG issues; as a result, over 11,000 European companies were required to report on a set of ESG issues. The NFRD was criticized for not going far enough with metrics and technical standards. In comparison, CSRD requires approximately 50,000 European companies to report specific information about their sustainability performance using the more robust set of ESRS.

European Sustainability Reporting Standards[5]

The ESRS are the mandatory standards (Figure 8.1) that companies within the scope of the CSRD must use for their sustainability reporting. The development of the ESRS is mandated by the CSRD; the task of providing technical advice to the European Commission through draft ESRS falls to EFRAG.

Like the development of other standards, the ESRS will be released over time. Set 1, comprising sector-agnostic standards, was published in 2023. Sustainability reporting under the ESRS addresses a combination of general as well as ESG information:

Key areas of disclosure include policies, targets, actions and action plans (including transition plans), and resources related to material sustainability issues. Where applicable, the ESRS also require disclosure of datapoints

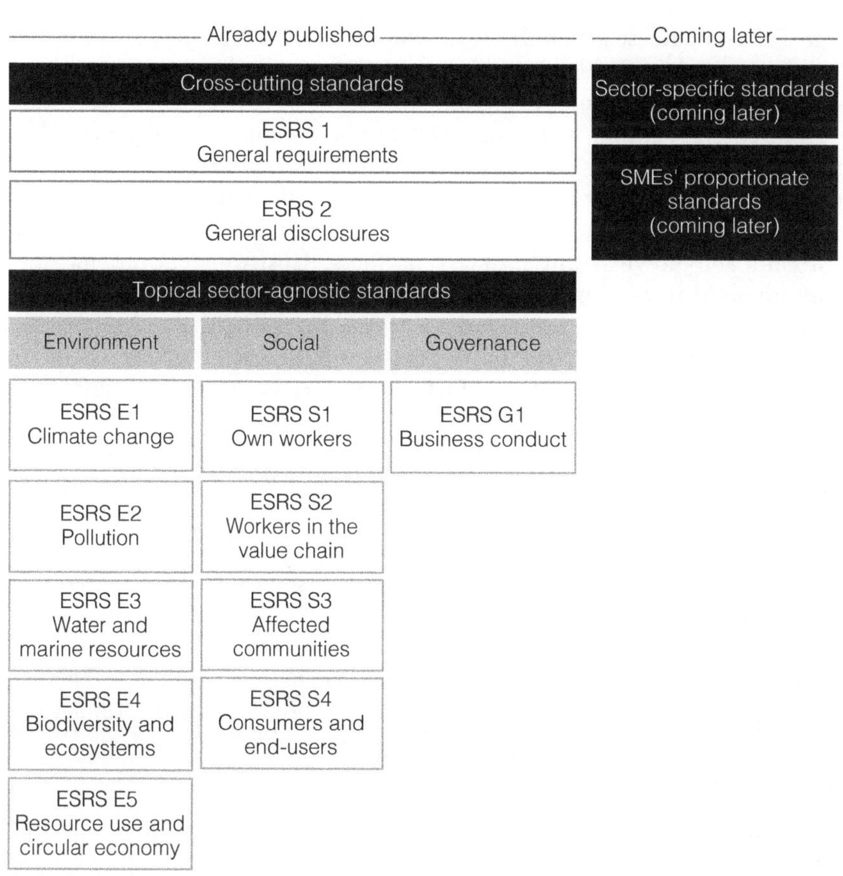

FIGURE 8.1   European Sustainability Reporting Standards (ESRS) summary.
Source: Ernst & Young denkstatt / https://denkstatt.at/en/esrs-standards-explained//
last accessed Aug 20, 2025.

associated with other EU legislation, such as those from the EU Taxonomy Regulation (to be discussed in Chapter 9).

The ESRS are distinct from other standards, like ISSB and GRI, but EFRAG makes an effort to avoid double-reporting where possible. For example, an interoperability document is anticipated to clarify where ESRS and IFRS sustainability standards align.

Corporate Sustainability Due Diligence Directive[6]

The CSDDD extends beyond reporting sustainability information—it imposes constraints on firm conduct, addressing adverse human rights and environmental impacts within a firm's value chain. The CSDDD applies to large EU companies, generally those with over 1,000 employees and net turnover exceeding €450 million. The final text, adopted in April 2024, was estimated to cover around 5,000 companies.

The core obligation under the CSDDD is to conduct due diligence. This involves engaging with stakeholders, identifying and assessing potential adverse impacts, and preventing, mitigating, or eliminating those impacts wherever possible. Due diligence obligations extend to the company's upstream and downstream business partners. Upstream entities include those involved in raw materials, production, and product/service development; downstream activities include distribution, transport, and storage—services related to the disposal of products are excluded.

These initiatives—EFRAG, CSRD, ESRS, and CSDDD—collectively support the European Green Deal. The CSRD and the ESRS encourage (or mandate) companies to integrate sustainability into their core business strategies and operations, implicitly suggesting action in addition to the core act of reporting. The CSDDD complements these reporting requirements by imposing concrete conduct obligations. For example, while the ESRS require companies to *report* on their due diligence processes, the CSDDD *mandates* that companies *perform* these due diligence steps. Both require companies to look beyond their own immediate operations to identify and address impacts and collect data from their upstream and downstream partners. Finally, EFRAG serves as a key *technical advisor* on what should be reported and how.

Omnibus 2025: Pushback[7]

Despite noble intentions, the combination of the ESRS, the CSRD, and the CSDDD introduced a lot of complexity into the EU market and increased the reporting burden for covered European companies. For example, the measures use different size-based cutoff points to determine which measurement and reporting requirements should apply to which companies, causing confusion and hindering adoption. An Omnibus package of legislative revisions, released in February 2025, includes many proposed changes to reduce the reporting burden and streamline requirements.

Corporate Sustainability Reporting Directive (CSRD). The CSRD thresholds would be relaxed to align with the original thresholds in place for CSDDD compliance. Harmonizing the reporting thresholds removes roughly 80% of companies from scope for the CSRD. Implementation would be delayed by several years, and firms that have already started complying with the CSRD (Wave 1 in the Implementation Timeline row in Table 8.1) *would no longer be required to do so* and would be free to halt compliance efforts.

European Sustainability Reporting Standards (ESRS). The ESRS would be streamlined by reducing mandatory datapoints, prioritizing quantitative

TABLE 8.1 Corporate Sustainability Reporting Directive (CSRD) Proposed Changes

Category	Existing Language/ Requirements	Proposed Changes
Reporting Thresholds	Four-wave implementation covering various company sizes including small- and medium-sized enterprises (SMEs) and companies with 250+ employees.	Mandatory reporting limited to large companies with 1,000+ employees and meeting financial thresholds (€50 million turnover or €25 million balance sheet). Removes around 80% of companies from scope.
Non-European Union (EU) Companies	Net turnover >€150 million in EU with qualifying subsidiary >€40 million turnover.	Increased to €450 million EU turnover with qualifying subsidiary/branch >€50 million turnover.
Implementation Timeline	Wave 2: Jan 1, 2025; Wave 3: Jan 1, 2026; Wave 4: Jan 1, 2028.	Wave 2 delayed to Jan 1, 2027; Wave 3 deleted; Wave 4 remains Jan 1, 2028 with modified scope.
Value-Chain Reporting	Value-chain cap applies only as limit in European Sustainability Reporting Standards (ESRS), protecting SMEs.	Extended to protect all companies with up to 1,000 employees, applied directly to reporting company.
Taxonomy Reporting	All in-scope companies must report taxonomy alignment.	Companies with >1,000 employees and <€450 million turnover only disclose if voluntarily claiming alignment.

over more onerous narrative reporting, and removing sector-specific standards (Table 8.2).

Corporate Sustainability Due Diligence Directive (CSDDD). No change to the companies which would have to comply with the CSDDD, since the original thresholds would be used for the CSRD (see above). The major simplification here is in mostly limiting due diligence to direct (Tier 1) relationships, plus slowing the cadence of due diligence assessments from annual to once every five years (Table 8.3).

If enacted, the recommended Omnibus changes are estimated to save over €6 billion in administrative costs.

TABLE 8.2 European Sustainability Reporting Standards (ESRS) Proposed Changes

Category	Existing Language/ Requirements	Proposed Changes
Mandatory Datapoints	Current set of mandatory disclosure requirements.	Reduction in mandatory datapoints by removing less important ones, prioritizing quantitative over narrative, further distinguishing mandatory vs. voluntary.
Sector-Specific Standards	Sector-specific disclosure requirements for certain industries.	Elimination of sector-specific standards to avoid increased disclosure requirements; focus on sector-agnostic standards.
Standards Revision	Current first set of European Sustainability Reporting Standards (ESRS).	Commission committed to simplifying ESRS through future delegated act.
Assurance Requirements	Limited assurance required, with reasonable assurance by 2028.	Targeted assurance guidelines to be issued; removes Commission's empowerment to adopt reasonable assurance standards by Oct 1, 2028.

TABLE 8.3 Corporate Sustainability Due Diligence Directive (CSDDD) Proposed Changes

Category	Existing Language/ Requirements	Proposed Changes
Implementation Timeline	Member States transposition by Jul 2026, application from Jul 2027.	Transposition delayed to Jul 2027; first wave application delayed to Jul 2028.
Due Diligence Scope	Value-chain due diligence across multiple tiers.	Limited to direct (Tier 1) business partners, with exceptions for plausible information of impacts beyond Tier 1.
Stakeholder Definition	Broader stakeholder engagement requirements.	Definition pared back to include only directly affected individuals and communities; reduced stages requiring engagement.

Category	Existing Language/ Requirements	Proposed Changes
Periodic Assessments	Annual assessments of due diligence effectiveness.	Extended from one year to five years, with ad hoc assessments only when significant risks arise.
Business Relationship Termination	Obligation to terminate business relationships as last resort.	Obligation to terminate removed; requirement to suspend relationships remains.
Financial Penalties	Minimum 5% of global turnover penalty cap.	Minimum cap removed; Member States must ensure fines are effective, proportionate, and dissuasive.
Civil Liability	Specific European Union (EU)-wide civil liability regime.	EU-wide regime removed; companies subject to liability under Member State laws.
Climate Transition Plans	Requirement to "put into effect" climate transition plans.	Requirement removed, aligning with Corporate Sustainability Reporting Directive (CSRD); companies must include implementation actions in plans.

GOVERNMENT REGULATION: OTHER COUNTRIES

The EU regulations, notwithstanding the push to simplify through the Omnibus proposal, represent the most ambitious and coordinated regulatory effort with regards to corporate measurement and disclosure of sustainability information. Many other countries are in various stages of developing their own regulatory approaches; this section provides a glimpse into some of these developments.

United States

The United States enjoys a complicated political relationship with sustainability initiatives, as shown by the extreme swings in policy and posture between Democrat and Republican administrations since President Obama was first elected in 2009. The Securities and Exchange Commission (SEC) had adopted climate disclosure rules in March 2024, but the change in administration prompted the agency to retract those rules.[8] Neither the NYSE nor NASDAQ exchanges have mandatory sustainability disclosure requirements as of this writing.

China[9]

China is developing its own sustainability standards and disclosure requirements, releasing an initial version of the "Sustainability Disclosure Standards for Enterprises—Basic Standards" toward the end of 2024. The standards set out general provisions, disclosure objectives, and information quality requirements, a first step toward China's planned national sustainability disclosure standard system. Also in 2024, China unveiled a mandatory sustainability disclosure regulation that will apply to companies listed on its three largest stock exchanges (Beijing, Shanghai, Shenzhen). This regulation requires the largest listed companies to report on a variety of ESG factors, including climate change and biodiversity, starting from 2026.

India[10]

India's Business Responsibility and Sustainability Report (BRSR) framework, in effect since 2023, requires the top 1,000 listed companies to report on 98 mandatory and 42 voluntary indicators. There are nine categories of indicators following the National Guidelines for Responsible Business Conduct; alignment with GRI and the Task Force on Climate-related Financial Disclosures (TCFD) is at least partially addressed.

United Kingdom[11]

The Streamlined Energy and Carbon Reporting (SECR) requires large UK companies to disclose energy use, carbon footprint, and greenhouse gas (GHG) emissions in their annual financial reporting. TCFD-aligned disclosures are required for large firms. The United Kingdom is also developing its own Sustainability Reporting Standards (SRS), aligned with the ISSB.

Australia[12]

Australia has finalized the Australian Sustainability Reporting Standards (ASRS) and implemented mandatory reporting of climate-related risks and emissions across their entire value chain. The mandatory climate reporting requirements, including TCFD, will be phased in over three years, starting in 2025.

Singapore[13]

The approach to corporate reporting requirements in Singapore is different from other countries discussed here—regulations are generally implemented through listing requirements rather than issued by a government agency. For example, in 2021, the Singapore Exchange (SGX) introduced a list of 27 metrics across ESG issues that listed companies in certain sectors were expected (though not mandated) to disclose. With the introduction of ISSB standards and the launch of the CSRD in Europe, the SGX took the opportunity to update its policy. Beginning in FY25, all issuers will be required to disclose Scope 1 and Scope 2 GHG emissions and TCFD-aligned disclosures. Scope 3 emissions are expected to be phased in over time, with the largest companies starting in FY26. It also introduced a timeline for the largest private companies to begin reporting Scope 1 and Scope 2, effective FY27. However, the threshold is quite high (annual revenue of at least S$1 billion and total assets of at least S$500 million) so the number of affected firms will be small.

SUSTAINABILITY REGULATORY FRAMEWORKS: INTERVIEW WITH MERVYN TANG, SCHRODERS

In conversation with James Cheo

James
What is the state of play of the global sustainability regulatory framework?

Mervyn
I will categorize regulatory regulations into a few subsets. First, there is corporate level disclosure, things like International Sustainability Standards Board (ISSB) and SGX listing rules. Those focus on increasing the standardization and the expectations of disclosure of companies—and an extension to that are fund disclosure and fund regulations like the Sustainable Finance Disclosure Regulation (SFDR), MAS [Monetary Authority of Singapore]' ESG requirements for retail funds, SFCs [Securities and Futures Commission of Hong Kong] listing requirements, and then also taxonomies. Beyond that, there are the climate risk regulations like the Taskforce on Climate-related Financial Disclosure (TCFD) requirements which adds an extra layer of rules for investment funds. Then you've got green bonds guidelines, which can make use of taxonomies—at least in the EU [European Union]

(Continued)

(Continued)

and will be coming through elsewhere. You've got another layer which is the fiduciary duty, due diligence expectations, which governs what the asset manager can do. Regulations are interrelated and evolving as such, but not necessarily always coherent. For example, corporate disclosure requirements are not evolving quickly enough to support fund disclosure, so you don't have the corporate data to apply to fund regulations.

In the global landscape, where, depending on which region or which jurisdiction, there are developments and focus on specific things, Singapore has clearly shown that they're much more focused on transition, with transition planning guidelines and taxonomy coming through, ahead of other places. On stewardship codes, Japan and South Korea stewardship codes have taken more of a precedence over other sets of regulations. In terms of the mix of regulations and global harmonization, the EU took the first step but I think when the EU took the first step with things like SFDR with taxonomy, the rest of the world is kind of taking lessons from the challenges, for example, Article 8 and Article 9 of SFDR. The industry has found SFDR very challenging to implement and the challenges have been highlighted by a wide set of asset managers, as well as asset owners. It has got to the point where the EU is also reviewing how to think about it. Whereas the MAS and SFC have taken much more pragmatic approaches in terms of defining what is a sustainable fund and what do you disclose as opposed to principal adverse impact indicators that are very specific but not that useful in practice. Lots of things are happening, sometimes in a bit of a disjointed manner with a regional bent around different places.

REGULATIONS AND STANDARDS: INTERVIEW WITH FANG EU-LIN, PwC SINGAPORE

In conversation with James Cheo

James
How do you see regulations and standards evolving going forward?

Eu-Lin
Europe is leading the way on regulations. The EU [European Union] taxonomy is a classification system that helps identify "environmentally sustainable" economic activities to make sustainable investment decisions. Companies that fall under the scope of the Corporate Sustainability Reporting Directive (CSRD) have to report in their annual reports to what extent their activities are covered by the EU taxonomy (taxonomy-eligibility) and comply with the criteria set in the taxonomy delegated acts (taxonomy-alignment). Other companies that do not fall under the scope of CSRD can decide to disclose this information on a voluntary basis to get access to sustainable financing or for other business-related reasons.

Globally, how regulators and standards will evolve will depend on five decision points that countries must take. First, on materiality, should countries decide on either financial or impact, or double materiality? Second, should the countries decide to apply to standards to listed or nonlisted companies, or both? Third, should the focus be only on environment, or look entirely with environment, social, and governance [ESG]? Fourth, for GHG [greenhouse gas] emissions, should it be for Scope 1, 2, and 3, or for all? Fifth, on assurance, should it be limited or reasonable?

Europe is leading with the world with the most comprehensive and strictest standards. Over time, the only way is forward, and I think most jurisdictions will converge to the European standards; the question will be how fast it will happen.

James
What are the challenges going forward? Is there any silver bullet to greenwashing? Can sustainability assurance solve it?

Eu-Lin
Sustainability assurance is not the silver bullet to eliminate greenwashing entirely, but sustainability assurance helps a lot to reduce greenwashing risk.

Due to the different skillsets from financial auditing, the main challenge will be for existing financial auditors to upskill and provide effective sustainability assurance. The industry will need the right people and it takes time and experience to build up sustainability capability and capacity.

SUMMARY

If a company can't measure its relationship with people and planet, how would anyone know what changes it should (be asked to/required to) make? For this reason, measurement and disclosure of sustainability-related information lies at the foundation of responsible corporate behavior. Without a compelling business case to justify the effort to measure and report the information, many companies still fail to disclose key information.

Regulatory action that compels disclosure is on the legislative agenda for countries around the world. This chapter pays special attention to the efforts of the European Union through its interlocking mechanisms of EFRAG, CSRD, ESRS, and CSDDD. The ambition level is high, but so is the resulting administrative burden, leading to some pushback and uncertainty in the reporting requirements that will take effect post the next round of legislation. Important emitters like the United States, China, and India, plus the United Kingdom, Australia, and Singapore, occupy very different points in the spectrum. Their reporting requirements offer varying combinations of proprietary vs. global standards and apply to a mix of large/small and public/ private companies. This variation is to be expected given the stark differences in local, political, and economic context. While it may be tempting to call for all companies to report on everything, increased measurement and disclosure of material issues for "large" firms would be a much-needed step in the right direction.

CHAPTER 9

Defining Green: Greenwashing and Taxonomies

"**W**hat is green?" While that sounds like a silly question,[1] in the case of environmental sustainability, the question is far more practical: defining which business activities count as "green" makes it easier to identify when firms might be "greenwashing." This chapter considers greenwashing and the regulatory response in four parts. First, it summarizes the role of regulation in financial markets and historically important regulations, before continuing to an exploration of greenwashing. Armed with an understanding of the various forms of greenwashing, this chapter looks at how regulators define what qualifies as "green" through what is referred to as a "taxonomy." We will also look at other legal mechanisms, including lawsuits, that suggest the market may be less willing to tolerate undesirable corporate behavior such as greenwashing.

FINANCIAL MARKET REGULATION: A REVIEW

Financial market regulation historically has been driven by the need to respond to financial crises and ensure market stability. The stock market crash of 1929, followed by the banking panics of the early 1930s, marked a significant turning point. The resultant economic turmoil contributed to the onset of the Great Depression, leading to an expansion of US federal oversight. Key legislation from this period includes:

- Glass-Steagall Act of 1933, which established the Federal Deposit Insurance Corporation (FDIC) and separated commercial banking from investment banking.
- Securities Act of 1933, aimed at ensuring transparency in the securities market by mandating the registration of securities with the federal government.
- Securities Exchange Act of 1934 created the Securities and Exchange Commission (SEC), tasked with protecting investors by enforcing securities laws and overseeing the securities industry.

After the flurry of regulation in the 1930s, the landscape remained relatively stable until a wave of US deregulation began in the 1980s. This shift reduced government oversight and intervention in financial markets, a change which arguably contributed to subsequent financial crises such as the Dot-Com Bubble of 1999–2001 and the Global Financial Crisis of 2008. Regulatory responses included the Sarbanes-Oxley Act of 2002, which laid the groundwork for corporate governance reforms, and the Dodd-Frank Act of 2010, which sought to prevent future systemic risks by imposing stricter regulations on financial institutions.

Financial market regulation is not limited to the United States. Since the creation of the European Union (EU), the aim of European financial regulation has been to harmonize regulations across member countries, e.g., establishing the European Banking Authority (EBA) to improve the regulation and supervision of financial institutions across the EU. Additional directives, like the Markets in Financial Instruments Directive (MiFID II), were intended to strengthen investor protections and improve the functioning of financial markets. Asian financial markets have also undergone significant regulatory transformations, influenced by both domestic needs and international standards. Countries like Japan and China have introduced reforms aimed at increasing the stability and transparency of their financial systems.

In many of the cases above, regulation was issued in response to "bad behaviors" which often led to a crisis. The recent emphasis on sustainability has coincided with (or contributed to) another set of bad behavior, perhaps even a crisis, around false claims and deceptive practices: greenwashing.

CORPORATE GREENWASHING

People who want to be seen a certain way sometimes exaggerate or lie to develop or maintain their reputation. Companies, which of course are run by people, sometimes do similar things. At the extreme there are examples of financial fraud, e.g., Enron and Wirecard to name a couple. There are also cases of operational fraud, e.g., Volkswagen and Sino-Forest, where the fraud isn't confined to the financial accounts but instead appears in the "real world" of products and business operations.[2]

When it comes to sustainability, issues arise when companies purport to have a more positive relationship with people and planet than is truly the case. Deceitful behavior related to sustainability issues is called "greenwashing," "social washing," "impact washing," and even "rainbow washing" when making use of the rainbow-colored United Nations Sustainable Development Goals (SDGs).

Greenwashing may be far more commonplace than expected; in 2020, studies by the EU of environmental claims in marketing materials found that 40% of green claims lacked supporting evidence and 53% provided vague, misleading, or unfounded information. A sweep of 500 websites in 2020 by an international group including the UK's Competition and Markets Authority found that 40% of websites were using misleading practices. Two common techniques used by companies include[3]:

- misleading claims, e.g., an oil company marketing its fuels as "carbon-neutral";
- attention deflection, e.g., shifting the blame to consumer behavior or "greenlighting" by overemphasizing green attributes with a *de minimis* contribution to the firm's carbon footprint.

Any internet search for a term like "greenwash checklist" will return many different lists and frameworks, including relatively well-known ones like "Sins of Greenwashing"[4] from TerraChoice (now part of UL Solutions). In a scholarly attempt to summarize the best ideas available into a single structure, a 2022 paper[5] in the peer-reviewed journal *Sustainability* developed the framework in Table 9.1.

Reading through the list of greenwashing claims in the first column, readers might have something in mind—like this 2021 example from personal care company Innisfree that might fit in "IV. Lies" (Figure 9.1).[6]

Without judging the curious (skeptical?) individual who *carefully* cut through the bottle to see what was inside, once the interior plastic bottle is revealed it is hard not to see this as a deliberate attempt to mislead customers. Not all cases of greenwashing are so blatant or so easy to identify, and hopefully the list of claims in the table above helps readers become more discerning when it comes to evaluating corporate environmental claims.

TABLE 9.1   Integrated Framework of Greenwashing

Types of Claims Used in Greenwashing	Description of Greenwashing	Indicator Questions (How to Recognize Greenwashing)
I. Selective Disclosure	Claim is based on a narrow set of attributes and distracts consumers from the organization's greater environmental impact.	I.1 When making/supporting a claim about the product/organization's environmental impact, has the organization failed to consider the entire organization/product/service's life cycle within its area of influence OR failed to assess the cumulative environmental impacts of its or its products' activities? For countries, does the claim cover only territorial emissions/footprints/impacts omitting (a) imported ones or (b) emissions from international aviation and shipping? I.2 While publishing the claim, has the organization failed to disclose all information regarding social and/or environmental performance on the specific aspect the claim refers to? I.3 Does the claim (a) fail to relate to aspects that are significant in terms of the product/service/organization's environmental impact OR (b) result in an undue transfer of negative impacts? I.4 Does the claim (a) communicate a specific type of product/service/policy as "more green," compared to competitors, even though there is no evidence that the product is "greener" than the usual production/service/policy OR (b) refer to "better" (recycled/certified/sustainable/less carbon intensive/etc.) products/services, while the organization fails to communicate the ratio of "better" vs. "conventional" products/services? I.5 Is the organization's claim to have net-zero emissions not based on reducing its own emissions to the full extent possible, and/or it relies on offsetting rather than reductions in its own emissions? For countries, are projects outside a country's national boundaries included in a nation's accounting as offsets?

Types of Claims Used in Greenwashing	Description of Greenwashing	Indicator Questions (How to Recognize Greenwashing)
II. Empty Claims	Making claims/ policies that either exaggerate achievements, or fail to live up to them.	II.1 Has the claim (a) promised some positive improvement (to environment/local communities, etc.) that has not been fulfilled OR (b) stated or implied environmental benefits if the benefits are negligible/short-term/disregard Indigenous/marginalized populations? II.2 Are there strong indications that the overall marketing budget is larger than the budget set aside for environmental improvement mentioned in the claim? II.3 Does the claim deflect attention to minor issues or lead to creating "green talk" through communication that (a) overstates the organizations' actual commitments, OR (b) lacks any concrete action with significant and measurable impact?
III. Irrelevant	Proclaiming accomplishments that are irrelevant or already required by law/competitors.	III. Is the public misled to believe the claim is a result of voluntary sustainable actions when it, or much of it, is compulsory by law and/or also required of competitors?
IV. Lies	Claims are outright lying.	IV. Is the claim contradicted by scientific consensus?
V. Just Not Credible	Claim touts environmentally friendly attributes of a dangerous or highly controversial practice/product/ service/policy.	V. Does the claim try to make the public feel "green" about a choice that is either dangerous (to health/environment) or highly controversial with potentially long-term ecologically harmful consequences or adverse impacts on natural resources?

(*Continued*)

TABLE 9.1 *(Continued)*

Types of Claims Used in Greenwashing	Description of Greenwashing	Indicator Questions (How to Recognize Greenwashing)
VI. Corporate Responsibility in Action	Claim does not reflect consistent organizational practice.	VI. Are the products/procurement practices/vision or public policy positions in conflict with the claim?
VII. Dubious Certifications and Labels	Claim has certifications that are prone to greenwashing.	VII.1 Is it true that the label/seal attached to the claim is not verified by an independent body? VII.2 Has the organization failed to clearly define and communicate publicly (a) the scope of certification, i.e., what is and what is not assessed in terms of products and/or processes AND (b) information (or its readiness to disclose information) about standards, inspection guidelines, audit reports, details of complaints including investigation summaries, and contact details of certification bodies? VII.3 Has the organization using a voluntary certification scheme (e.g., retailer/producer) failed to apply an effective due diligence policy that is regularly updated to ensure that the product claim is genuine? VII.4 Has the organization responsible for the voluntary certification scheme (i.e., standard owner and/or nongovernmental organization [NGO] helping to set it up) failed to ensure that (a) other stakeholders can effectively challenge the standard owner or the certification bodies through adequate and accessible complaint and objection procedures OR (b) it is able to meaningfully control, challenge, or sanction the certification bodies? VII.5 Is the organization making/supporting the claim associated with/consistently contributing to voluntary certification schemes or committed to multistakeholder initiatives that (a) certify business as usual OR (b) certify products that do not meet its standards OR (c) certify activities that have been implicated in illegality/environmental destruction/human rights abuse within its scope of certification?

Types of Claims Used in Greenwashing	Description of Greenwashing	Indicator Questions (How to Recognize Greenwashing)
VIII. Political Spin	Claim boasts of green commitments, while the organization lobbies against environmental laws.	VIII.1 Has the organization that makes the claim or that helps a corporate entity to make a claim (a) lobbied for blocking/weakening of pro-environmental laws and regulations OR (b) sent any such submissions to politicians/governmental agencies? VIII.2 Is the organization affiliated with think tanks, trade associations, or other groups that spread environmental science disinformation and/or block environmental action in contradiction to its claims?
IX. Co-opted Endorsement	Claims that greenwashing organization's activities are endorsed by other organizations.	IX.1 Does the organization (a) help publicize/endorse another organization's claim that is a greenwash OR (b) make a contrary green claim to the harmful activities it supports from other organizations? IX.2 While receiving payment (through partnership, donation, or a membership fee for one of its programs) from another organization which greenwashes, does the organization endorse that greenwash claim?
X. No Proof	Claim cannot be substantiated by easily accessible supporting information.	X. Does the claim contain statements that are not based on robust, independent, verifiable, and generally recognized evidence?

(Continued)

TABLE 9.1 *(Continued)*

Types of Claims Used in Greenwashing	Description of Greenwashing	Indicator Questions (How to Recognize Greenwashing)
XI. Vagueness	Claim is poorly defined/broad so its real meaning is misunderstood.	XI.1 Has the claim failed to specify whether it refers to the product/packaging/service or just a portion? XI.2 Do the words of the claim (other than in XI.3) have unclear/ambiguous meaning that mislead people about the organization's/product's/service's environmental footprint/impact? XI.3 When making a net-zero/carbon neutrality claim, has the organization (a) failed to measure, track, and regularly publish its emissions according to the latest Intergovernmental Panel on Climate Change (IPCC) guidance (e.g., Scope 1 and 2 emissions—and Scope 3 emissions to the furthest extent possible) OR (b) based its claim on an unsubstantiated single point target without a clear strategy, implementation planning process, and interim targets OR (c) failed to develop and publish a long-term strategy with a decarbonization pathway that prioritizes reducing its own emissions? XI.4 Is the claim based on implementation methodologies that are (a) not clear nor transparent and/or (b) do not have robust metrics?
XII. Misleading Symbols	Claim uses visuals and symbols that induce a false perception of the organization's greenness.	XII. Does the claim have an overall presentation designed to evoke an environmental sensitivity that (a) overstates the achieved environmental benefit OR (b) has no connection with the product/service/organization?
XIII. Jargon	Claim uses jargon/ information that consumers cannot understand/verify.	XIII. Does the claim use technical language/complex scientific jargon that makes it difficult for people to understand?

Source: Adapted from / https://www.mdpi.com/article/10.3390/su14084431/s1.

FIGURE 9.1 An example of greenwashing?
Source: Eco-Business/ https://www.eco-business.com / last accessed on August 18, 2025.

ANTI-GREENWASHING LEGISLATION

To protect consumers from greenwashing and other sustainability-related deceptive practices, several jurisdictions are planning or have passed different versions of anti-greenwashing legislation. Some notable examples include:

- **European Union.** The EU is finalizing its EU Green Claims Directive which will require companies to provide evidence supporting their voluntary green claims in consumer-facing communications. The EU has also amended its Unfair Commercial Practices Directive to include a list of deceptive environmental claims in the definition of unfair commercial practices. Germany and France have national anti-greenwashing laws.[7]
- **United Kingdom.** Introduced the Green Claims Code,[8] stating that environmental claims must be backed up by data.
- **India.** The Central Consumer Protection Authority (CCPA) published the "Guidelines for Prevention and Regulation of Greenwashing and Misleading Environmental Claims" in 2024.[9]
- **Australia.** The Australian Association of National Advertisers (AANA) developed the Environmental Claims Code[10] which stipulates that sustainability claims be realistic, achievable, and evidence-based to reduce greenwashing.
- **Canada.** Amended its Competition Act to add substantiation requirements for companies making environmental claims.

As some readers may have experienced already, it is one thing to have a regulation in place, and another thing altogether to see the regulation enforced. As these new anti-greenwashing regulations take effect, companies will be increasingly discouraged from greenwashing when they see the regulations are being enforced. The Sabin Center for Climate Change Law at Columbia University in the United States maintains a database of climate change litigation.[11] As of this writing, of the 250 cases against corporates located outside the United States, 88 were for misleading advertising. This list includes all known cases, including those which have been dismissed; however, companies have already been found guilty of greenwashing. For example, in 2024, a Dutch court ". . . ruled that KLM's claims suggesting that flying can be or is becoming sustainable, as well as advertising suggesting that its 'offsetting' products reduce or compensate for the climate impact of flying are misleading and therefore unlawful."[12] More such verdicts could have a profound effect on corporate behavior, provided the penalties are economically meaningful.

FINANCE GREENWASHING: EUROPEAN UNION TAXONOMY

Particularly relevant following Chapter 7 and the discussion of sustainability-related financing instruments, companies may also greenwash through their financing choices. There are multiple layers to this issue. First, there may be a question about how the proceeds will be used, e.g., are green projects really green? Second, even if proposed projects are sustainable, do they achieve the anticipated results? And third, did the company really need to use a sustainability instrument for financing, or could it have financed the project(s) through working capital or other more traditional means?

Answering the second question is the most straightforward. Use-of-proceeds bonds require annual reporting on how the funds were used, and where possible, on the impacts of those projects. Sustainability-linked bonds (SLBs) and sustainability-linked loans (SLLs) set and disclose progress against key performance indicators (KPIs)/sustainability performance targets (SPTs). Such disclosures allow stakeholders to monitor the issuer, at least to a certain extent. What may frustrate investors is the lack (or size) of penalties for misuse of funds or missed targets—use-of-proceeds bonds have no penalty mechanism other than reputational consequences, and, as described in Chapter 7, the penalty for missing an SPT depends on the pre-determined step-up/step-down.

Now, let's consider the first question, are green projects really green? Financial regulators in many countries and jurisdictions have responded to claims of greenwashing by establishing lists of business activities that are allowed to be called "green." The first major taxonomy was developed by the European Union. First proposed in 2020, the EU Taxonomy establishes technical screening criteria with which to evaluate six broad categories of business activities; those which meet the criteria are considered green[13]:

- climate change mitigation;
- climate change adaptation;
- the sustainable use and protection of water and marine resources;
- the transition to a circular economy;
- pollution prevention and control;
- the protection and restoration of biodiversity and ecosystems.

The Taxonomy has been adding more detailed activities and adjusting performance thresholds over time. As an example, one of the activities aligned with mitigation is reducing emissions from automotive transport. Conceptually, if the baseline is an internal combustion engine (ICE)-powered vehicle burning petrol (gasoline) or diesel, any activity that reduces emissions from the baseline could be considered green—but the taxonomy is more nuanced than that.

Before 2024, the technical criteria for investments in vehicular transport required tailpipe carbon dioxide (CO_2) emissions to be below 50 g CO_2/km to qualify as green. Under this definition, a fleet operator converting from ICE to hybrid or low-emission ICE vehicles would be eligible to finance the purchase of new vehicles using a green bond, provided the new vehicles had tailpipe emissions below the threshold. However, the EU is committed to reach climate neutrality by 2050, and the largest member states have made a concerted effort to build out the charging infrastructure necessary to support increased adoption of fully electric vehicles. Therefore, following the 2024 update to the Taxonomy technical criteria, only zero tailpipe emission vehicles—full electric vehicles (EVs)—can be considered green.

In the EU Taxonomy, aligned activities must satisfy four criteria:

- Making a substantial contribution to at least one environmental objective.
- Doing no significant harm (DNSH) to any of the other five environmental objectives.
- Complying with minimum safeguards.
- Complying with the technical screening criteria.

"DNSH" is an important caveat designed to prevent companies from claiming green status for activities that make a substantial contribution to one environmental objective but have a negative impact on another. An example of this could be a company that plans to invest in flood protection for one of its distribution centers (positive for adaptation), but the investment would damage an ecologically diverse wetland area abutting its facility (negative for protection and restoration of biodiversity and ecosystems).

The "minimum safeguards" criterion ensures "alignment with the OECD [Organisation for Economic Co-operation and Development] Guidelines for Multinational Enterprises and the UN Guiding Principles on Business and Human Rights, including the principles and rights set out in the eight fundamental conventions identified in the Declaration of the International Labor Organization on Fundamental Principles and Rights at Work and the International Bill of Human Rights."[14] In other words, while the Taxonomy is inherently designed around environmental objectives, these safeguards introduce an element of social objectives that cannot be ignored.

The EU Taxonomy provides some assurance to stakeholders that projects selected for sustainable financing are, in fact, green. Just because a project qualifies as green, however, doesn't guarantee that financing for these projects adds a lot of value—the amount of value may be up for debate. As discussed in Chapter 7, a recent study of green bonds in the United States showed that only 2% of green bond projects are associated with clearly novel green features.[15] A strict view of measuring value created might look down upon providing financing for investments that are already familiar to the issuer. Still, if the projects are aligned with the technical criteria embedded within a taxonomy, there is a case to be made for value in those projects.

FINANCE GREENWASHING: INTERNATIONAL TAXONOMIES

After the introduction of the EU Taxonomy in 2020, international regulators began to issue their own taxonomies. By mid-2025, at least 15–20 countries or jurisdictions have issued some form of taxonomy or announced that they are in the process of doing so (Figure 9.2). The countries include Mexico, South Africa, Colombia, South Korea, Zambia, and New Zealand. Five of the Association of Southeast Asian Nations (ASEAN) member states—Indonesia, Malaysia, Philippines, Singapore, and Thailand—have issued taxonomies, and the ASEAN Secretariat has issued a combined taxonomy based in large part on Singapore's entry.

Since different countries start from different positions on emissions and other sustainability issues, taxonomies in any two countries may differ greatly. The ASEAN Taxonomy is a good example on multiple levels. The first ASEAN country to create its own taxonomy was Singapore (2022). When first issued, the Singapore taxonomy was among the first to incorporate technical criteria for transition activities, and it adopted many of the same criteria as used in the EU Taxonomy.

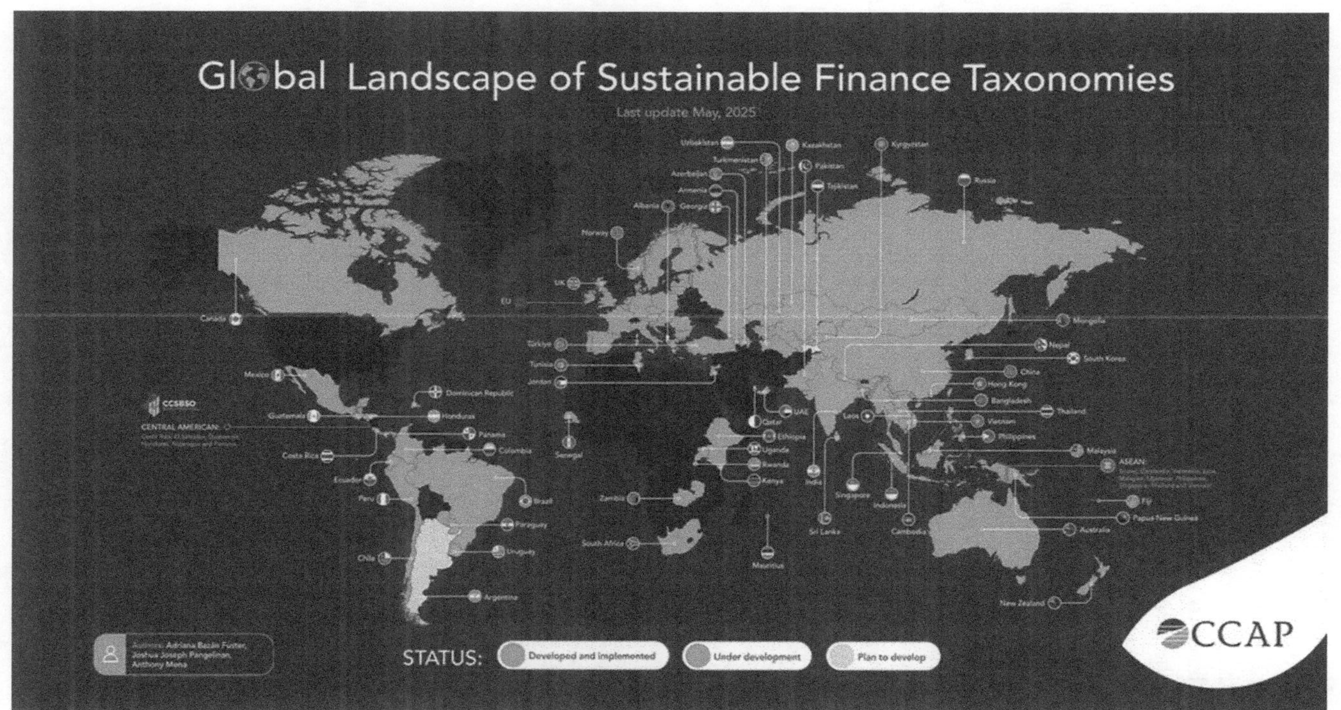

FIGURE 9.2 Global landscape of sustainable finance taxonomies, 2025.
Source: Center for Clean Air Policy (CCAP) / https://www.ccap.org/post/the-next-wave-global-trends-in-sustainable-finance-taxonomies / last accessed Aug 20, 2025.

Compared with its ASEAN neighbors, however, Singapore started from a very different baseline. A much smaller nation by land area and population, its power generation comes predominantly from natural gas rather than coal, which is common in larger neighbors like Indonesia. Singapore also did not have to worry about a large economically sensitive population which could be negatively impacted by a shift away from coal and other extractive industries. Creating a taxonomy which could be applied across ASEAN therefore presented meaningful challenges. In the end, the regulators agreed on an approach that balances the developed and less-developed economies in the region:

- A traffic lighting system to acknowledge that some activities should be permittable today to assist with the transition to a low(er) carbon economy.
- A dual-track system that allows member nations to choose the approach that best meets their needs:
    - Detailed descriptions of business activities aligned with traffic lighting, most closely aligned with the Singapore Taxonomy.
    - A more judgment-based classification system allowing regulators to assign levels of green to activities based on the existing local context.
- Specific consideration for social aspects (Figure 9.3).

Social Aspects		Definition
	Promotion and Protection of Human Rights	Promotion of human rights and fundamental freedoms, in line with the ASEAN Human Rights Declaration (AHRD) and the Phnom Penh Statement on the Adoption of the AHRD (ASEAN, 2012).
	Prevention of Forced Labour and Protection of Children's Rights	Promotion of labour rights and prohibition of forced labour, including but not limited to exploitation, trafficking in persons, violence and abuse, in line with the ASEAN Declaration on the Protection of the Rights of Migrant Workers and the ASEAN Consensus on the Protection and Promotion of Rights of Migrant Workers (ASEAN, 2012).
	Impact on People living Close to Investments	Management of investment-related impacts to people (including children) living in at-risk areas by encouraging inclusive and targeted measures to reduce the impact of investments on vulnerable populations and strengthen institutional capacity to address the needs of people affected, in line with the ASEAN Declaration on Strengthening Social Protection (ASEAN, 2013).

FIGURE 9.3 Key social aspects.
Source: ASEAN Secretariat / https://asean.org/wp-content/uploads/2024/12/ASEAN-Taxonomy-Finalised-Version-3-4.pdf / last accessed Aug 20, 2025.

Working together, the ASEAN member states were able to create a science-based taxonomy that incorporated the most nuanced elements available while respecting the different levels of economic development across the region. For that reason, explicitly recognizing the social elements of sustainability projects is far more important to other ASEAN states than it is to Singapore. As local companies and banks continue to work together, identifying sustainability improvement projects and financing the implementation, following frameworks like the ASEAN Taxonomy, will help reassure stakeholders that their capital will be put to good use.

And now we return to the third question posted at the beginning of the section "Finance Greenwashing: European Union Taxonomy": did the company really need to use a sustainability instrument for financing, or could it have financed the project(s) through working capital or other more traditional means? For investors motivated by sustainability, this is an important question. If a company could have financed a project through "normal" means, why would it have raised capital using a sustainability instrument like a green bond or SLB? As discussed in Chapter 7, these bonds are more costly, both in terms of issuing cost and monitoring expense, and it's unclear that the issuer should expect any benefit in the form of a lower interest rate (greenium). One thought might be that the company hopes to "look good" through its use of sustainability financing, not that the financing makes a difference in the company's ability to pursue desirable projects. As we will discuss in Chapter 12, the onus is on investors to do their homework and decide how much they care if their capital makes a difference in whether the project happens—a concept known as "additionality."

INTEGRATING SUSTAINABILITY: INTERVIEW WITH MICHAEL TANG, SGX

In conversation with James Cheo

James
How does the Singapore Exchange integrate sustainability?

Michael
For some time now, there has been a recognition that the sustainability performance of a company would have a correlation to the financial performance of the company. This is a key reason why, as a securities market regulator, we need to make sure that there is sufficient sustainability information for investors to make decisions.

(Continued)

(*Continued*)

Since 2011, we have asked companies to consider reporting on sustainability performance. But this was a voluntary requirement. In 2015, with the Paris Agreement, there's a lot more global acceptance that climate action requires all nations to act. And that would have an impact on capital markets.

In 2016, we introduced sustainability reporting for the first time as a listing requirement. At that time, we made the requirement flexible in order to suit the needs of companies. We require a sustainability report to be published, but companies can choose the most appropriate types of frameworks and targets for their business.

In 2021, we introduced a phased approach to mandatory climate reporting based on the recommendations of the Task Force on Climate-related Financial Disclosures TCFD) following a public consultation. This is a first step to better prepare issuers for reporting against anticipated global baseline sustainability reporting standards to be developed by the International Sustainability Standards Board [ISSB], which build on existing work of leading sustainability reporting organizations, including the TCFD.

That's our journey and how sustainability is incorporated into our listing requirements and framework.

James
How does the world stack up on sustainability standards?

Michael
Different countries are at different pace of adopting reporting requirements on sustainability. There is a common baseline requirement, but each country may differ on the specific matrix or information. For example, the US introduced specific climate reporting requirements. The US has taken the approach of designing their own set of reporting metrics and indicators and have required Scope 1 and Scope 2 to be disclosed, but not Scope 3 at this stage. The EU [European Union] of course also has its own set of standards. Their own European sustainability reporting standards are a much more comprehensive set of disclosure requirements, more prescriptive, and consider Scope 1, 2, and 3.

For the rest of the world, the ISSB is the baseline set of standards. The ISSB was endorsed by the International Organization of Securities Commissions (IOSCO). The next stage is for individual jurisdictions to adopt ISSB standards into their own requirements. For now, there might be deviation, but I believe that the trend is to have convergence around common international standards. Just look at the International Financial Reporting Standards [IFRS] and how it has evolved over the years and taken a similar trajectory. While there's a set of international standards, it's still dependent on individual markets to adopt it. Initially, not all markets may fully adopt the IFRS. However, over time, more countries will converge.

James
What are some positive and negative examples on sustainability reporting?

Michael
There are examples of good and bad reporting practices. In 2023, we commissioned the NUS [National University of Singapore] Business School, to look at all the sustainability reports with recommendations on how companies can do better. On the reporting itself, we looked at whether the company has disclosed the requisite information. In that respect, some areas are not so well suited for securities market regulations, because our primary concern is disclosure. We can set the reporting requirements in terms of what to disclose, but whether a target is sufficiently robust or whether a company is using energy efficiently is something that other stakeholders will need to opine on, as these involve some form of merit judgment on the company's performance. Similarly for financials, as a regulator, we say that a company must report on revenues, profits, and losses, for example, against the IFRS. But we do not say that you need to achieve this amount of profits in order to be a good company. So that's up to the rest of the ecosystem to judge.

James
What are the main sustainability tools for the exchange?

Michael
Disclosure is the main tool. Giving more information to stakeholders like investors will help them make better decisions and perhaps bring about change. I think the other powerful tool is that we've made the Board responsible for sustainability. Putting the responsibility on a board to take charge of sustainability means that the Board would then need to consider all these KPIs or governance frameworks to make

(Continued)

(*Continued*)

sure that the ESG targets are met. Apart from the hard tools, I would say that we also embark on a lot of market development efforts to raise the capacity and awareness on sustainability topics.

James
What sustainable products development have been developed by the exchange?

Michael
Equities are our mainstays, but the Singapore Exchange [SGX] is also a global listing platform for bonds, particularly wholesale bonds. We launched the SGX Group Sustainable Fixed Income initiative about two years back to give regulatory recognition to green bonds, social bonds, and sustainability bonds that meet certain prescribed requirements. The issuer will select a set of sustainability principles that is recognized by SGX, and also provide a review that would confirm compliance with these principles. Issuers getting this recognition must also make post-issuance reports on the use of the proceeds. The recognition allows issuers to differentiate themselves from other issuers.

On exchange-traded funds (ETFs), we see more ETFs with a sustainability theme. For example, the iShares MSCI Asia ex-Japan Climate Action ETF is listed on SGX. I think the proliferation of these instruments shows that there is investor interest in sustainability instruments and that hopefully would then become feedback for companies and a price signal for companies to know that there are benefits to be had.

James
How does the exchange mitigate the risk of greenwashing?

Michael
Greenwashing is a topical issue for regulators. The bigger question is what is sustainable. Taxonomy does help in setting these standards. The marketing of the terms "green" and "environmentally friendly" is under some scrutiny. The EU has recently rolled out a Greenwashing Directive to say that if you are going to use some of these terms you need to back it up. In Singapore, and maybe in Asia, the bigger challenge has been getting companies to disclose more information about their own sustainability performance.

James
How do you make small nonlisted companies with lesser resources disclose their sustainability?

Michael
We need to be proportionate for the smaller companies. In Singapore, we are extending the reporting mandate beyond listed companies. The Accounting and Corporate Regulatory Authority (ACRA) has announced that they want to look at climate reporting for nonlisted companies. We will start with the large companies, but that would slowly trickle down to smaller companies. As more companies report on sustainability, that is going to be the trajectory. We must be proportionate to give time for companies to build up the capacity.

James
The future role of exchange. How do you see the exchange enabling sustainable finance in the future?

Michael
We are focusing a lot on disclosure. When we get more high-quality sustainability data, we get better price discovery. So that is the baseline. With more data comes the ability to create more sustainable products. The exchange provides a platform for sustainable finance. For now, a lot of the sustainable financing takes place through the banks, perhaps for ease of execution. It's much easier for a bank to control the deal, to negotiate individually with borrowers with the right structure. But at some point in time, the capacity of banks is going to be outstripped by the demand. That's where capital markets can step in. For example, the exchange can enable securitization deals, when traditionally bank-backed projects, such as infrastructure projects, can be securitized into tranches and listed on the exchange. For maximum impact, the entire financial system can and should be transformed to incentivize and facilitate sustainable finance.

SUMMARY

There is a long tradition of companies trying to exploit the financial system (through legal means or otherwise) and regulators playing catch-up by adding new rules. With the increased awareness of sustainability and the rise of specialized financing instruments, greenwashing and its relatives are among the recent examples of undesirable corporate behavior; regulators are beginning to address this problem through a mix of legal statutes, taxonomies, and enforcement action. Anti-greenwashing legislation makes it clear how companies are expected to support their environmental claims, protecting consumers from misleading statements or those which attempt to deflect attention from the truth.

With respect to financing decisions, the EU Taxonomy and more recent international examples help define which business activities may already qualify as "green," which may not be green but can aid in the transition, and which are not aligned with a sustainability outcome. When combined with legal action, like the lawsuit against KLM for unsubstantiated environmental claims, the world may finally be able to anticipate an inflection point in corporate behavior.

CHAPTER 10

Taxes and Carbon Markets

Every few years, governments which are signatories to the Paris Agreement are required to submit a nationally determined contribution (NDC) describing their emissions reductions goals and initiatives. While some portion of emissions stem from government-controlled entities, in many economies it is the private sector that is responsible for much of the emissions. In Chapter 9, we discussed how regulators create disclosure requirements to encourage certain corporate behaviors. These changes in behavior are in part required because companies have been able to conduct their business without paying for the negative externalities they generate.

A negative externality is a term from economics that refers to ". . . the indirect imposition of a cost by one party onto another."[1] For example, imagine a company that dumps toxic chemicals into a river. From the company's perspective, it minimizes its own expenses by avoiding the cost of proper waste disposal. Meanwhile, downstream from the company, the local river life (fish, birds, other animals) has died, and local inhabitants are getting sick; but the company might not care unless *someone makes it pay for the damage it causes*—the negative externality.

Greenhouse gases (GHGs) are a classic example of a negative externality. Historically, coal-burning utility companies have not been asked to pay for the damage they cause, either from the lead and mercury by-products or the contribution to global warming from the carbon dioxide (CO_2) released into the atmosphere. Economist William Nordhaus was awarded the 2018 Nobel Prize in Economic Sciences for his development of an "integrated assessment model" (Figure 10.1):

> . . . *a quantitative model that describes the global interplay between the economy and the climate. His model integrates theories and empirical results from physics, chemistry and economics. Nordhaus' model is now widely spread and is used to simulate how the economy and the climate co-evolve. It is used to examine the consequences of climate policy interventions, for example carbon taxes.*[2]

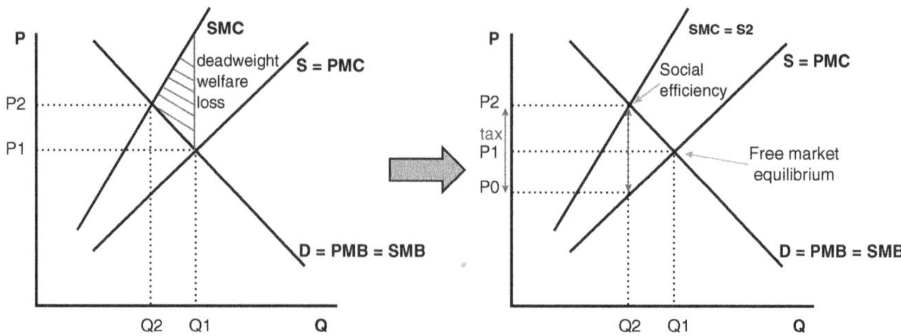

FIGURE 10.1   Diagram for negative externality.
Source: EconomicsHelp.org / https://www.economicshelp.org/blog/805/economics/ diagram-for-negative-externality/ / last accessed Aug 20, 2025.

As Nordhaus developed his model, he was able to estimate the cost of GHG emissions, i.e., the negative externality. As with other externalities, the government can play a corrective role by putting a price on pollution to raise the cost of production, which in turn results in a lower quantity at equilibrium.

The left-hand diagram shows what happens with an uncorrected negative production externality. In a free market, equilibrium occurs where private marginal cost (PMC) = private marginal benefit (PMB), or Q_1. When there is a negative externality, the socially optimal equilibrium occurs where the social production and demand curves meet (SMC = SMB) at Q_2. The negative externality leads to overconsumption and deadweight welfare loss (shaded).

To correct for this deadweight loss, a tax equal to the cost of the negative externality is introduced in the right-hand diagram. The price increases from P_1 to P_2 and demand decreases from Q_1 to Q_2 as companies and consumers alike account for the full costs of the negative externality.

Following this hypothetical scenario, the rest of this chapter explores mechanisms governments may use to address the negative externality of GHG emissions, either by directly establishing a price for pollution, by creating market-based financial incentives for decarbonization, or through collaboration with another nation-state.

POLLUTION TAXES

Pollution taxes are imposed by governments to force companies to account for the negative externalities of pollution, e.g., health issues and climate change, by making polluting activities more expensive for businesses and consumers. Such taxes can be applied across different types of pollution:

- *Solid waste* taxes address the disposal and management of solid waste.
- *Wastewater* taxes are based on the volume and toxicity of wastewater discharged.
- *Air pollution* taxes apply to emissions that degrade air quality, e.g., sulfur dioxide (SO_2) and particulate matter (PM; the most harmful type is less than five microns in size, referred to as PM5).
- *Hazardous chemicals* taxes are imposed on harmful industrial chemicals that pose significant environmental or health risks.
- *GHG emission* taxes are based on the carbon content of fossil fuels and other sources of emissions, e.g., methane emissions from animal husbandry.

Within these categories, pollution taxes can be further differentiated based on their design:

- *Emissions taxes* are levied directly on the quantity of pollutants emitted, providing a direct incentive for pollution reduction at the source. They may be difficult to monitor.
- *Product taxes* are applied to polluting products, such as fossil fuels. They may be easier to manage but less effective across an entire produce life cycle.

Policymakers may believe that pollution taxes can not only incentivize emissions reductions but also generate revenue for environmental investments and social programs. Critics argue, however, that these taxes lead to increased costs for consumers, disproportionately affecting low-income households. As countries refine their approaches to pollution taxation, the focus remains on creating systems that are environmentally effective, economically viable, and socially equitable.

Carbon Taxes

Putting a price on emissions corrects for the underpricing of the externality, integrating the cost of environmental harm into the pricing of goods and services, and encouraging the adoption of more responsible practices. The Nordic countries were among the first to implement carbon taxes in the early 1990s and boast some of the highest tax rates globally. While over 30 carbon tax and trading systems are operational at the national, subnational, and regional levels, the global average price of emissions remains notably low at less than US$5 per metric ton, a figure considerably below what is necessary to compel companies to change their operations.

These taxes are commonly imposed on fossil fuels in proportion to CO_2 emissions when burned, or on goods and services based on emissions released during their production. A carbon tax should extend universally to all fuels and sectors, yet many economies have started with artificially low tax rates and limited coverage by sector or firm size. Examples include:

- **Canada.** Canada's carbon tax system illustrates a complex interaction between federal and provincial policies. As of 2022, provinces like Alberta, Saskatchewan, Manitoba, and Ontario were subject to the federal fuel charge, while others like Quebec and British Columbia had their own systems, leading to a fragmented approach to carbon pricing. Companies pay the carbon tax but pass on much of the tax to their customers. The government uses the accumulated tax revenue to pay for environmental initiatives and returns the rest to individual taxpayers to compensate for higher prices.
- **Norway.** Norway introduced a carbon tax in 1991, which has undergone significant rate increases and gradual removal of exemptions over the years. This tax varies by sector and includes a CO_2 tax on mineral products, offshore petroleum operations, and waste incineration emissions. The Norwegian government has proposed further increases to the carbon tax, aiming to raise it to NOK2,000 (around US$190–200) per metric ton by 2030, compared to 2025 levels of NOK766.
- **Singapore.** In 2021, Singapore became the first Association of Southeast Asian Nations (ASEAN) country to introduce a carbon tax. Originally set at a low price of S$5 per metric ton of greenhouse gas emissions (just over US$3), it rose to S$25 in 2024 and is set to increase again to S$45 in 2026. It applies to facilities—as opposed to companies—emitting at least 25,000 metric tons of carbon dioxide equivalent (CO_2 e) per year, a level intended to impact roughly 50 companies responsible for 90% of national emissions.

The design of the tax and the method of revenue allocation significantly affect public acceptance and the behavioral outcomes associated with pollution taxes. Revenue recycling, where tax revenues are returned to citizens or invested in green initiatives, can mitigate regressive impacts on lower-income households and enhance overall public support. For instance, a visible dividend check may transform perceptions of the tax from a penalty to a mechanism that rewards sustainable practices, increasing acceptance and participation among citizens.

Carbon Leakage: Carbon Border Adjustment Mechanism[3]

Assume a European Union (EU) building developer can choose between two potential suppliers of steel with the same embodied carbon: a local mill also in the EU, and another mill from a non-EU country with no carbon tax. The EU-based supplier pays the EU carbon tax, and as result its steel is more expensive than that from the foreign supplier with no corresponding carbon tax. All else being equal the developer might choose to purchase from the foreign supplier instead of the local supplier to avoid paying the EU carbon tax.

To avoid this so-called "carbon leakage," or carbon arbitrage, the EU introduced the Carbon Border Adjustment Mechanism (CBAM). Designed to level the cost of carbon embedded between domestic and imported goods, the mechanism initially applies to six hard-to-abate, carbon-intensive industries.[4] Firms importing these goods from other markets would declare the value of the carbon embedded in the product and pay a tax equal to the difference between the export market's carbon price and the equivalent price in the EU. Even before implementation scheduled for 2026, revisions to CBAM have been included in the EU Omnibus proposal that would limit its reach to a smaller number of larger companies and delay implementation by a year or more—similar to the changes proposed for the Corporate Sustainability Reporting Directive (CSRD).

Emerging economies have spoken out against the CBAM, saying that it is unfair to impose developed-country tax levels on emerging markets and amounts to a form of "green protectionism." In a way, it is reminiscent of the wave of offshoring that shifted manufacturing jobs from the United States to China to exploit lower labor costs—here the cost differential is carbon, not wages. It is expected to be a matter of interest to the World Trade Organization (WTO).

CARBON MARKETS

Carbon markets have become a crucial tool in addressing climate change, integrating the cost of carbon emissions into economic decisions. Two different market mechanisms, regulated and voluntary, serve different purposes as described in the following sections. By putting a price on pollution, both market mechanisms create financial incentives for reducing emissions while encouraging innovation in cleaner technologies. However, carbon credit markets also face significant integrity risks, and overcoming issues such as environmental integrity and the quality of carbon credits is crucial for the growth and effectiveness of carbon markets.

Carbon credits are generated by projects that mitigate GHG emissions, with one credit corresponding to a metric ton of CO_2e. The concept of a credit is especially important for companies in hard-to-abate industries (e.g., airlines) that may find it difficult to reduce their emissions to net zero by 2050, the level required to be aligned with the Paris Agreement. By purchasing a credit, the high-emissions company pays for a project somewhere else that will avoid, reduce, or remove one metric ton of CO_2e—this is called offsetting.

Under the Science Based Targets Initiative (SBTi) methodology, permanent removals and storage (Figure 10.2) can be included in a net-zero target. While more controversial and a source of recent debate, some forms of "beyond value chain" mitigation may also be included.

Regulated Carbon Markets

Regulated (or compliance) carbon markets are systems where governmental organizations issue carbon emission allowances for domestic firms and sectors. There are two common methodologies used to price carbon:

- **Cap-and-trade.** Authorities set an upper limit (the "cap") on the total amount of GHG that an industry is permitted to emit. The cap is reduced over time by a predetermined rate. Each allowance (sometimes called a permit) allows its owner to emit one metric ton of CO_2 or similar GHG. Allowances are allocated to firms, after which the firms are able to buy and sell unused allowances in the market. At the end of the year, firms must return allowances equivalent to their GHG emissions for the year, incentivizing firms to reduce their emissions lest the costs of purchasing allowances in the market become too expensive.
- **Baseline-and-credit.** Baseline emission levels are defined and credits are issued to companies which reduce their emissions below the baseline level.

The EU Emissions Trading System (ETS)[5] is the largest emissions trading scheme globally and a cornerstone of European climate policy. The EU ETS operates on a "cap-and-trade" system that covers industries representing nearly 40% of the EU's GHGs. Since its introduction in 2005, emissions from covered sources (electricity and heat generation, industrial manufacturing, aviation, and maritime transport) have declined 48%, aided by higher input prices and declining prices for renewable energy (Figure 10.3).

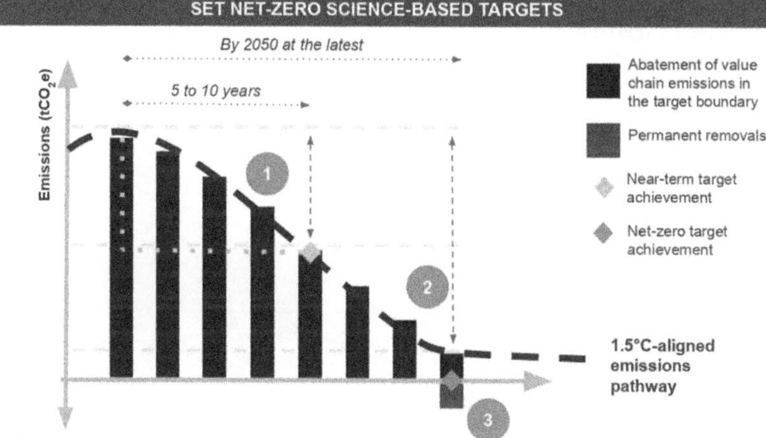

1   **Near-term SBTs**: 5-10 year emission reduction targets in line with 1.5°C pathways.

2   **Long-term SBTs:** Target to reduce emissions to a residual level in line with 1.5°C scenarios by no later than 2050.

NEUTRALIZATION

3   **Neutralization of residual emissions:** GHGs released into the atmosphere when the company has achieved their long-term SBT must be counterbalanced through the permanent removal and storage of carbon from the atmosphere.

<u>Recommendation 10 - Neutralization milestones</u>: *Companies should disclose information such as planned milestones and near-term investments that demonstrate the integrity of commitments to neutralize unabated emissions at net-zero.*

BEYOND VALUE CHAIN MITIGATION (BVCM)

<u>Recommendation 9 - Beyond value chain climate mitigation</u>: *Companies should take action or make investments outside their own value chains to mitigate GHG emissions in addition to their near-term and long-term science-based targets. For example, a company could provide annual support to projects, programs and solutions providing quantifiable benefits to climate, especially those that generate additional co-benefits for people and nature. Companies should report annually on the nature and scale of those actions.**

** Please see "Above and Beyond: An SBTi report on the design and implementation of beyond value chain mitigation (BVCM)".*

BVCM Goals

Goal 1: Deliver additional near-term mitigation outcomes to achieve the peaking of global emissions in the mid-20s and the halving of global emissions by 2030.

Goal 2: Drive additional finance into the scale-up of nascent climate solutions and enabling activities to unlock the systemic transformation needed to achieve net-zero by mid-century globally.

BVCM Principles

FIGURE 10.2   Four key elements make up the Net-Zero Standard framework. *Source:* Jones Lang LaSalle IP, Inc. / https://files.sciencebasedtargets.org/production/files/SBTi-Net-Zero-Standard-Event-slides.pdf / last accessed Aug 20, 2025.

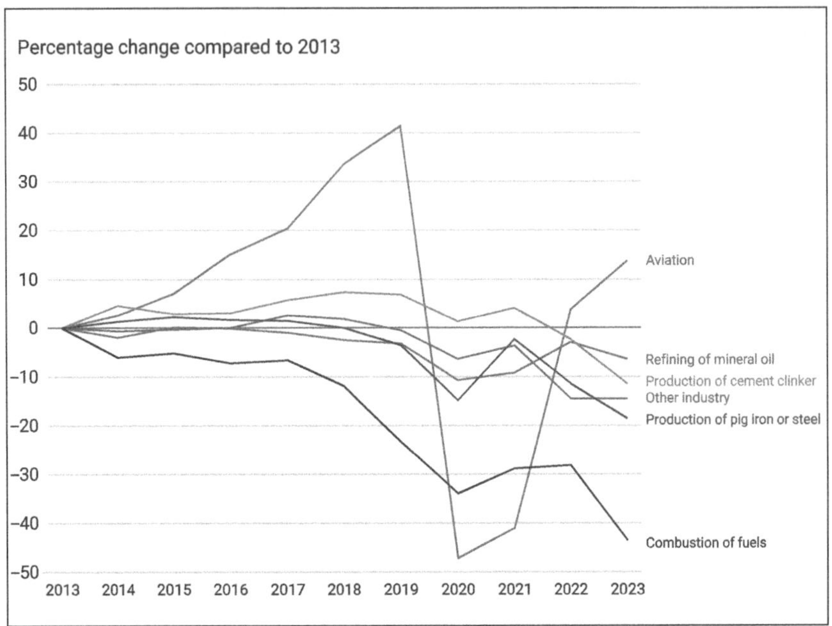

FIGURE 10.3 European Union (EU) carbon permits since late 2021.
Source: European Environment Agency / https://files.sciencebasedtargets.org/
production/files/SBTi-Net-Zero-Standard-Event-slides.pdf / last accessed
Aug 20, 2025.

The cap is reduced at a rate of 4.3% per year through 2027, and 4.4% beginning in 2028. The cost of carbon, while initially low, has remained above €60 per metric ton since late 2021 (Figure 10.4).

As of this writing, the World Bank lists 80 different compliance mechanisms, including 37 ETSs, including in the EU, the United Kingdom, New Zealand, South Korea, Canada, and China.[6] At present, ETSs operate on a largely independent basis, but international cooperation could lead to linkages between compliance carbon markets and a consistent global carbon price over time.

Voluntary Markets

The voluntary carbon market (VCM) is a self-regulated market that enables participants to offset their emissions by purchasing credits associated with projects intended to avoid, reduce, or remove GHGs (Figure 10.5).

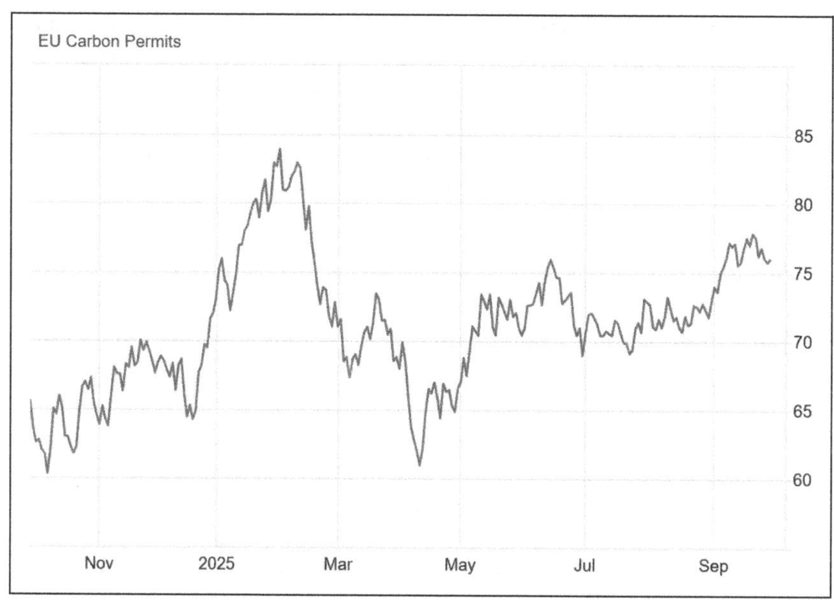

FIGURE 10.4 Changes in emissions covered by the European Union (EU) Emissions Trading System (ETS) by sector, 2013–2023, relative to 2013.
Source: Modified from https://tradingeconomics.com/commodity/carbon (Left).

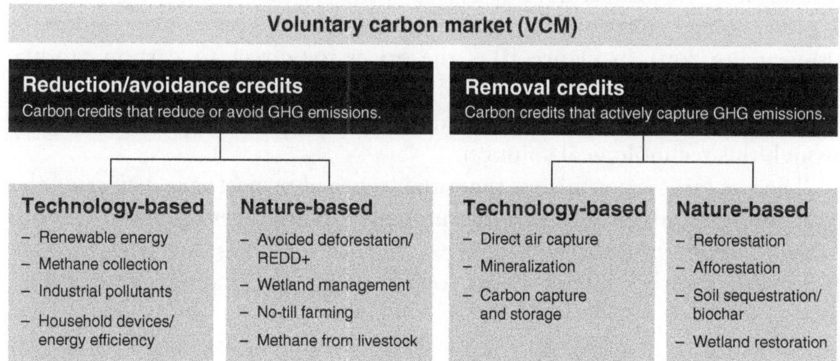

FIGURE 10.5 Voluntary carbon market (VCM).
Source: EYGM Limited /https://www.bankofsingapore.com/managed-resources/
pdf/BOS-EY-ESG%20report%20on%20Carbon%20Credits_2023.pdf / last
accessed Aug 20, 2025.

Reduction/avoidance credits focus on emission reduction or prevention, including deforestation avoidance and providing fuel-efficient cookstoves. Removal credits involve capturing and storing carbon from the atmosphere through projects such as reforestation, coastal area restoration, direct air capture, and carbon capture, utilization, and storage. Other eligible project types include methane capture, tree plantations, wind farms, and solar-powered lamps, as well as various nature-based solutions (NBSs).

Key participants along the life cycle of a project from inception to issuance (and trading) of credits include:

- *Developers* who design and implement projects for emission reduction, prepare project documents, and follow established methodologies.
- *Standards-making bodies* (e.g., Verra, Gold Standard) that establish requirements, procedures, and tools for project stakeholders to develop projects and verify emission reductions/removals.
- *Verification agencies* that validate project design and verify carbon reduction claims by conducting feasibility studies and calculations.
- *Registries* that provide transparency by tracking the transfer and retirement of carbon credits.
- *Legal entities* that request registration of a project and credit issuance.
- *Financial institutions* that provide financing and facilitate trading.

Market pricing for credits, each representing the same one metric ton of CO_2e, varies widely. Aside from common investment attributes, such as the reputation of the project developer, one of the primary drivers is confidence that the claimed emissions mitigation is both real and permanent (at least a 100-year horizon). In Figure 10.6, the prices for direct air carbon capture and storage (DACCS, often simplified to DAC) are by far the highest, reflecting the greater confidence in the measurement of mitigation outcomes through this technological solution.

There is far less confidence that other types of projects are delivering the stated mitigation outcomes. A recent paper in the peer-reviewed journal *Nature Communications* analyzed 65 scientific studies covering projects representing nearly 1 billion metric tons of CO_2e. The findings are striking:

> We estimate that less than 16% of the carbon credits issued to the investigated projects constitute real emission reductions, with 11% for cookstoves, 16% for SF_6 destruction, 25% for avoided deforestation, 68% for HFC-23 abatement, and no statistically significant emission reductions from wind power and improved forest management projects.[7]

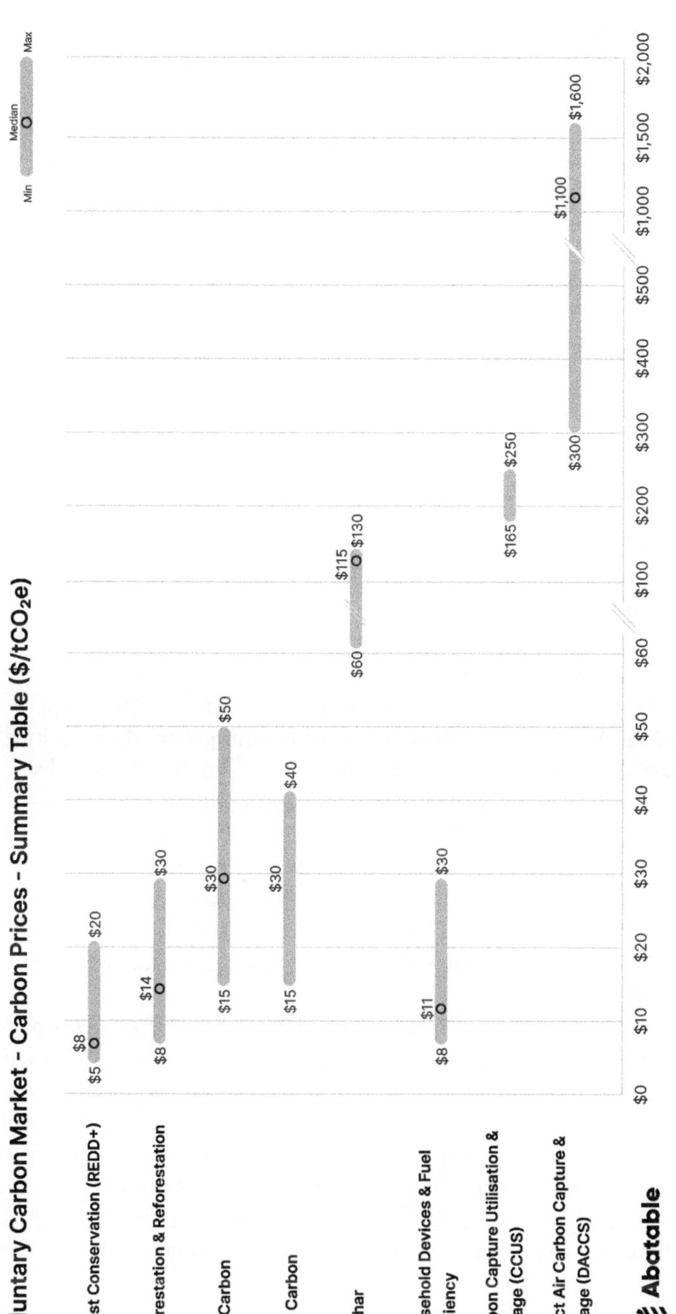

FIGURE 10.6 Voluntary carbon market: carbon prices, August 2022.
Source: Zero Imprint Ltd / https://abatable.com/blog/carbon-credits-pricing/, data as of August 2022 / last accessed Aug 20, 2025.

Critics argue that some companies exploit the VCMs by purchasing low-integrity credits to claim they are on the path to net-zero, while the difficult work of real emissions reduction is left for the future. Self-regulatory bodies, verification agencies, and other participants are working hard to rectify these integrity issues. Even if questions remain about the veracity of voluntary offsetting, many projects remain worthwhile—planting trees[8] and replacing charcoal cookstoves could hardly be called "bad" for climate—as long as the claimed amount of carbon mitigation is within reason.

ARTICLE 6 CARBON MARKETS

The earlier sections on "Pollution Taxes" and "Carbon Markets" describe how companies can use carbon credits as part of an emissions reduction strategy, either on a compliance or voluntary basis. But credits and offsetting are not limited to companies; Article 6 of the Paris Agreement includes mechanisms for Parties to cooperate on a voluntary basis to help achieve their respective NDCs.

Article 6.2 introduces Internationally Transferred Mitigation Outcomes (ITMOs) as the unit of trade. Both parties must maintain a current NDC and possess a recent national inventory report. Parties are required to submit initial reports, annual information, and regular updates, detailing the cooperative approach, and ITMO metrics including emissions mitigation data. Critically, both parties to the ITMO must adjust their emissions levels to reflect the transfer or receipt of mitigation outcomes, preventing double-counting.

Article 6.4 and the associated Supervisory Body establishes the Paris Agreement Crediting Mechanism to maintain accounts for pending actions, holdings, retirements, and cancellations. This body will also issue Article 6.4 Emission Reductions (A6.4 ERs) for verified mitigation achievements which can be utilized toward Parties' NDCs or other international mitigation efforts.

Unfortunately, as of this writing, Article 6 has not yet been completely finalized and implemented. However, some countries are moving forward to sign bilateral Article 6.2 ITMOs. As a small but developed country, Singapore presents an interesting case study. Lacking the physical resources[9] to develop significant renewable energy capacity on its own, Singapore has become one of the world's most active proponents of Article 6.2 ITMOs with seven such agreements signed as of June 2025.[10] The first agreement with Papua New Guinea was finalized in December 2023, followed by Ghana, Bhutan, Peru, Chile, Rwanda, and Paraguay.

Using the Papua New Guinea arrangement as an example, Singapore takes two additional steps to fight climate change. First, the project developers will contribute an amount equal to 5% of the deal value (in A6.4 ERs) to support the host country's adaptation actions. Second, Singapore will retire 2% of the emissions at issue, permanently removing those credits and ensuring that they cannot be traded or reused in the future. Article 6 has an important role to play in realizing global climate ambitions, and it will be interesting to see what happens after all is signed and implemented.

SUMMARY

Companies have overproduced and society has overconsumed for decades, resulting in a climate crisis of our own making. As government steps in to address the negative externality of greenhouse gas emissions, we should expect things to change if the price on pollution is high enough. Whether through taxes or carbon markets, companies will be under increasing pressure to pay for their emissions or make changes; individuals, too, will see prices for items go up and will need to decide whether and where to change their behavior. Whether the mechanism is a carbon tax, regulatory or voluntary carbon markets, or national-level agreements through Article 6 of the Paris Agreement, every action matters. The degree to which companies implement internal carbon pricing similarly should be of great interest to investors wishing to assess the sensitivity of companies to higher carbon prices.

Sustainable Investing

Companies in the "real economy"—fabricating items and performing services—are not the only entities with a role to play in addressing sustainability issues like climate change. They are merely the most directly involved, since real economy activities create emissions in the first place. But making changes to operations are rarely without cost, and companies need to pay for these changes somehow. Some sustainability issues may present meaningful financial or operational risks to companies, such as a firm with physical assets located near the coast or near a floodplain. Investors, therefore, are increasingly focused on the financial implications of sustainability issues for companies.

Although the words used to describe these activities may be new ("ESG," "sustainability," "DEI"), the act of investing is not. The Principles for Responsible Investment (PRI) say that sustainable investing does not mean a wholesale rejection of traditional investing, but rather that investors incorporate issues of sustainability systematically throughout the investment process.

Part Four describes how investors make their investment decisions in practice. In Chapter 11, we examine environmental, social, and governance (ESG) ratings which serve as a bridge between corporate sustainability disclosures and investors. Chapter 12 explores the different strategies that investors follow when incorporating sustainability information into their investment decisions. One of these strategies, impact investing, is sufficiently different from the others that it receives its own chapter (13). We examine some of the key differences in sustainable investing across asset classes, e.g., public vs. private equities, in Chapter 14. Finally, Part Four concludes with Chapter 15 on greenwashing and regulations for investors.[1]

Interpreting Corporate Sustainability Disclosures: Environmental, Social, and Governance Ratings

As companies measure and disclose increasing amounts of information regarding their sustainability-related activities and impacts, this information becomes the raw material from which investors make their investment decisions. This should come as no surprise—after all, investors routinely use financial statements to perform their financial analyses, e.g., using 10-K and 10-Q filings to estimate the "fair value" of a stock based on projected future cash flows.

In the same way, we shouldn't be surprised that another artifact of the traditional investing landscape has blossomed in the garden of sustainability: experts. Or, as they more commonly appear, "ratings" from experts. Many readers will be familiar with equity and debt analysts who work for investment banks and appear on business television shows to pronounce a stock is a "buy, hold, or sell." There are even ratings on mutual funds, although not exactly following the same format. After a brief summary of the traditional types of ratings, the remainder of this chapter describes the new kid on the ratings block, "ESG ratings." We will summarize the Big Three (MSCI, Refinitiv, and Sustainalytics) plus a few others of note, and end with a review of the many limitations of ESG ratings.

ANALYST RATINGS

Investing can be a decidedly independent, solitary activity. Popular accounts often glamorize the individual without much recognition for the network of other actors that have a role to play. Certainly, for professional investors working at investment firms, it makes intuitive sense that others may be involved, e.g., analysts supporting the portfolio manager, or traders who take care of buying and selling at the best possible prices. Even "mom and pop" investors are in some way beholden to others, whether financial columnists, a Reddit group, or a couple of friends at the gym. The fact is that investors of all stripes tap into a network of information providers.

A valuable part of that information network is an influential group of firms and experts whose jobs it is to provide their well-researched opinions on potential investments.[1] In the world of stock investing, these are called "research analysts" or "equity analysts." They may work for global investment banks like Goldman Sachs or UBS, regional banks like DBS (Singapore) or BTG Pactual (Brazil), or one of many independent specialist firms. Equity analysts typically create their own forecasts for a company's future financial performance. By comparing the current price of a stock, and the value of the company that it implies, with the forecast value, analysts may decide that the stock appears to be under- or overvalued. If the value discrepancy is large enough, the analyst may issue a rating of "buy" or "sell"; one of the most common ratings is "hold," or its equivalent, reflecting both the difficulty of accurately forecasting the future and the relative efficiency of major stock markets.[2]

Let us consider a simplified example. An analyst working for a large, multinational bank specializes in the airline industry. One of the stocks they cover is Thai Airways. Their research suggests that the value of the company should be US$466.18 million; current stock prices, however, indicate that the market believes the company is only worth US$396.25 million,[3] a difference of −15%. In this case they might choose to publish a rating of "buy," reflecting their conviction that the market is currently (and temporarily) underpricing Thai Airlines' stock. However, if the current valuation was US$412.76 million, instead, and the underpricing was only −4%, that might not be enough of a difference to warrant a "buy" rating—in this case the imprecision of forecasting might mean that a valuation estimate within ±4% is nothing to be excited about. In that case they might rate the stock a "hold."

Similarly, bond investors will be familiar with credit ratings. There are important differences between stock and bond analysts and their ratings. First, the market for credit ratings is far more concentrated than for stocks, with three firms—Fitch, Moody's, and S&P—enjoying an oligopoly in this market. Second, the nature of the analysis is quite different. Whereas an equity analyst is tasked with forecasting the future value of an entire firm, a credit analyst's concern is the creditworthiness of the company. Even more specifically, the credit analyst is responsible for assessing the risk that a company (the "issuer") will default on a specific bond.

Let's assume that Thai Airways has issued a 10-year bond for THB1.5 billion, with an interest rate of 5.16%.[4] A Moody's credit analyst will analyze the company's financials to estimate the risk that Thai Airways might have to default on the interest payments or might not be able to return the full principal amount. As described above, equity analysts generally have three options when publishing their ratings: buy, hold, or sell. The major credit ratings agencies, however, use a more granular ratings system shown in Table 11.1.

TABLE 11.1 Credit Rating Tier Definitions

Moody's	S&P	Fitch	Creditworthiness[7][8]
Aaa1 Aaa2 Aaa3	AAA+ AAA AAA−	AAA+ AAA AAA−	An obligor has **extremely strong** capacity to meet its financial commitments.
Aa1 Aa2 Aa3	AA+ AA AA−	AA+ AA AA−	An obligor has **very strong** capacity to meet its financial commitments. It differs from the highest-rated obligors only to a small degree.
A1 A2 A3	A+ A A−	A+ A A−	An obligor has **strong** capacity to meet its financial commitments but is somewhat more susceptible to the adverse effects of changes in circumstances and economic conditions than obligors in higher-rated categories.
Baa1 Baa2 Baa3	BBB+ BBB BBB−	BBB+ BBB BBB−	An obligor has **adequate** capacity to meet its financial commitments. However, adverse economic conditions or changing circumstances are more likely to lead to a weakened capacity of the obligor to meet its financial commitments.
Ba1 Ba2 Ba3	BB+ BB BB−	BB+ BB BB−	An obligor is **less vulnerable** in the near term than other lower-rated obligors. However, it faces major ongoing uncertainties and exposure to adverse business, financial, or economic conditions which could lead to the obligor's inadequate capacity to meet its financial commitments.
B1 B2 B3	B+ B B−	B+ B B−	An obligor is **more vulnerable** than the obligors rated 'BB', but the obligor currently has the capacity to meet its financial commitments. Adverse business, financial, or economic conditions will likely impair the obligor's capacity or willingness to meet its financial commitments.
Caa1 Caa2 Caa3	CCC+ CCC CCC−	CCC+ CCC CCC−	An obligor is **currently vulnerable**, and is dependent upon favourable business, financial, and economic conditions to meet its financial commitments.
Ca1 Ca2 Ca3	CC+ CC CC−	CC+ CC CC−	An obligor is **currently highly vulnerable**.
	C+ C C−	C+ C C−	The obligor is **currently highly vulnerable** to nonpayment. May be used where a bankruptcy petition has been filed.
C	D	D	An obligor has **failed** to pay one or more of its financial obligations (rated or unrated) when it became due

Source: https://en.wikipedia.org/wiki/Bond_credit_rating.

In this case, the credit analyst believes that Thai Airways is financially sound and poses a low risk of default; Moody's has issued a rating of Baa1,[5] reflecting moderate credit risk according to its rating criteria.

Comparing our two examples, there are several important differences to note. First, there are far more firms publishing stock ratings than credit ratings agencies. Second, equity ratings schemes are less complicated than credit ratings. Third, however, equity ratings are based on more complex information encompassing the whole firm and its future cash flows, while credit ratings are narrowly focused on a specific bond issuance and the potential risk of default. Overall, bond ratings appear "simpler" compared with equity ratings, and analysis bears this out. Even allowing for the greater number of ratings categories in use, bond ratings from the three big ratings agencies are very highly correlated.[6] From this perspective, once an investor knows the credit rating assigned by one of the credit ratings agencies, the ratings issued by the other two agencies are unlikely to add a significant amount of new information.

Finally, there is the question of which analysts issue ratings for which companies, and why. Equity analysts within larger brokerage firms are usually considered a "cost center," i.e., unprofitable based on their own revenues and expenses. They publish ratings for the benefit of two different sets of clients, both internal and external. Analyst ratings represent information for their colleagues in the sales and trading businesses (internal) and their investing clients (external). Analyst ratings are also important for companies (external) and the analysts' colleagues in investment banking (internal). If an influential analyst decides to cover a stock, and the coverage (including the rating) is positive, then that might lead more investors to buy the stock, potentially increasing the stock price. Investment bankers benefit from having a good analyst covering the stock of a company for which the bankers wish to do deals. Faced with this complex set of internal and external dynamics, the important element for this discussion is that analysts and their employers decide themselves which firms to cover and which firms to ignore[7]—no one pays them for coverage.[8]

The fixed-income market works differently, potentially with separate ratings for the company overall and for each individual bond. Credit ratings agencies (Fitch, Moody's, and S&P) provide both types of ratings. The business model, however, is different: most of the time, companies pay the ratings agencies to issue a rating for each bond. This apparent lack of independence came under scrutiny following the 2008 Global Financial Crisis. In hindsight, credit ratings on some mortgage-backed securities (MBS) did not reflect the true risk of the underlying subprime loans. Although AAA-rated subprime securities performed better than expected, the failure of credit ratings agencies to accurately assess risks in weaker securities contributed to crisis.[9]

ENVIRONMENTAL, SOCIAL, AND GOVERNANCE RATINGS

Exxon is rated top ten best in the world for environment, social & governance (ESG) by S&P 500, while Tesla didn't make the list! ESG is a scam. It has been weaponised by phony social justice warriors.[10]

—Elon Musk via Twitter (now X), MAY 19, 2022
https://x.com/elonmusk/status/1526958110023245829

As companies began to follow standards, like the Global Reporting initiative (GRI), to measure and disclose their sustainability information, a new kind of rating emerged: environmental, social, and governance (ESG) ratings. While some CEOs may take issue with the rating for their company—or the whole system, if you're Elon Musk—ESG ratings are now a important part of the sustainability landscape. The original intent was to create a complementary view of a company compared with a typical equity analyst's rating, focused exclusively on its sustainability characteristics. The pioneer in this space was KLD. Founded by Peter Kinder, Steve Lydenberg, and Amy Domini, KLD launched the Domini 400 Social Index in 1990, the very first ESG index. Initially focused on product-based exclusions and companies with strong community, employee, and environmental practices, KLD later expanded its methodology to include governance and climate-related factors. In 2009, KLD was acquired by RiskMetrics, which in turn was acquired by MSCI in 2010, marking the start of the firm's dominant position in the ESG ratings business.[11] Since then, many independent firms have launched competing ESG ratings, either covering a broad set of issues in a slightly different way, or specializing in a narrow set of issues with greater depth than other firms.

Over time, MSCI, Refinitiv, and Sustainalytics have gathered the lion's share of the market, but there are many ESG ratings and ranking agencies, each with its own methodology for evaluating a company's ESG performance:

- **MSCI.** MSCI acquired both Innovest and KLD, two of the earliest ESG data vendors. MSCI ESG Ratings are built on Innovest's methodology, which focuses on financial materiality and industry-specific assessments.
- **Refinitiv.** Refinitiv's ESG scores are based on an analysis of public information disclosed by companies in reports and on websites, as well as through direct contact with the company. Refinitiv's arrives at its ESG scores using a roll-up of ~400 metrics.

- **Sustainalytics.** Now part of Morningstar, Sustainalytics provides ESG risk ratings using industry-specific criteria and covering preparedness, disclosure, and performance. Sustainalytics allows companies to review their ESG Company Feedback Report prior to publication.
- **ISS ESG.** Institutional Shareholder Services (ISS) provides a variety of ESG ratings solutions to help investors incorporate ESG insights into their investment research. The ISS Governance Quality Score is often available on Yahoo!Finance. ISS's methodology takes into consideration numerous governance factors, including board structure, compensation, shareholder rights, and audit and risk.
- **Bloomberg.** Bloomberg launched its ESG Data Service in 2009, offering ESG metrics and disclosure scores for more than 11,500 companies in over 80 countries, with historical data going back to 2006. Bloomberg uses analysts to standardize reported data disclosed by companies, using ~120 ESG indicators, with scores updated annually.
- **Moody's–V.E.** Moody's acquired Vigeo Eiris (V.E), a research agency that uses 38 sustainability criteria based on international standards. V.E is based in Europe, but is now positioned as a global ESG player.
- **S&P Global.** S&P Global provides corporate sustainability assessments, utilizing the Carbon Disclosure Project (CDP) Climate Change Questionnaire in its methodology, and also offers Trucost ESG analysis.
- **JUST Capital.** JUST Capital is a nonprofit organization that tracks and engages with large corporations and investors on their performance on public priorities. JUST Capital polls Americans to determine what issues matter most.

Pause for a moment and think about how you would create a rating system for corporate sustainability performance. What information would you need? How would you assess the performance? How would you assign weights to E, S, and G? Holding this mental model in your mind, consider the following information on the three largest ratings agencies, MSCI, Sustainalytics, and Refinitiv.

MSCI

The MSCI rating scheme follows the familiar bond rating system where AAA represents the highest rating (lowest risk) and CCC represents the lowest rating (highest risk). To arrive at these ratings MSCI follows a funnel-like process:

1. Gather as much sustainability-related data as possible, including data disclosed by the company, as well as data from other sources.
2. Consider the material risks facing the company.

3. Evaluate how well the company is managing its risk exposure.
4. Analyze the exposure the company has to a list of critical issues (this list is updated every year).
5. Combine the information in the preceding steps to create the final ratings.

Visually the process is represented in Figure 11.1.

Detailed information on MSCI's ratings methodology is available on its website, which, as of this writing, appears here: https://www.msci.com/esg-and-climate-methodologies.

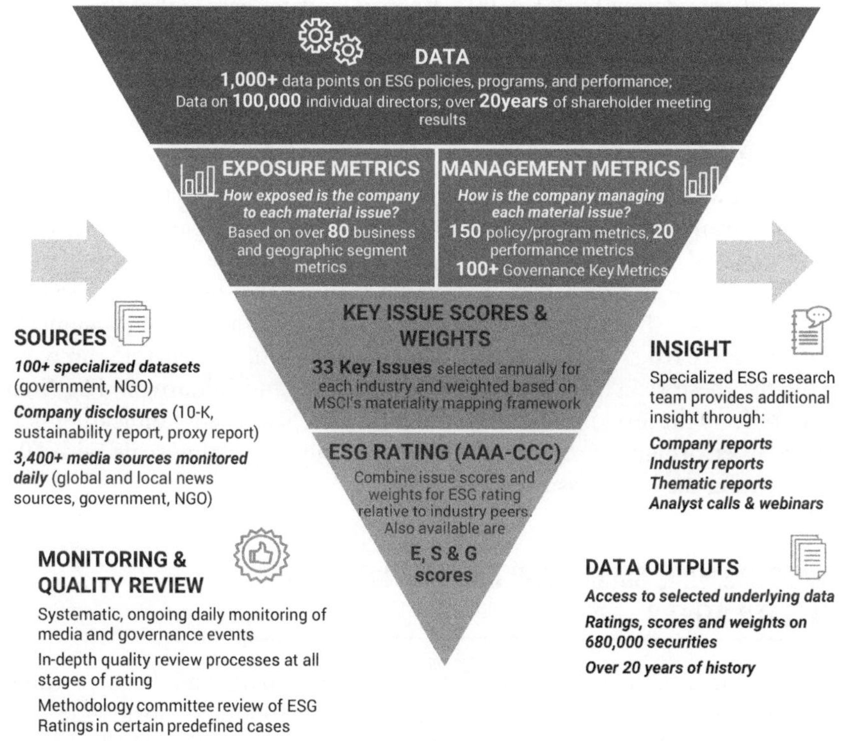

FIGURE 11.1 MSCI environmental, social, and governance (ESG) rating framework and process overview.
Source: MSCI Inc. / https://www.msci.com/esg-and-climate-methodologies. / last accessed Aug 20, 2025.

Refinitiv

Refinitiv ESG Ratings, formerly known as ASSET4, provide a comprehensive evaluation of companies' ESG performances. The ratings are based on over 630 ESG metrics, with 186 material metrics used to calculate scores across ten thematic categories, such as emissions, human rights, and shareholder management. Companies are assessed on an academic grading scale from A+ to D−. Refinitiv's methodology emphasizes materiality, weighted by industry to ensure that the most relevant ESG factors are prioritized. Additionally, the ESG controversy (ESGC) score adjusts ratings to reflect the impact of negative media coverage. The ratings cover over 12,500 companies globally, with historical data dating back to 2002. Regular updates ensure that the ratings reflect the latest available information, while controversy adjustments help account for media bias, particularly for larger companies.[12]

Sustainalytics

As the "newest" of the big-three ratings agencies, Sustainalytics considered its competitors and identified what they considered to be a gap in the market. Sustainalytics' ESG Risk Ratings measure the extent to which a company's economic value is exposed to ESG risks using a two-dimensional framework: Exposure and Management. Exposure assesses a company's vulnerability to ESG risks, while Management evaluates how well the company mitigates these risks through policies, practices, and initiatives. The final score reflects the level of unmanaged risk, with a lower score indicating better ESG performance.[13] Sustainalytics uses a numeric rating scale with "0" representing the best possible score (zero risk).

ENVIRONMENTAL, SOCIAL, AND GOVERNANCE RATINGS: SELECTED OTHERS

By year-end 2024, the market for ESG ratings data had become quite crowded, with estimates suggesting there were hundreds worldwide and approximately 30–40 operating within the European Union (EU) alone.[14] Some of the more established ratings providers include:

- **CDP.** The Carbon Disclosure Project (CDP) was the first organization to leverage investor pressure to drive corporate environmental disclosure. Its disclosure system integrates best reporting standards, including the International Sustainability Standards Board (ISSB) and the Taskforce on Nature-related Financial Disclosures (TNFD), providing comprehensive data to support informed environmental decision-making for businesses, investors, and governments.[15]

- **ISS.** Institutional Shareholder Services (ISS), a proxy advisory firm, provides guidance for shareholders on how to cast their votes. In addition, ISS issues stand-alone ratings on corporate Governance practices, similar to the Governance pillars of composite ratings from firms like MSCI.[16]

- **FTSE4GOOD.** The FTSE4GOOD Index Series is designed to measure the performance of companies demonstrating strong ESG practices. It serves as a tool for investors to create sustainable investment products, benchmark portfolios, and assess companies' alignment with evolving ESG standards.[17]

- **GRESB.** GRESB (Global Real Estate Sustainability Benchmark) provides standardized and validated ESG data assessing the sustainability performance of real estate and infrastructure portfolios worldwide. As a benchmark provider using company-submitted data, GRESB is the one organization that simultaneously functions as a standard for corporate reporting and a ratings provider for investors.[18]

ISSUES WITH RATINGS

Any product with many features and potential configurations will find it difficult to satisfy everyone's needs at the same time. Such is certainly the case with ESG ratings. Perhaps because KLD chose to emulate the bond rating nomenclature, investors developed an expectation that ESG ratings should behave like bond ratings—few ratings agencies and high correlations between them. In other words, they wanted ESG information to be relatively easy for investors to process. This is most certainly not the case today.

Consider bond ratings again for a moment. A bond rating is predominantly based on audited financial information provided in a standardized format, plus the terms of the bond itself as described in a prospectus. Sustainability information, however, includes all manner of unaudited data, in varying units (kilograms of carbon dioxide [CO_2] emissions, hours, megaliters, etc.), and presented in a myriad of formats. The objective of a credit rating is to assess default risk, full stop. The objective of an ESG rating, however, encompasses a far wider range of potential risks, as well as opportunities. As a result, the correlations between different ratings providers range from merely weak to quite low, an effect sometimes referred to as "ratings disagreement" and well documented in an influential academic paper published in 2022.[19]

After measuring the amount of disagreement between leading ESG ratings providers (MSCI, Refinitiv, Sustainalytics), the authors extended the analysis to identify the *sources* of disagreement. Broadly speaking, they highlighted three main areas:

- what is measured;
- how it is measured;
- relative weighting of measures.

RATING AGENCIES: INTERVIEW WITH MITCH REZNICK, CFA, FEDERATED HERMES

In conversation with James Cheo

James
When the agencies rate conventional bonds, the ratings are quite similar. But now with different rating agencies rating on green bonds, is it very different?

Mitch
Rating agencies have been in business for 120 years. And credit analysis probably goes back 1,000 years. So, there's substantial correlation between the ratings. With the green bonds, and the assessment services, [they] are all relatively new, but they have different nomenclature for conveying the same thing, which is, they are all guided by the ICMA [International Capital Market Association] principles, and even the banks are guided by the ICMA principles when they create these bonds. Rating agencies are creating interpretations based on a set of universal principles. And there's some convergence there. The part that that I worry about is, they pay for the rating, and if the rating is going to be very poor, they don't get the ratings. So, there's an element of you need a certain assessment to get into the market, but you never see anyone fail, or very rarely. That's particularly true in the sustainability-linked markets.

I do have concerns about conflicts of interest—the verification services might be guiding a company [on] how to issue and then they rate it at the same time.[20] Nevertheless, I'm more concerned about the ESG rating market than the green bond assessment market, because at least in the green bond assessment market, you have a framework that we can lean to, whereas the ESG rating market is just the wild, wild west.

A good example of how the same incident may be treated very differently by different ESG ratings providers comes from the Wells Fargo account opening scandal of 2016.[21] In this incident, employees opened new accounts for existing customers without their permission, all in an effort to meet their sales targets. The scandal cost the chief executive officer (CEO) his job, and would clearly impact the firm's ESG rating—but where? One ratings agency penalized the firm under the governance pillar; another ratings agency under social and the issue "information to customers." What seems like a relatively straightforward questions may be subject to interpretation where ESG ratings are concerned.

In addition to this rather lengthy list of methodological issues and potential biases, there is another important issue lurking in the background: materiality. A sensational (by finance standards) article in *Bloomberg Businessweek* in 2021 stated it very clearly:

> *...[t]here's virtually no connection between MSCI's "better world" marketing and its methodology. That's because the ratings don't measure a company's impact on the Earth and society. In fact, they gauge the opposite: the potential impact of the world on the company and its shareholders. MSCI doesn't dispute this characterization. It defends its methodology as the most financially relevant for the companies it rates.*[22]

ESG ratings are deliberately constructed around *financial* rather than *impact* materiality.

So what? Bond ratings are also focused on financial risks, and since ESG ratings are loosely modeled on bond ratings, why should this be a surprise? The issue may stem from the fact that people are used to associating default risk with *financial* materiality but think of *impact* materiality (Make the world a better place! Treat the environment well! A great place to work!) when it comes to issues of sustainability. When a company has a AAA credit rating, we can believe it's unlikely to default. When a company has a AAA *ESG rating*, however, it is possible that people will think about the company's impact on people and planet before the financial risks.

Even if this is the case, is it important? When investors use ESG ratings in their investment process and subsequently portray their funds as being focused on providing capital to "sustainability leaders", then it's a problem because that's not what ESG ratings are for. We will discuss this problem in more detail when we discuss investor greenwashing in Chapter 15.

There are other issues at work, two of which we will discuss here. The first concerns who pays for the ratings data. In the bond market the issuer pays. While this model presents its own challenges,[23] for the purposes of this discussion the important takeaway is that investors pay very little for credit ratings data. For ESG ratings, however, the investor often must pay a very substantial subscription fee. Investors would prefer to pay for information that is important to stock returns, and they are accustomed to spending money on services such as Bloomberg, Refinitiv, and FactSet. While there are competing vendors available, most investors will use a single service because historical pricing data and company financials are relatively commoditized—and because subscriptions can cost well over $100,000 per year.

With ESG ratings data, however, differences in the ratings methodologies means that the data are *not* commoditized, so investors face a two-part challenge. First, investors need to compare different ratings providers to determine which service(s) would best complement the investor's research process. Second, it may be the case that different ratings data can be used for different things, which might suggest the investor should subscribe to multiple ESG ratings providers—an expensive and time-consuming endeavor. Investors might prefer to have a single "golden source" for ESG ratings data for multiple reasons, and the fact that this is not possible is frustrating for them.

Another potential problem concerns firm selection and the use of modeling/estimated data. ESG ratings providers choose the companies for which they will publish ratings; there is no mandatory list of companies to rate, no requirements from regulators or exchanges to fulfill. Ratings providers therefore seek to balance breadth of coverage (how many companies are rated) with the depth or thoroughness of coverage (which may be expensive). In their 2022 paper, Berg et al. show that the number of companies rated by the six largest agencies ranges from 9,662 (MSCI) to 1,665 (S&P Global).[24] Ratings providers have been criticized for bias, selecting companies to rate based on how accurately the ratings provider believes its methodology will predict stock price performance. Ratings providers have also developed models to complete the data for companies for which certain data elements may not be available. For example, if Company A in the hospitality industry does not report its water usage, a ratings provider might use water usage data from other hospitality companies to estimate the water usage for Company A. If the modeled data are eventually found to be inaccurate when Company A begins disclosing the data, then the ratings agency can just update its agency data. However, the data used by investors to make their investment decisions may have been inaccurate (or used without appreciating its source) with potentially negative impact on investment performance.

On balance this may seem like a rather esoteric point, but it has powerful implications for investors: sometimes the data are modeled, not actual. Some investors have responded by creating their own proprietary ratings methodology, others just buy the most commonly-used ESG ratings data. There is no easy answer.

RATING AGENCIES: INTERVIEW WITH MERVYN TANG, SCHRODERS

In conversation with James Cheo

James
On ESG data, data quality depends on the company's disclosure. If you overlay that with ESG, third-party rating agencies, where are we in the state of things?

Mervyn
When you're analyzing a company, you're looking at a lot of different data points. That's not just what the companies disclose. You might be looking at Glassdoor reviews and scrap[ing] the information on the Internet for employee satisfaction, for example. And so, there's a lot of macro system-level data that is not what the company disclose[s]; you'll never have standardization of such data. If you are an Investment Analyst, you'll be finding different data sources, you'll be looking at government policy and macro data to give you an understanding of the carbon pricing and other issues affecting the industry. There'll be more subjective data like controversies. A company like Boeing, with its safety incidents, that's going to be a subjective call that you have to make on the ESG internal rating and process.

Taking a step back, there's more standardization of how carbon emissions data, such as Scope 1 and 2, is being collected. How do you assess a sector decarbonization pathway? How [do] you think about a net-zero transition plan? That allows some degree of coherence across different asset management, different asset owners, and how they analyze ESG. However, what you'll never get is the overall assessment of sustainability becoming totally standardized.

In the same way, you look at broker reports for financial information; there'll be buy, sell, hold, and different views on valuation. That's the same for ESG, you will have different views on how sustainable a company is. There will be different views on the forward-looking aspects of the sustainability profile of the company. We just need to document that and have the right information, the right arguments, to really understand why there are differences in opinion.

(Continued)

> (*Continued*)
>
> Supply-chain data are getting better as more companies are tracking their operations through [their] supply chain[s]. For example, a palm-oil company uses data to track potential risks of deforestation on their global operations. There'll be certain sets of information that will become more standardized, but I don't think you'll get standardizations of the third-party ratings and asset managers approaches on sustainability.

REGULATION

Equity analysts that publish ratings on public companies may be subject to regulation in different jurisdictions. In the United States, for example, the Securities and Exchange Commission (SEC)'s Regulation Fair Disclosure (FD) was passed in 2000 at the peak of the Dot-Com Bubble. As the bubble burst, it came to light that certain sell-side analysts maintained public ratings that were positive, while privately they were very negative on the stock. For example, Merrill Lynch analyst Henry Blodget rated the stock of InfoSpace (INSP) a "buy," but in internal emails he called the company a "piece of sh*t."[25]

Around the same time, analysts sometimes issued ratings on stocks that they and their family members might have owned personally. In an effort to avoid such conflicts of interest, Regulation FD required publicly traded companies to disclose material nonpublic information to all investors simultaneously, rather than selectively sharing it with certain individuals or entities, such as securities market professionals or shareholders likely to trade on the information.[26]

So, what does this have to do with ESG ratings? At the end of 2024, the EU announced that it will be regulating providers of ESG ratings.[27] This regulation mandates that ESG rating providers operating within the EU must be authorized and supervised by the European Securities and Markets Authority (ESMA). It applies to ESG ratings issued by providers operating in the EU, including those established outside the EU if they distribute their ratings to EU-based financial institutions or public authorities.

SUMMARY

ESG ratings act as a bridge between companies and investors. ESG ratings agencies, loosely following the model created by credit ratings agencies, use a proprietary methodology to measure and score companies on a set of sustainability-related issues. These issues are essentially "intangibles" more than they are concrete line items following approved accounting standards. As such, ESG ratings agencies enjoy considerable flexibility in how they construct their ratings. While this results in a diverse set of ESG ratings that ultimately reflect the many ways in which investors may evaluate corporate intangibles, the lack of consensus creates more work for investors.

As we shall see in Chapter 12, investors have developed a wide range of strategies that incorporate aspects of sustainability alongside traditional financial elements. The degree to which ESG ratings factor into these strategies is another way that the strategies differ from one another. As with so many aspects of sustainability and investing, there is no "right" answer, but certain strategies are more or less appropriate for investors with different return objectives and beliefs, and preferences for sustainability.

CHAPTER 12

Sustainable Investing Strategies

Investors, as owners of firms, have long been concerned with good governance and social concerns—elements of what we refer to today as sustainable investing. To better appreciate sustainable investing, this chapter begins with a necessarily brief summary of some important attributes of traditional investing before explaining the most common strategies used in sustainable investing: screening, environmental, social, and governance (ESG) integration, thematic investing, and active ownership.

TRADITIONAL INVESTING

A useful starting point for our discussion of traditional investing is the efficient-market hypothesis (EMH), which posits that stock prices accurately reflect all available information. If that is the case, it will be extremely difficult to consistently outperform the market. Instead, investors would be better off using *passive* investment strategies that seek to replicate the performance of broad market indices as closely as possible and at the lowest possible cost. However, research shows that investors frequently exhibit irrational behavior, leading to market inefficiencies. If markets are somewhat inefficient, then the door opens to a competing strand of traditional investing, *active* investing, where investors attempt to beat the market through superior investment skill.[1]

The "passive vs. active" debate is an old one in the halls of finance. However, investors took sustainability issues into consideration for religious or ethical reasons long before the EMH was described by University of Chicago professor Eugene Fama in 1970.[2] As practiced today, sustainable investing follows a more specialized set of techniques and tools that we will discuss in this chapter. These techniques share important underlying characteristics with "traditional" investing: in both cases we speak of strategies, asset classes, and implementation options. We look first at these shared characteristics before discussing the sustainable investing strategies later in the chapter.

Strategies

An investment strategy refers to the process through which an investor decides which investments to make. For larger or professional investors this appears at the tail end of a higher-level process setting out broader investment objectives, risk tolerance, and allocation to different asset classes.[3] Once an investor has decided where to allocate capital—a fund investing in global health care stocks, for example—then an investment strategy might be described in this way:

> The investor aims to achieve a long-term annualized return of 6–10% by investing in a diversified portfolio of global health care stocks. The strategy will allocate 70% of the portfolio to large-cap health care companies with a track record of strong financial performance and stable dividend yields. The remaining 30% will target mid-cap and small-cap health care innovators, focusing on biotechnology and medical device companies with high growth potential. Investment decisions will rely on fundamental analysis of company financials, competitive positioning, and management quality, complemented by ongoing monitoring of industry trends, regulatory developments, and R&D progress. Risk is managed through a maximum 5% position size per stock. (source: author's own)

At a very granular level, no two strategies will be the same due to differences in the people making the investment decisions. However, there are a few common ways of classifying strategies based on what type of information is important to the decision-making process: fundamental, quantitative, and technical.

Fundamental investing emphasizes information about the company, its financial statements, its business strategy, and its competitive positioning among other things. Investors following a fundamental process may also read news articles and attend management presentations to stay abreast of corporate developments. Investment decisions often reflect an investor's experience and judgment in addition to the math used to forecast future earnings of the company.

Quantitative information goes beyond the fundamental financial information about the company. For example, point-of-sale scanner data, social media traffic, and other data that can be linked to a company are now available for investors to use in their decision making. As the amount of data available in the world increases every day, so too does the opportunity for quantitative investors to combine new datasets with company information. Once an investor identifies a set of signals that appears to be a good predictor of future returns (strong "backtest" performance) they can create a rules-based approach to manage a portfolio based on those signals—with only limited human intervention.

Technical information reflects the historical price, time, and volume for a given index or security. For example, technical analysis might consider the 200-day moving average (200DMA) for a stock. To calculate the 200DMA, an investor would look back in time for the past 200 days and calculate the average price. Doing this for every 200-day period in the past five years would create a trend line that reflects lagged performance for the stock. By adding a shorter-term average like the 50-day moving average, the analyst would then be in a position to identify periods of strengthening (50DMA > 200DMA) or weakening (50DMA < 200DMA) momentum as shown in Figure 12.1 for Vestas Wind Systems. In this chart, the 50DMA (100.250 on y-axis) broke below the 200DMA (145.047 on y-axis) on July 16, 2024, suggesting weakening performance ahead—which in this instance turned out to be the case.

There are other ways to classify traditional investing strategies according to attributes of the stocks. Some investors may have a bias in favor of growth companies (high revenue growth) or value stocks (cheap as measured by price-to-book value, for instance). Another strategy focuses on stocks within specific market capitalization bands, i.e., small stocks or large stocks. Of course, what is considered "small" will be very different in Germany vs. Vietnam, for example. These attributes may be combined as well, as in a small-cap value fund.

Finally—although by no means exhausting the set of possible investment strategies—some investors try to profit from stocks going *down* rather than up by "shorting" the stocks.[4] Most retail-accessible mutual funds or unit trusts are prohibited by regulation from shorting stocks because the strategy is risky and because due diligence is more complicated (hence deemed inappropriate for the average retail investor). Nevertheless, many so-called "hedge funds" incorporate short selling into their investment process. They may do so based on a combination of fundamental, quantitative, or technical information, and they may apply their strategy to growth or value stocks, or small or large stocks, or stocks in different sectors or countries—there are many possible strategies.

Asset Classes

The term "asset class" refers to investments that "exhibit similar characteristics and are subject to the same laws and regulations."[5] The most traditional asset classes are stocks, bonds, and cash; anything other than these three are referred to as "alternative investments" or simply "alternatives" for short.[6] This broad classification includes a dizzying array of possibilities, including:

- commodities
- hedge funds

FIGURE 12.1 Vestas Wind Systems: 200-day and 50-day moving averages for stocks.
Source: Adapted from https://www.barchart.com/stocks/quotes/VWS.C.DX/interactive-chart. Retrieved 30 Jan, 2025.

- private equity and venture capital
- real estate and infrastructure
- private credit
- collectibles
- digital assets

Because different asset classes represent anything from an ownership stake in a company (stocks) to a metric ton of copper (commodities), their prices may not be equally affected by the same factors. For example, three stocks trading on the stock exchanges of New York, London, and Tokyo are still stocks; if global markets decline then they are all likely to decline as well (though perhaps by different amounts). But if global markets decline that doesn't necessarily mean that infrastructure investments will decline as well. This characteristic is valuable when building portfolios, since holding assets with low correlation in a portfolio (referred to as "diversification") helps reduce risk.[7]

Implementation

Implementation is where investment strategies are applied to different asset classes to create products for investors. Public markets investing is the realm of single stocks and bonds, mutual funds and exchange-traded funds (ETFs), and (for the more adventurous) options and currencies. (see Table 12.1). While there are many potential combinations of strategies and assets,

TABLE 12.1   Application of Investment Strategies

	Public Markets			Private Markets	
Strategy	Equity	Bonds	Commodities and Currencies	Equity	Debt/Lending
Fundamental	Growth equity	High-yield	Fundamental commodity/ currency trading[8]	Private equity, venture capital	Private credit
Quantitative	Statistical arbitrage	Yield curve arbitrage	Currency pairs	n/a[9]	Quantitative credit risk
Technical	Momentum and technical trading	Trend trading	Technical trading/ commodity trading advisors (CTAs)	n/a	n/a

quantitative and technical strategies mostly apply to public assets which usually have sufficient price transparency to support quantitative and/or technical analysis.

Investing in public assets, such as stocks and bonds, is made somewhat easier because regulations exist to protect the public. For this reason companies are required to disclose audited quarterly financial statements, providing investors a consistent, mostly trustworthy source of information with which to make investment decisions.[10] These assets also trade on stock exchanges where the prices are more transparent than for private companies.

Private assets, e.g., private equity and venture capital, present a unique set of risks since private companies are not subject to the same reporting and disclosure requirements as public companies. In many jurisdictions private markets investments are restricted to institutions and so-called "qualified" or "accredited" individual investors. Often, this just means that the individual has sufficient income or wealth to be considered knowledgeable enough to make riskier investments (which may or may not be the case).

SUSTAINABLE INVESTING STRATEGIES

In contrast to traditional investing, described above, sustainable investing incorporates ESG factors into the investment decision-making process. In this way, sustainable investing takes a broader perspective on risks and opportunities, particularly in the context of issues like climate change.

There is no single, universally agreed term for "sustainable investing"; readers may encounter the terms "responsible investing" or "socially responsible investing" as well. While oversimplifying a bit, investors may approach what we call "sustainability" today with different objectives in mind:

- **Do no harm.** When investors apply their values, beliefs, and preferences to their investing, they often intend to *avoid* investments that could harm others according to that investor's definition of "harm." Faith-based institutions and individuals with religious beliefs may decide to avoid allocating to companies that operate in a manner inconsistent with those beliefs, e.g., Muslim investors may avoid producers of alcoholic beverages.[11] In the early 1980s, investors sold their investments[12] in South African companies as a way of protesting against *apartheid*. More recently, as people become more aware of climate change, fossil fuel companies are often added to the list of undesirable industries.

- **Create benefits for stakeholders.** Some companies may, through their day-to-day operations, deliver benefits to their stakeholders. When the stakeholders in question are the customers or beneficiaries of a firm's products or services, there are many possible examples in the areas of health, education, housing, and access to financial services.
- **Contribute to solutions.** The final category of objectives includes those who believe their capital can directly contribute to solving problems in the world. Development finance institutions (DFIs) like the World Bank or the Asian Development Bank (ADB) were established to invest in emerging economies and represent some of the earliest solutions-focused investors operating at large scale. One of the challenges to meeting this lofty objective is to prove that an investment *created* the solution, also referred to as "causality."

SUSTAINABLE INVESTING: INTERVIEW WITH MERVYN TANG, SCHRODERS

In conversation with James Cheo

James
How would institutional investors think about sustainable investing?

Mervyn
There is a huge range of different institutions in terms of the level of sophistication. On one side of the spectrum, there are institutions required to follow some set of rules. For example, in Singapore, there is a need for insurance companies to adhere to MAS [Monetary Authority of Singapore] environmental risk management guidelines, with transition scenarios and assessment to physical risk and to show how stewardship is done in the portfolio. So, there's the kind of regulatory-focused institutional asset owners who are just having to fulfill what is required. Another example would be in Hong Kong, with the MPF [Mandatory Provident Fund] guidelines requiring examples of ESG [environmental, social, and governance] integration. In the MPF's Request for Proposal (RFP) and the due diligence questionnaires, there is a requirement to provide examples of how ESG integration is done. A lot of those are compliance-driven where the focus is to meet a certain set of requirements.

(Continued)

(Continued)

There is a smaller pool of institutions which are driven by stakeholder or client demand. For example, pension funds in Australia have specific needs for sustainability requirements driven by their members, and they do want to express that. You may have insurers who are trying to take a lead when it comes to showing what they've done in sustainable investment and showing that they have committed to decarbonization, as part of the group level where their CEO wants to push a certain direction.

The most common conversation is decarbonization, just because many asset owners have set net-zero targets and that net-zero target can come in different forms. For example, it could be using Weighted-Average Carbon Intensity (WACI), or it could be using carbon footprint or temperature alignment. Typically, it's a 2050 end goal and then some set of interim goals. The question they are asking is not do I need to invest in a climate fund, it is more about how do I measure the emissions of my overall portfolio, and then, how do I manage that in a way that adjusts over time, and how do I want that pathway to look?

Some asset owners have looked to reallocate to a lower-carbon portfolio over time and increase that share to decarbonize. Others are having a conversation with their asset managers to have an emission reduction pathway as part of their mandate to achieve their decarbonization pathway.

The most advanced, I think, institutions now have implemented some of those decarbonization processes, and they realized that it can tilt away from emerging markets, for example, harder to decarbonize sectors like steel or cement and thinking now more about transition. In particular, among Asia-Pacific asset owners, they're thinking, how do I find methodologies and frameworks to invest in companies that are may be high carbon now but will decarbonize in the future. They could use targets and projections; there are a lot of different ways of looking at that. And so, transition investment is of increasing interest.

The other set, in terms of climate-related investments, are climate solutions or technologies which are going to enable system-wide decarbonization. We are seeing investment products in both public and private assets there. So, it could be direct infrastructure investment in wind and solar. It could be battery technology investment, even hydrogen. Hydrogen is an increasing area of interest, because it could be a scalable investment for a hard-to-decarbonize sector. Climate solution is a big bucket. What institutions are less focused on are general sustainable funds.

Some institutions, who are in an earlier stage in their ESG integration journey or ESG approach, may take a simple approach like allocating a certain percent to green bonds or sustainable funds. Those are the ones who probably hadn't thought about the details [of] what they actually want to achieve from a sustainability perspective, like they just wanted to showcase that they have an allocation to a sustainable climate portion of their investments. I think the more advanced ones are thinking about what kind of sustainable outcome they want to achieve, and how that fits alongside other objectives. A few institutional asset owners are putting aside money for impact, even those that may not have looked at this before. It requires a different skill set of in-house analysts to think about incorporating impact into investments, but then there is experimentation among some of the institutions on the impact side as well.

Screening

In traditional investing, when someone says that they are a "value investor," that implies that they are only interested in companies that represent a good value—cheap according to some measure of firm value. They would, therefore, "screen out" any stock that is more expensive than their desired valuation level. Within sustainable investing there are three common screening strategies: negative, norms-based, and positive screening. While they all describe a programmatic way to select some assets while excluding others, only one of them is relatively similar to the "value investor" screening.

Negative screening describes how sustainability-minded investors exclude some investments—for this reason it is sometimes referred to as "exclusionary screening." The value investor uses a concrete measure of "value" to conduct their screen, but negative screening is very different. In this strategy, the investor is more interested in making sure that investments are consistent with a set of values, beliefs, and/or preferences. Common screens include fossil fuel companies, as well as so-called "sin stocks" such as companies associated with alcohol, tobacco, and gambling. Investors may wish to exclude other companies for what may be deeply personal reasons.

TABLE 12.2   Conglomerates in Emerging Markets

Conglomerate	Country	Industries
Tata Group	India	Automotive, steel, information technology, telecommunications, hospitality, consumer goods
Vingroup	Vietnam	Retail, real estate, health care, education, automotive
Ayala Corporation	Philippines	Real estate, banking, telecommunications, water infrastructure, power generation, education

This leads to an important observation about negative screening: there is no right or wrong set of screens. One investor may be against birth control for religious reasons, another may be against the consumption of farmed animal protein, and a third may want to avoid weapons manufacturers. Investors can and do disagree (sometimes vehemently) with each other's choice of exclusions, but to say that one investor is wrong while the other is right seems harder to defend. For investment managers, this presents a challenge. On the one hand, the manager would like to offer products that appeal to as many investors as possible, but this is difficult when investors may have different values, beliefs, and preferences. In practice, managers may offer multiple funds using different sets of screens, e.g., one with fewer restrictions and one with more.

How to define and apply the screens may also be a challenge, especially in emerging markets where many public companies have multiple lines of business. For example, the firms in Table 12.2 might be hard to evaluate in a simple screening methodology.

This leads to another way to examine a fund's negative screening policies, namely how *restrictive* the policies are. In the most restrictive application, the manager may apply a zero-tolerance standard, i.e., a company with any revenue at all from an excluded activity would be excluded. A less restrictive policy, however, might set a revenue threshold for excluded activities, e.g., less than 5% of revenue from Arctic drilling. Combining these two aspects of setting screens—the number of industries excluded, and how restrictive each exclusion is—leads to the matrix in Table 12.3.[13]

Investing in funds with negative screening strategies, therefore, requires a bit of investigation to determine the degree to which the screening policies are aligned with the investor's values, beliefs, and preferences. Unfortunately, the information needed may be difficult to find. Mutual funds often include

TABLE 12.3   Restrictive Screening Policies

	Zero Tolerance	Threshold-Based
More industries excluded	Excludes companies with any involvement across multiple industries	Excludes companies that derive a significant portion of their revenue (e.g., > 5%) from multiple industries
	Example: Excludes all companies with any revenue from fossil fuels, tobacco, and gambling	Examples: Excludes companies earning > 5% revenue from fossil fuels, tobacco, and gambling
Fewer industries excluded	Excludes companies with any involvement in a limited number of industries	Excludes companies that derive a significant portion of their revenue (e.g., > 10%) from specific industries
	Example: Excludes all companies with any revenue from controversial weapons	Example: Excludes companies earning > 10% revenue from controversial weapons

terms like "enhanced" or "advanced" or even "leaders" in the names of their sustainability-oriented funds, but what do those terms mean? Investors need to read the fine print to find out exactly how the manager has set up the screens, e.g.:

- *Asset Manager A* employs an exclusionary approach with a zero-tolerance policy for specific industries. Their sustainability funds completely exclude companies engaged in thermal coal mining, oil and gas production, and controversial weapons manufacturing. Even if a company derives only a small percentage of revenue from these activities, it is still screened out.
- *Asset Manager B* applies a threshold-based screening model. Instead of outright exclusion, they allow investment in companies as long as revenue from restricted industries remains below a set limit (e.g., no more than 5% from fossil fuels or 10% from gambling or tobacco). Additionally, companies actively transitioning toward renewable energy or improving corporate governance may still be included.

SPECIAL TOPIC: DIVESTMENT

There is considerable disagreement about the efficacy of divestment as a means to influence corporate behavior. The practice involves selling off investments in companies or industries perceived to be incompatible with specific values or sustainability goals, particularly those contributing to climate change and social injustice. The arguments in favor of divestment include:

- Divesting from fossil fuel companies has the potential to reduce exposure to financial risks associated with stranded assets.
- Divestment allows investors to express their moral stance against companies engaging in practices that are socially or environmentally damaging. For example, protesting *apartheid* was a common rationale behind the movement to divest from South African stocks in the 1980s.

Critics of divestment have several forceful counterarguments:

- Divestment reduces investors' ability to influence company management because they no longer own shares or vote.
- The actual impact of divestment on business operations or stock prices is minimal, and in many cases corporate actions might only result in a transfer of assets to another owner rather than making substantive operational changes.

However compelling, these are less interesting than one of the most hotly debated questions: Does divestment result in a higher cost of capital for the divested firm? Advocates say yes, critics say no. What does academic research say? One recent paper[14] suggests that while it is possible that mass divestment could raise the cost of capital for heavily emitting industries, the *change* in the cost of capital would be economically insignificant (15 basis points [bps]).

Norms-based screening looks for companies that have adopted third-party standards for corporate conduct, such as those included in the United Nations Global Compact and the Organisation for Economic Co-operation and Development (OECD) Guidelines for Multinational Enterprises on Responsible Business Conduct.[15] These standards cover topics such as human rights, labor rights, environment, bribery, consumer interests, disclosure, competitive practices, and taxation. Companies are not required to adhere to these standards, but, instead, may elect to become a signatory to the standards and follow them on a voluntary basis. Where the information on signatory status is available, either through the standard-setter or disclosed by the company, investors can screen based on whether a company is a signatory.

Best-in-class, also known as *positive screening*, is the screening strategy that most closely resembles the value-investing screening described at the beginning of this section. While value investors use a measure of firm valuation (cheap vs. expensive) to screen for value stocks, best-in-class screening typically screens based on ESG ratings. Under this approach, the investor chooses one or more ESG ratings provider(s) and divides the rated companies into buckets, e.g., deciles or quartiles. The investor screens for the stocks that are in the best buckets (e.g., top quartile), leaving the investor with a shorter list of well-rated securities. Although technically one could say this is also a form of negative screening—removing the bottom quartiles—by convention this is considered positive screening because it helps the manager select the stocks that it will consider for investment. This strategy has some controversy associated with it due to the reliance on ESG ratings and the issues associated with the interpretation of those ratings described in the Chapter 11 section "Issues with Ratings."

Environmental, Social, and Governance Integration

ESG integration is the strategy which most closely resembles traditional investing, only with ESG information integrated throughout the process. As one investing industry group describes it:

> The purpose of integrating environmental, social, and governance (ESG) information into the investment analysis process is to reduce the financial risks and/or enhance the financial returns of an investment by identifying and valuing risks or opportunities that are not typically identified and valued using traditional financial data.[16]

Note that the net effect of sustainability-related information may be either to reduce risk or identify opportunities, or both. The challenge, therefore, is for traditional investors to make the shift to value companies in ways that are "not typically identified and valued using traditional financial data." This transition is difficult for many investors, yet fundamental and quantitative strategies readily accommodate sustainability-related information such as emissions data or ESG ratings. Quantitative analysts may include sustainability data as part of a longer-duration signal,[17] perhaps combined with other information. Note that technical analysis techniques are less relevant for sustainability data in isolation since most ESG data lack attributes analogous to price, time, and volume that are required for technical analysis.

For their part, fundamental analysts often consider sustainability data together with financial and other fundamental data in preparing a sustainability-adjusted estimate of fair value for the company. The analyst will consider potential costs the company may incur to address sustainability issues, as well as opportunities to generate incremental revenues from changes to existing products and services or altogether new offerings.

The website for the United Nations Principles for Responsible Investment (PRI) includes a set of case studies provided by investment managers that illustrate this type of analysis.[18] One such case study provided by Dutch investment manager RobecoSAM demonstrates how they incorporate material sustainability issues into both expenses and revenues for Infineon, a semiconductor manufacturing company (Figure 12.2):

> The equity analyst builds an economic value added (EVA) model, incorporating the information from the sustainability analyst by estimating the material sustainability issues' financial impact on the business value drivers (growth, profitability and risk). In the example of Infineon, the sustainability analyst suggested a positive impact

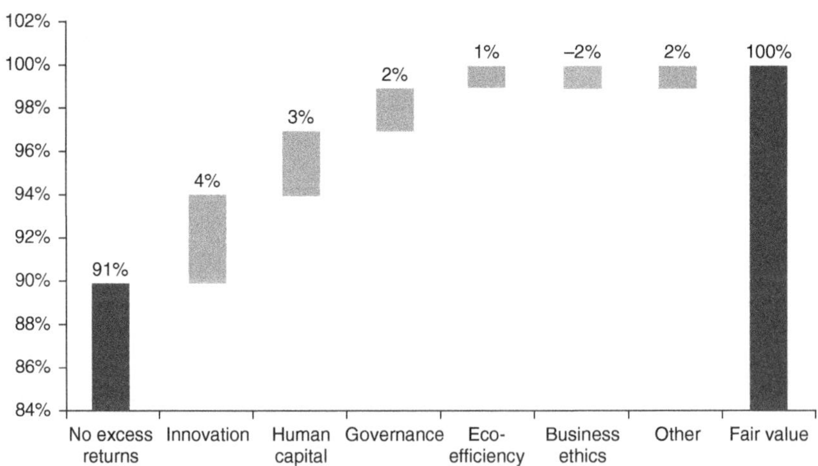

FIGURE 12.2 Infineon: financial and sustainability analysis.
Source: PRI Association / https://www.unpri.org/listed-equity/calculating-material-esg-issues-impact-on-fair-value/156.article / last accessed Aug 20, 2025.

on growth and profitability (driven by the strong capacity to innovate and the leading position in human capital management), and no impact on risk (WACC). Operational efficiency gains from environmental initiatives also increased the operating margin. With sustainability factors integrated, we applied an operating margin above the historic five-year average operating margin of the company, and assumed strong organic revenue growth. The negative impact on the risk profile from antitrust issues was off-set by proactive corrective actions around business ethics and the generally good performance in corporate governance, resulting in no adjustment to the risk assumptions.

To extract sustainability's contribution to the overall fair value of Infineon, we applied an excess return model. In this model, the fair value with industry average returns applied is subtracted from the analysed company's total fair value, leaving the excess returns, which are attributed to sustainability. This is then split proportionally according to the respective sizes of the positive and negative impacts identified previously.

For Infineon, innovation management, human capital management, corporate governance and operational efficiency gains from environmental issues have a positive 4%, 3%, 2%, and 1% impact on the fair value while business ethics has a negative 2% impact.

If this sustainability analysis sounds like more work than the traditional financial-only analysis, that's because it is! At a minimum, notice the reference made to separate equity and sustainability analysts in the first paragraph, hinting at the extra expense required to employ a larger investment team. If a firm is unable or unwilling to make this kind of investment in resources, investors may simply add ESG ratings to an existing investment process ("we think the stock is worth US\$32.50, and it has an ESG rating of AA by MSCI") instead of performing a more detailed analysis that truly integrates ESG issues into the fair value estimate itself. As we have already learned about ESG ratings, they are not a replacement for detailed analysis. At best, they offer a shortcut to think about the potential impact of ESG risks on a company, but without quantifying the financial impact of those risks.

The degree to which investors may have relied on ESG ratings can be seen in market-sizing data reported by the Global Sustainable Investing Alliance (GSIA). The data are self-reported through surveys of investment managers around the world, carried out through regional sustainable investing organizations.[19] According to the 2020 GSIA data, ESG integration was one of the largest—and fastest growing—strategies, especially in the United States where assets grew from US\$10,353 billion in 2016 to US\$25,195 billion in 2020.[20] With the 2022 report, however, the data showed a dramatic decrease in the assets associated with ESG integration, specifically in the United States. What happened?

According to the GSIA, the US organization responsible for collecting the data for this survey tightened up the definition of ESG integration as part of an effort to refine and standardize sustainable investment strategies. In its 2020 data collection, the US Sustainable Investment Forum (SIF) Foundation adjusted its methodology, specifically by extrapolating data from a different subset of respondents than in previous years. In 2022, this methodology was further refined to apply a stricter definition of ESG integration. The US SIF Foundation no longer included firmwide ESG integration claims unless specific ESG criteria were explicitly documented. As the GSIA 2022 Report states: "The revised methodology does not include the assets under management (AUM) of investors who stated that they practice firmwide ESG Integration but did not provide information on any specific ESG criteria they used (such as biodiversity, human rights or tobacco) in their investment decision making."[21] Additionally, several asset managers reported significantly lower ESG AUM in 2022 compared to 2020, in some cases by billions or even trillions of dollars, due to this stricter classification. These methodological changes were introduced to address concerns about greenwashing, ensuring only investments with clearly defined ESG integration practices were reflected in the reported data. With the more restrictive definition in place, US institutional investors changed their disclosures, resulting in the decrease in AUM associated with ESG integration (and other) strategies.

For those investment managers who remain committed to integrating ESG information throughout their investment process, there are many ways to accomplish this objective. Some firms create centralized teams of sustainability experts that support the portfolio managers across the organization. In other firms, the portfolio management teams develop their own ESG capabilities, resulting in a more distributed model than the centralized approach. For example, consider how two leading global investment managers, MFS (US) and Nordea (Denmark) integrate ESG into their investment process (Table 12.4).

Firms also differ in the degree to which they rely on third-party ESG ratings, either on a stand-alone basis or in combination, with some firms taking the extra effort to create their own, proprietary ratings using primary data disclosed by companies as discussed in Chapter 11. Some firms may limit their sustainability efforts to only sustainability-focused products, or only certain asset classes or regions. Given the many possible dimensions of sustainability, ESG integration is certainly subject to a high degree of variation across managers.

TABLE 12.4 Conglomerates in Emerging Markets

	MFS Investment Management (US)[22]	Nordea Asset Management (Denmark)[23]
Environmental, social, and governance (ESG) integration approach	Decentralized model: ESG integration is embedded within investment teams. Portfolio managers and analysts incorporate ESG factors directly.	Centralized model: Dedicated ESG committees oversee integration, engagement, and exclusion strategies.
Governance structure	Investment Sustainability Committee (ISC) and Proxy Voting Committee guide ESG policies and stewardship.	Responsible Investment Committee (RIC) and ESG Committee govern ESG strategies and implementation.
ESG data and tools	Use issuer-reported data, third-party research, and proprietary ESG analysis. ESG expertise is integrated across teams.	Portfolio managers have access to ESG data and tools. Relies on external ESG providers and internal research.
Engagement and active ownership	Portfolio managers and stewardship teams engage with issuers on ESG issues.	Direct company engagement, proxy voting, and investor collaborations drive active ownership.

ESG INTEGRATION: INTERVIEW WITH EMILY WOODLAND AND HEIDI YAP, BLACKROCK

In conversation with James Cheo

James
How does BlackRock incorporate ESG into its investment process?

BlackRock
At BlackRock, we define ESG integration as the incorporation of financially material ESG data into our firm-wide processes to enhance the risk-adjusted returns of our clients' portfolios. We do this for investments whether or not a product has a stipulated sustainable ESG specific objective, where we have the discretion to do so.

(Continued)

(*Continued*)

BlackRock's ESG integration framework permits a diversity of approaches across investment teams, strategies, and different client mandates. For passive, indexed portfolios, our duty is to track the index regardless of ESG or other considerations. But for all the portfolios in which we have discretion to take active investment decisions, the base case is the integration of ESG risks and opportunities, no different from other investment considerations. Portfolios that are on our sustainable or transition platform would use ESG factors as an explicit constraint or objective in the portfolio's construction.

There are three main pillars to how we build in ESG considerations, namely: (i) investment processes, (ii) material insights, and (iii) transparency.

So, first on the processes, we integrate ESG information in active funds and advisory strategies wherever it's applicable. And this means that every strategy needs to determine how and what ESG data could be financially material to assets invested. The portfolio managers are accountable for managing the exposure to these financially material ESG factors. They conduct active monitoring throughout the life of their portfolio and provide evidence on how they consider ESG materiality in their investment decision-making. We make this information available to our clients through our reporting that is aligned to international standards. In addition, the BlackRock Investment Stewardship team also engages with companies on the material risks and opportunities to enhance long-term value for our clients.

Now, on material insights, what we are continuously trying to do for our public market strategies is expand access to good quality ESG data through Aladdin, BlackRock's proprietary platform that consolidates and provides a range of data analytics to our own portfolio managers and to our clients. Our investment teams have a range of access to third-party data sets and internal materiality-focused ratings across the core Aladdin tools. They use that to identify financially material ESG data or information for their investment processes. On the private market side, it is also important for alternative strategy teams to integrate ESG considerations, but it is much less straightforward to obtain that data in private markets. It's a more opaque space with less data available off the shelf, and also less standardization of which ESG metrics are material or relevant to specific assets. We are trying to find ways to collect and aggregate data directly from the companies or from other fund managers, for instance, through ESG surveys.

On transparency, wherever relevant, we disclose this ESG integration, both practices as well as the outcomes and the results and relevant metrics, in our fund documentation or websites. We share BlackRock's approach to ESG integration through the various reporting frameworks applicable for asset managers, such as the Principles for Responsible Investment (PRI). We also release Taskforce on Climate-related Financial Disclosures (TCFD) reports which detail how climate-related risks and opportunities are integrated into Black-Rock's governance, strategy, investment processes, and metrics.

ESG INTEGRATION: INTERVIEW WITH MERVYN TANG, SCHRODERS

In conversation with James Cheo

James
How do investors integrate ESG into the investment process?

Mervyn
The larger asset managers can have in-house proprietary tools to design and scale ESG analysis and integration. The smaller asset managers may use third-party tools directly, like MSCI, Sustainalytics, or some other kind of ESG ratings and scores, and then they may make adjustment decisions around that as part of the overall integration approach. Most large asset managers have a proprietary approach, but asset owners need a way to compare—that's where the third-party scoring and analysis is often used.

When thinking about ESG integration, taking a single scoring approach will only ever get you so far. There is a need for different tools to think about different perspectives. Climate risk [and] transition risk analysis and carbon pricing sensitivity are going to be very different to overall sustainability. Exposure to positive or negative externalities is going to be very different to thematic or SDG [Sustainable Development Goal] alignment.

(Continued)

(Continued)

Positive externalities can be reflected in lower cost of capital due to decreased liability risks, while negative externalities can manifest in higher capital costs due to high energy intensity, water usage, or greenhouse gas emissions.

There's a need to use qualitative analysis as well. [The way] we have approached ESG integration is to create multiple different tools that our investors can use: for example, a tool to answer what's your exposure to climate solutions, and how do you think about how much avoided emissions are in your portfolio or what's your transmission risk exposure for another set of models, and aggregation of quantitative assessment of positive and negative externalities. There's a need for an analyst to make their own judgment, for example, when a carbon-intensity metric is not reflective of risks vs. peers due to business model differences. You may need top-down quantitative metrics as a way of giving you a kind of cross-cutting perspective. But then you need the qualitative [metrics] to distinguish and understand the actual profile of that company.

Therefore, enhancing traditional financial analysis with extensive ESG-derived metrics gives a fuller financial picture, which can inform a more realistic discount rate and allow for more informed earnings and cash-flow projections.

What we have found with different investment desks, for example, a long-short strategy or a quality strategy vs. a credit risk analysis, [is] they all have different analytical approaches, and the way they think about ESG differs. So, we can give them the same set of tools, and the way they apply the tools can differ based on the actual overall investment approach. It is very hard to mandate a process on ESG integration that is a one-size-fits-all [solution] and apply [it] across a diversified firm.

Thematic Investing

Thematic investing is much as it sounds: investing in assets that are exposed to a theme. Note that sectors and themes are not the same thing. Sectors refer to companies in the same line of business, e.g., semiconductor equipment manufacturing, information technology (IT) services, or electric utilities. The General Industry Classification Standard, or GICS, describes 11 sectors at a rather high level; the more granular groups of specific competitors are referred to as industry groups, industries, and subindustries.[24] For example, the hierarchy within the health care sector can be seen in Table 12.5.

TABLE 12.5 Health Care Sector Hierarchy

35	Health Care	3510	Health Care Equipment & Services	351010	Health Care Equipment & Supplies	35101010	Health Care Equipment
						35101020	Health Care Supplies
				351020	Health Care Providers & Services	35102010	Health Care Distributors
						35102015	Health Care Services
						35102020	Health Care Facilities
						35102030	Managed Health Care
				351030	Health Care Technology	35103010	Health Care Technology
		3520	Pharmaceuticals, Biotechnology & Life Sciences	352010	Biotechnology	35201010	Biotechnology
				352020	Pharmaceuticals	35202010	Pharmaceuticals
				352030	Life Sciences Tools & Services	35203010	Life Sciences Tools & Services

Source: Modified from https://www.spglobal.com/marketintelligence/en/documents/gics-mapbook-brochure.pdf, pp. 36–37.

With this perspective in mind, thematic investing becomes clearer: themes cut across multiple sectors. According to the wealth management arm of UBS, their longevity theme provides a good example: "We distinguish between drivers of longevity (companies in pharmaceuticals, medical technology, and health care services) and beneficiaries (consumer goods, financial services, real estate, and industrial sectors) that benefit from the evolving needs of an aging population."[25] Investing in sustainability-related themes may also apply to different asset classes and include multiple investment strategies. For example, a mutual fund investing in public equities exposed to the theme of increased electrification might include electric vehicle (EV) manufacturers, charging point operators, grid infrastructure, and battery storage companies. A venture capital fund focused on the same theme might invest in earlier-stage private companies working on the same issues, perhaps trying to disrupt the public incumbents.

A scan of financial information providers Morningstar (www.morning star.com) and Pitchbook (www.pitchbook.com) reveals ETFs[26] following a variety of different themes (Table 12.6).

TABLE 12.6   Exchange-Traded Fund (ETF) Themes

Theme	Fund Name	Ticker (US)
Clean energy	iShares Global Clean Energy ETF	ICLN
	First Trust NASDAQ Clean Edge Green Energy ETF	QCLN
	Invesco WilderHill Clean Energy ETF	PBW
Water resources	Invesco Water Resources ETF	PHO
	Invesco S&P Global Water Index	CGW
	First Trust Water ETF	FIW
Robotics and automation	Global X Robotics & Artificial Intelligence ETF	BOTZ
	ROBO Global Robotics and Automation Index ETF	ROBO
	iShares Robotic and Artificial Intelligence ETF	IRBO
Cybersecurity	First Trust NASDAQ Cybersecurity ETF	CIBR
	ETFMG Prime Cyber Security ETF	HACK
	Global X Cyber Security ETF	BUG
Genomics and biotechnology	ARK Genomic Revolution ETF	ARKG
	iShares Genomics Immunology and Healthcare ETF	IDNA
	Global X Genomics & Biotechnology ETF	GNOM

Depending on what options are available on a brokerage account platform, investors may have the opportunity to choose between many different potential themes across asset classes. The distinction between asset classes becomes important when considering the ultimate objective of investors. Where the objective is to use capital to make a difference in the world, thematic investments in venture capital may be the best fit since younger firms may need capital to trial or scale promising new technologies. In contrast, thematic investments in public equities may be more aligned with "financial returns first"—incremental buying and selling of stocks has limited to no effect on the degree to which a public company contributes to solutions for people or planet.[27]

THEMATIC INVESTING: INTERVIEW WITH EMILY WOODLAND AND HEIDI YIP, BLACKROCK

In conversation with James Cheo

James
How do you think about long-term sustainability trends or themes? How do you construct them? Where do you see the opportunities?

BlackRock
Research is at the center of the investment approach and process. BlackRock's Investment Institute researches structural trends shaping the economy, markets, and asset prices. And we assess how those trends can affect the long-term value on an individual company and how they unfold over time.

We are focused on mega forces, which are the big, structural changes that are poised to create big shifts in profitability across economies and sectors, which will affect investing now—and far in the future. The five mega forces we are tracking are demographic divergence, digital disruption and AI [artificial intelligence], geopolitical fragmentation, future of finance, and low-carbon transition. Specific to the transition to a low-carbon economy, BlackRock has put together input-driven, probabilistic forecasts of how the transition might unfold, which are described in our transition scenarios.

(Continued)

(*Continued*)

The starting point is a little different from the scenarios set out by other providers, which are based on outcomes or warming pathways. Our input-driven forecast describes the opportunities as well as risks for investments, and helps us shape the investment thesis around the longer term.

Structural shifts associated with the low-carbon transition—technological innovation, consumer and investor preferences for lower-carbon products, and shifts in government policies—are reshaping production and consumption and spurring capital investment. This is creating investment opportunities. For example, average annual spend in the energy system through 2050 is estimated to reach US$4 trillion per year, up from US$2.2 trillion over the last decade. There's a big gap that needs to be closed. One finding is that the transition is unfolding at different speeds across different sectors and regions. And this means that if you can identify the sectors that are aligned to the necessary capital expenditures needed from a region and market perspective, early action may be rewarded.

THEMATIC INVESTING: INTERVIEW WITH JEREMY HALL, BROOKFIELD

In conversation with James Cheo

James
How do you decarbonize heavy-emitting industry and make it an investment opportunity?

Jeremy
Decarbonizing heavy-emitting industries is complicated due to both their scale and the earlier stages of the underlying technologies. The opportunity set among industries is wide—including cement, steel, chemicals, transportation, and more—but what they have in common is that they are all irreplaceable and serve critical functions of the economy.

Cement's share of global emissions is estimated at up to 8%, with no cost-effective replacements. Most of its emissions result from chemical reactions in the manufacturing process, not from energy consumption. [The] cement industry is one the largest use cases for carbon-capture technologies.

Another heavy-emitting industry is steel which relies heavily on coal, which is used in blast furnaces to turn iron ore into molten steel. There are a few low-carbon alternatives in the transition of steelmaking. The reduction of gases themselves—typically carbon monoxide and hydrogen produced from the burning of natural gas or coal—are replaced by clean hydrogen produced by solar- or wind-powered electrolysis. When burned, hydrogen produces water instead of greenhouse gases. However, green steelmaking is not yet cost-effective.

On impact and investments, investors who are willing to deploy their capital for the transition of heavy-emitting industries—instead of pursuing divestment policies—can potentially drive greater reductions in real economy emissions. At Brookfield, we plan to go where the emissions are by partnering with industrial companies and innovators through long-term offtake contracts. We are not an investor in unproven technology but looking at developing low-carbon solutions through proven technology. Such investments fund the underlying assets that then supply the output to the partnering industrial companies.

James
How about investing in renewable energy?

Jeremy
We have been in the clean energy business of owning, operating, and developing renewable power facilities. Global annual spending on renewables continues to set records, with capacity additions led by increases in solar and incremental wind. We've been doing renewables before it became "trendy" as we felt that renewable assets were just great investments. They're also good for the economy as they are low-capex investments.

When we talk about additionality, we are making our renewable energy generation more efficient. For instance, in our wind farms, we are increasing the size of the rotor diameters allowing wind turbines to sweep more area, capture more wind, and produce more electricity. Hence, we have the expertise to re-turbine our assets to get an immediate uplift of energy capacity. Over the years, our wind turbines have grown—in both height and blade lengths—and could generate more energy.

(Continued)

(Continued)

James
The energy demand due to artificial intelligence will only increase. Is this an opportunity for transition?

Jeremy
The energy demands of data centers will only accelerate. AI is highly energy intensive, and requires more electricity than older technologies, resulting in greater power demand from both existing and new data centers. Current electrical grids are already having trouble keeping pace.

Brookfield has collaborated with Microsoft to support their customer demand with the build-out of over 10.5 gigawatts of renewable energy capacity. This [is a] first-of-its-kind global framework agreement that will accelerate the expansion of renewable energy capacity to contribute to Microsoft's sustainability goals, with the potential to expand the scope and development capacity within the target regions of the US and Europe, and beyond to Asia-Pacific, India, and Latin America.

From an investment perspective, growing AI data center demand will not be easily met with new supply, creating a supportive outlook for data center real estate rent growth and valuations.

Active Ownership

The *active ownership* strategy—also referred to as *ESG engagement*—refers to instances when investors attempt to catalyze changes within a company and its management team that lead to improvements in sustainability disclosures and/or the sustainability of business practices. The investor can gain the attention of company management either because it is a large investor (like a leading global investment manager) or already has a meaningful financial stake in the company's equity or debt.[28] Due to their smaller average investment amounts, individual investors are unlikely to be able to engage with management in this way. The important question is then one of efficacy: what does ESG engagement entail and what does it accomplish?

There are two primary parts of an engagement strategy. The first is that shareholders should exercise their vote. It may seem surprising that voting needs to be included as active ownership, but not all shareholders make an *active* decision on each proposal up for vote in a shareholder meeting. To begin with, shareholders may decide not to vote because nonvoted shares are counted as voting in favor of management's proposals. If an investor only intends to support management, then it might not bother to vote its shares. In the United States, voting participation varies significantly between investor types; while approximately 91% of institutional investors vote their shares, only about 29% of individual (retail) investors do so.[29] Shareholder services companies like ISS and Glass Lewis support shareholders by providing a recommended voting action; shareholders can subscribe to a voting service that follows those recommendations without any additional analysis required on the part of the investor.

In comparison, active ownership implies deliberate analysis of proposals submitted to a shareholder vote. Some investment managers follow policies of always voting in favor of proposals linked to environmental or social issues, for example, and disclose their voting policies and activity to their investors as in the following example from LGIM (Figure 12.3). In 2023, LGIM voted on 148,794 resolutions globally, including 3,713 shareholder proposals.[30] LGIM takes the extra step of disclosing how they voted, including 22% of votes made against management recommendations (Figure 12.4).

It should be noted that shareholder votes are not necessarily binding and the company can decide to ignore the voting results. Some votes, however, *are* binding, such as when voting for nominees to the Board of Directors, or when the company has received an offer to be acquired. The extent to which shareholder votes are binding varies by country. In the United States and Canada, most shareholder resolutions are advisory, meaning companies are not legally required to implement them, though ignoring strong shareholder support may carry reputational risks. In contrast, many European countries treat shareholder resolutions as binding, while in Australia, votes may be nonbinding or binding depending on specific regulatory requirements.[31]

Being an "active owner" means voting based on the investment manager's own analysis of the pros and cons of each measure. But how much of a difference does voting really make? Research finds that shareholder voting is an effective governance tool, as dissenting votes are linked to changes in board composition and the withdrawal of mergers and acquisitions (M&A) deals.[32] Even in cases where votes are advisory rather than binding, strong shareholder opposition can influence corporate reputation and market pressure on management. For this reason, many institutional investors emphasize shareholder engagement as part of an active ownership strategy.

Beyond voting, the largest institutional investors may enjoy sufficient market power that they can engage with companies that they do not own yet; for everyone else, ownership may be a prerequisite to arranging a meeting with company management. The investor needs to have a clear goal in

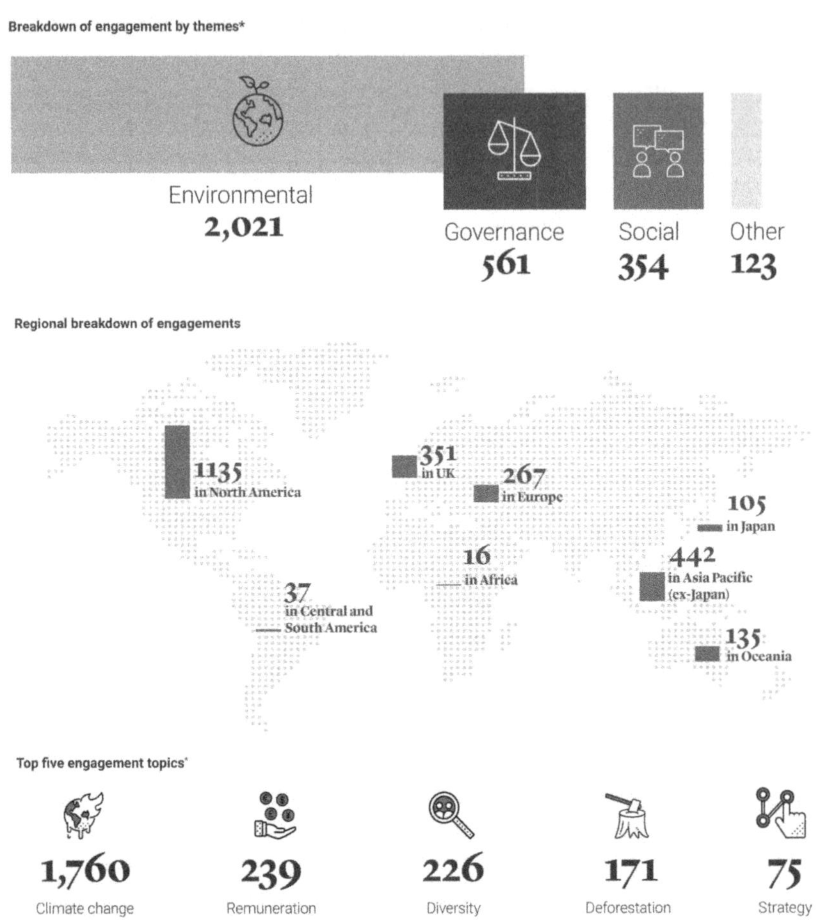

FIGURE 12.3   Active engagement in numbers.
Source: Legal & General Investment Management (Holdings) Limited / A
https://am.landg.com/asset/4a7df4/globalassets/lgim/_document-library/
responsible-investing/active-ownership-report-2023---full-report.pdf, p85 /
last accessed Aug 20, 2025.

mind for the meeting, and where sustainability issues are involved, investors
commonly peruse one of two different topics: the measurement and reporting of sustainability-related information, and the sustainability of certain
business practices.

With respect to measurement and reporting, institutional investors may
be looking for more detailed information than the company has chosen to
provide. For example, an emerging markets equity investor was interested in

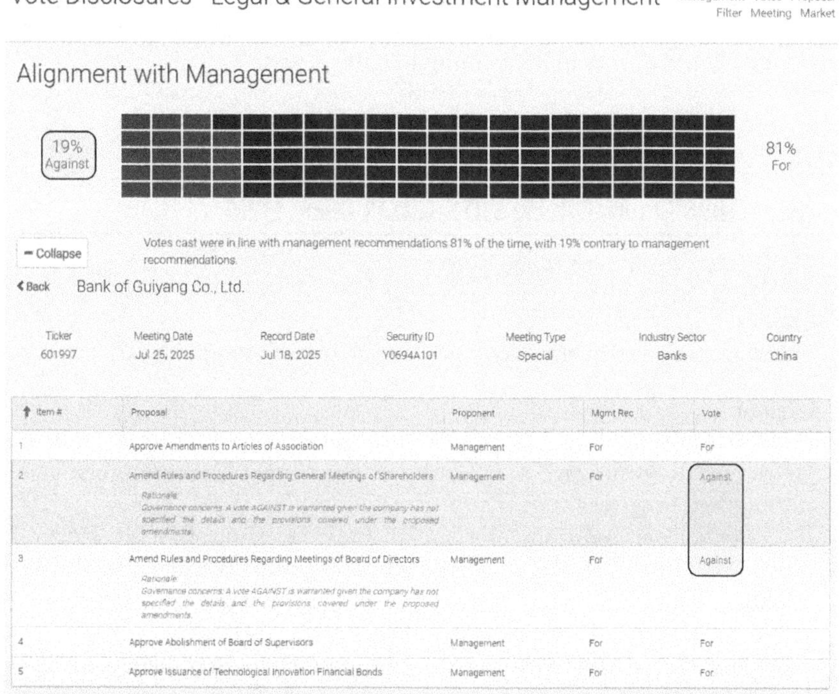

Item #	Proposal	Proponent	Mgmt Rec	Vote
1	Approve Amendments to Articles of Association	Management	For	For
2	Amend Rules and Procedures Regarding General Meetings of Shareholders *Rationale* *Governance concerns: A vote AGAINST is warranted given the company has not specified the details and the provisions covered under the proposed amendments.*	Management	For	Against
3	Amend Rules and Procedures Regarding Meetings of Board of Directors *Rationale* *Governance concerns: A vote AGAINST is warranted given the company has not specified the details and the provisions covered under the proposed amendments.*	Management	For	Against
4	Approve Abolishment of Board of Supervisors	Management	For	For
5	Approve Issuance of Technological Innovation Financial Bonds	Management	For	For

FIGURE 12.4 LGIM voting disclosure.

Source: Legal & General Investment Management (Holdings) Limited / https://vds.issgovernance.com/vds/#/MjU2NQ==/ (highlighting added for emphasis) / last accessed Aug 20, 2025.

the stock of a firm which is a large bottling company for soft drinks and other beverages. One of the largest material environmental issues in the beverage industry is water management, including how much water is withdrawn from aquifers every year and how much is recharged back into the aquifer. This investor liked the business prospects and financial performance of the company but observed that management provided no information on water management in its sustainability reports. This was especially relevant since many of its bottling plants were located in known areas of high water stress. The first step of the investor's engagement with the company was to seek greater transparency on its water management practices.

Improved disclosures may lead to a second level of engagement, seeking operational changes to address sustainability issues. When the bottling company began to disclose its water usage data, the investor then identified potential water risks due to excessive water withdrawals relative to the replenishment activity undertaken by the company. Further engagement conversations encouraged the company to reevaluate and improve its water management practices in areas of high water stress.

STEWARDSHIP: INTERVIEW WITH TRISTA CHEN, LGIM

In conversation with James Cheo

James
How does stewardship play a part in the investment process?

Trista
Stewardship is a key component of responsible investing, which is essential to mitigate risks, unearth investment opportunities, and strengthen long-term returns for clients.

We believe environmental, social, and governance (ESG) factors—such as climate change, social inequality, and executive pay—are financially material. So, we see responsible investing as the incorporation of ESG considerations into investment decisions.

The way we look at stewardship is not just about a specific investment strategy. It cuts across the broader asset classes, because when we engage using our investments stewardship approach, we are not just thinking to drive change for a specific company, we want to aim for a market change. When we talk about investments stewardship, it is about engagement with the companies and policymakers. So, in the Singapore context [it] can be MAS [Monetary Authority of Singapore], it can be Ministry of Environment, or it can be SGX [Singapore Exchange] related to corporate disclosure requirements. For example, in the Asia market, to address the climate conversation, aside from engaging with companies, we also need to engage with policymakers. Our engagement with policymakers is vital to our aim of raising climate policy in key markets in which our clients invest, because many sustainability challenges, including climate change, require systemic policy reform. We also engage with peers. We want to bring like-minded people together to join forces to go the same [way], especially with the combined scale and size of our investments.

Broadly speaking, our stewardship process is that we first identify themes—like climate, nature, people health, governance, and digitization—that are important to our clients. We ask pertinent questions like what are the changes we are driving? What are our expectations of our investing companies and how to measure them? What will be the proposed consequences if the change is not evidenced, such as voting? This is a very structured procedure that we communicate publicly about our expectations through our thematic policies disclosures.[33]

We have a proprietary methodology to derive an LGIM ESG score[34] so companies will know how they are scored against our expectations. In our annual active owner's report[35] and quarterly engagement report,[36] we go in depth on how we engage, not just within the investment stewardship team, but also with our investment teams to drive change in different jurisdictions.

James
How do you identify companies to engage with?

Trista
We have a fiduciary duty to our clients to act on themes that matter to them, themes like climate, nature, people health, governance, and digitization. With a global view, we bring it down to which geography and sector are the most relevant. So, that will be a materiality kind of approach. And then we'll drill down to the companies.

The company filtering process is deliberate, and the engagement campaign is intentional. And often, we will need to know whether we have the existing relationship with a company that influences how likely they will be engaged. We need to explain why we want to engage with them. In our experience, about 80% to 90% of companies are willing to talk to us. That's when we set an engagement plan.

We hold directors to account for their management of climate risk. For example, in our latest Climate Impact Pledge Report,[37] during the 2024 proxy season, 455 companies were identified as subject to voting sanctions for not meeting our minimum standards. In addition, 14 companies remain on our divestment list, including two additional companies from 2024.

Our Climate Impact Pledge covers 5,000+ companies across 20 "climate-critical" sectors. More than 100 companies are now covered in our qualitative deep dive engagement; these are companies we believe can be "dial-movers" on climate action in their sectors, given their size and potential to galvanize action in their sectors.

(Continued)

(*Continued*)

In 2023, we updated our Deforestation Policy and engaged with over 160 companies on the topic.[38] This was the first year we applied specific deforestation vote sanctions. We were also involved in multiple engagements with the UK's key water companies, their major shareholders, and industry regulators.

The biggest lever is to understand the carrot-and-stick approach. For example, in the EU deforestation law, commodities imported to the European Union need to satisfy a low deforestation requirement. Our engagement approach is to turn the stick into carrot, to find win–win; the goal of deforestation is aligned to the access of a bigger market. In our engagement, we have to find what's in it for the companies, for climate change. For example, using circular economy solutions could open up new markets for the companies.

James
What are the toolkits for engagement?

Trista
We have different toolkits for engagement: proxy voting, pre-vote declaration, and shareholder resolution.

We declare our vote,[39] either for or against, with a rationale, so as to send a strong message to the company of our expectations. Exercising voting rights is a powerful engagement tool with which to hold company boards to account and raise market standards; it is used extensively by our Investment Stewardship team. Importantly, the team votes with one voice across all of our clients' investments where we have discretion, because it operates independently from–but in collaboration with–our portfolio managers.

For example, under our Climate Impact Pledge, our Investment Stewardship team analyzes each company covered in the qualitative engagement in depth using public information, based on the framework set out in our net-zero sector guides,[40] and then engages in detail with these companies to understand to what extent their strategy is aligned with a transition to net zero and to encourage further action. We publish our sector guides on our website,[41] which helps companies understand our expectations and the questions we are likely to ask them. These guides outline our expectations and "red lines" for each sector. If a company fails to meet our "red lines" we may apply a vote sanction, usually a vote against the chair, at its next AGM [annual general meeting].

When change is insufficient over time and engagement has not been fruitful, we may also divest from that company in applicable funds.

Divestment is itself part of the engagement effort because it is used to signal dissatisfaction with the pace of change while being accompanied by further engagement activity or attempts. Divestment is not the end goal because we believe that when we remain as shareholder, it will give us the opportunity to engage a company further and drive change.

We normally do not engage ahead of the AGM because we consider engagement should happen outside of the peak season. A company should already reflect their understanding of what our expectations are when they publish their financial statements. So, that's the way that we look at voting.

We can file shareholder resolutions. The purpose of shareholder resolutions are two-fold. One is to bring a closed-door conversation, to get the company to respond to our engagement with consequence. The intention for the closed-door conversation is to get the company on board to make the changes, so shareholder filing might not be intended to be made public if the issues can be resolved. It is a lever we use as the engagement.

Our engagements have a clear expectation, engagement time frame, [and] escalation pathway. Sometimes, we engage just to get information, but once the information is acquired, we can choose to move on because the company is on track, or we can use information to share with the industry to provide a sectorial or geographic view of a certain agenda. Sometimes, after information is acquired, we will start the direct engagement and collaboration with a very set specific agenda and that is normally a multiyear journey. Sometimes, we'll send a letter to the Chairman of the Board to express our expectations as shareholder.

James
How do you think about social and governance from a stewardship perspective?

Trista
We placed 354 votes on social issues globally.[42] In 2023, we completed our expanded engagement campaign on ethnic diversity. We started a focused engagement campaign with a clear escalation strategy to get 15 global food retailers to reduce income inequality within their

(Continued)

(Continued)

operations and supply chains. In December 2023, we published our first Human Rights Policy.[43]

Globally, we opposed 52% of all pay-related proposals in 2023 due to the companies not meeting our minimum standards for fair and appropriate long-term performance-based pay.

James
What are the success stories of engagement and stewardship?

Trista
In our recent active ownership reports, you will find one specific case about China Mengniu Dairy. They have been in our climate engagement for a number of years. When they couldn't meet our expectations, we first divested from the company in 2021[44] after years of active engagement. Despite the divestment, we continued to engage with them, and we were very explicit, saying that in order for you to get off our divestment list, this is our deadline consideration per the sector guide. One is the net-zero 2050 and the other one is no deforestation commitment because they import a large amount of soybean for animal feed. The company was quite receptive to the conversation because they want to be recognized as doing good. China Mengniu came forward with their carbon-neutral statement by 2050 last year. We recognize this is ambitious enough in the China context though it's not a net zero. In addition, they put up a no deforestation commitment. In evaluating the progress they have made, we were encouraged by the progress [that] has [been] made, and we took the company off the Climate Impact Pledge divesting list in 2023.[45] This is a very powerful and strong example of how engagement is driving change. While we are pleased with their progresses, we have clarified that we would like them to seek approval of their net-zero targets by the SBTi [Science-based Targets Initiative], and that we encourage them to report their Scope 3 emissions.

We believe taking these steps and improving disclosures enables investors and the market to assess risks and opportunities related to deforestation and price these more accurately. Appropriate pricing of climate-related risks and opportunities in the market can also be an important incentive for change.

The success of engagement is not always getting what we want; getting our message across is more important. In the case of McDonalds, as stated in our active ownership report, it has substantial influence in the beef industry being the largest beef purchaser in the US. We view that the company has a significant role to play in reducing anti-microbials in their meat products through supply-chain management, because most antibiotics used are not for humans but for animals. The overuse of antibiotics in animals would have implications on consumers who are subject to antimicrobials through food consumption. It is important to note that we did not ask the company to ban the use of antibiotics in their supply chain, but to comply with the WHO [World Health Organization] guidelines. We see large companies like McDonalds having a role to play in this.

James
Do you think that stewardship is an afterthought?

Trista
Stewardship is financially material to our client. It is not the trade-off and it's not that if we make profits, then we start thinking of stewardship. I think one of the challenging parts of investment stewardship is that if you actually do well, it may not reflect on the balance sheet.

Taking a step back, stewardship is a key part of responsible investing, which is essential in seeking to improve long-term returns [and] unearth potential opportunities, and aims to mitigate risks by fostering sustainable markets and economies. When we allocate capital, we conduct extensive research into potential environmental and societal outcomes across our investments. ESG factors are financially material, albeit not all to the same degree. And patience is required, because the time horizons of ESG outcomes and investment returns are not always aligned.

STEWARDSHIP: INTERVIEW WITH EMILY WOODLAND AND HEIDI YIP, BLACKROCK

In conversation with James Cheo

James
How do you conduct investment stewardship?

BlackRock
Investment stewardship is one of the ways in which BlackRock fulfils its fiduciary responsibility to our clients to advance their long-term economic interests. We do this through engaging with the companies our clients are invested in, voting proxies for those clients who have given us authority, and encouraging sound corporate governance and business practices as an informed, engaged investor. In our experience, companies that effectively manage material risks and opportunities in their business models, including those related to sustainability, are better positioned to deliver durable, long-term financial performance. High standards of corporate governance, and strong boardroom and executive leadership, enable companies to be resilient and adaptable through the macroeconomic and societal challenges that can impact their financial performance over time.

Most of our clients are investing to meet long-term goals for retirement. Our BlackRock Investment Stewardship (BIS) team takes a long-term approach to engage company boards and management teams to understand how the companies are managing financial value creation and how that serves our clients' objectives. Engagement is a key mechanism for providing feedback or signaling concerns to companies about factors that affect long-term financial performance. Proxy voting is used to signal our support for, or raise our concerns over, a company's corporate governance or business model. We regularly share our perspective on topical and emerging stewardship issues that may impact clients' financial interests as long-term investors, and report on stewardship statistics to provide insight and transparency into the actions we are taking on behalf of clients.

One area that BIS focuses on is climate risk. The low-carbon transition is an investment factor that can be material for many companies and economies around the globe, but companies in various sectors may be affected differently. Through engagement, we encourage companies to disclose how they're managing the climate risks material to them, and we take the company's readiness and adequacy of action into account in future discussions, as well as, potentially, proxy voting.

Natural capital is another focus area. It's still more of a developing space, and BIS will look toward relevant public disclosures by companies to help them assess the extent of risk oversight that the companies have already put in place and to understand how the natural related impacts and dependencies are currently being managed. We're also engaging companies to integrate natural capital risk into their governance strategy.

STEWARDSHIP: INTERVIEW WITH MERVYN TANG, SCHRODERS

In conversation with James Cheo

James
How do you think about stewardship?

Mervyn
It's very difficult for any individual asset manager to attribute their own actions to an outcome—to say I had this meeting with this company, and then because of that meeting, they had this net-zero transition plan, or they have disclosed this much. This is because many other asset managers could be having that same discussion.

It's very hard to establish direct causality of any individual action. I think what you can do, however, is to start bringing together aggregated statistics. So, if I'm engaging with 2,000 companies in different sectors, have the companies I engaged with, overall, been more likely to set on transition plans or to decarbonize by a certain amount. And you can start putting that information together, and it will still be hard to go from correlation to causality, but you can start putting that information in a way which says, in aggregate, there has been a change in how companies are doing based on the priorities I've set.

The quantification of stewardship is improving amongst asset managers. So, [to] give you an example, we are starting to track the way we engage by having individual engagement objectives, followed

(Continued)

(Continued)

by milestones. So, milestone one would be we engaged a company; milestone two would be the company acknowledges; and milestone three would be the company has initiated the plan to do what we asked them to do; milestone four would be [the] company actually completed the action. And then we can start tracking what's the speed of when we first asked the company to set a net-zero transition plan to where they set one—is it quicker than companies that we haven't asked to set a net-zero transition plan. And once you have this huge database of thousands of engagements that we do across the firm, then we can assess whether we do stewardship more effectively or are there areas where we can't do it very effectively.

USE CASES AND COMBINATIONS OF STRATEGIES

The strategies described above represent different approaches to sustainable investing. Individually, they serve slightly different purposes and may appeal to investors with different objectives. Revisiting the framework used at the beginning of the chapter, we can distinguish between three different high-level use cases:

- **Avoid harm.** Avoid supporting companies whose business practices create some harm of concern to the investor, e.g., cigarette manufacturers.
- **Benefit stakeholders.** Invest in companies which create some benefits to stakeholders beyond their shareholders, e.g., Bosch. Unlike traditional shareholder-driven corporations, Bosch is majority-owned by the Robert Bosch Stiftung, a charitable foundation. Approximately 94% of its profits are reinvested into philanthropic initiatives, research, and environmental programs, rather than being distributed to private shareholders.[46]
- **Contribute to solutions.** A smaller number of companies go beyond creating benefits and are actively trying to solve the underlying problems, e.g., microfinance companies.

Investors may have other reasons for following one or more sustainable investing strategies, either preferencing or avoiding investments based on the investor's specific needs (Table 12.7).

TABLE 12.7 Sustainable Investing Strategies and Use Cases

Strategy		What It Means	Use Case
Screening	Negative screening	Avoid allocating capital to companies engaged in activities which are not aligned with investor values, beliefs, and preferences	Avoid harm
	Norms-based screening	Allocate capital to companies which commit to follow certain standards for corporate behavior	Avoid harm/ emphasize "good behavior"
	Best-in-class screening	Allocate capital to companies that are less exposed to ESG-related risks as measured by ESG ratings	Avoid risk
Environmental, social, and governance (ESG) integration		Incorporate sustainability risks and opportunities into fundamental investment decisions	Long-term capital allocation aligned with sustainability issues
Thematic		Allocate capital to companies exposed to sustainability-related themes	Profit by contributing to sustainability solutions
Active ownership		Use equity ownership to influence corporate disclosure and behavior through voting and engagement	Mitigate risks and contribute to solutions

These strategies do not need to be followed exclusively; many investment managers include different combinations of strategies in their investment process. A common combination includes three strategies, i.e., negative screening, ESG integration, and active ownership:

- First, screen out certain business activities.
- To select stocks for the portfolio, integrate ESG data throughout the investment process.
- Especially for portfolio holdings, engage with management on ESG issues.

CATEGORIES OF SUSTAINABLE INVESTING: INTERVIEW WITH EMILY WOODLAND AND HEIDI YIP, BLACKROCK

In conversation with James Cheo

James
What are the dimensions of sustainable investing?

BlackRock
BlackRock's sustainable investing platform consists of four categories: screened, uplift, thematic, and impact. We use screening to help clients to avoid certain issuers or certain activities that have higher perceived risks, or less desirable environmental, social, and governance characteristics. For instance, some of our products may exclude companies that have a certain threshold of revenue exposure to controversial weapons companies, coal, or exposure to certain governance controversies.

Our uplift category reflects products that have a commitment to investments that improve certain environmental, social, and governance characteristics relative to the product's or the portfolio's benchmark or reference universe.

And then a third category is thematic, and in this space, we target investments in issuers that have business models that are aligned to certain thematic trends or sustainability outcomes.

Lastly, we have the impact investments. These are portfolios committed to generate positive and measurable sustainability outcomes.

Across the portfolios, particularly the screening or the exclusionary categories, we also use active engagement to work with specific companies to understand how we should classify them and help them improve on sustainability issues.

TRANSITION INVESTING

As of this writing, a relatively new strategy is increasingly popular: transition investing. In the broadest terms, transition finance refers to investments in activities that are not *currently* aligned with the Paris Agreement but may represent *intermediate steps* that help a company achieve Paris-alignment at a future date.[47] An oft-cited example of the clean energy transition are investments that enable the early retirement of coal-fired power plants (CFPP).

CFPPs are among the most difficult GHG emission sources to phase out, despite their well-documented environmental and social harms. They remain the single largest source of carbon dioxide (CO_2) emissions worldwide, with approximately 2,000 CFPPs (around 5,000 units) in Asia alone emitting about 7.2 gigatons of CO_2 annually—accounting for roughly 20% of the 36.8 gigatons of total global energy-related CO_2 emissions.[48] Beyond CO_2, CFPPs release sulfur dioxide (SO_2) and nitrogen oxides (NOx) which react with the atmosphere to form acid rain and fine particulate matter, a major contributor to respiratory diseases. Additionally, CFPPs produce coal ash, a toxic by-product that can seep into groundwater, causing long-term contamination issues. This is particularly concerning in countries with poor waste disposal regulations, where coal ash frequently leaches into drinking water supplies.

Despite these environmental concerns, CFPPs remain a major energy source, particularly in developing economies which lack the necessary infrastructure to scale up renewables at the pace required. In addition, the high upfront costs of retiring coal plants and transitioning to alternative energy sources pose a financial challenge for governments and private sector investors alike.

Recognizing these challenges, the Asian Development Bank (ADB) has introduced the Energy Transition Mechanism (ETM) to support the early retirement of CFPPs and scale up investments in clean energy.[49] The ETM aims to create blended finance structures, combining public and private capital to buy out and decommission existing coal assets while simultaneously financing new renewable energy projects. In the Philippines, the ADB has endorsed a US$500 million investment plan to accelerate the country's coal transition, ensuring affected workers and industries receive economic support.[50] Similarly, in Indonesia, the ADB approved a US$500 million loan to help the country phase out coal and expand its renewable energy sector, aligning with Indonesia's target of net-zero emissions by 2050.[51]

So, what counts as transition? Taxonomies, described in Chapter 9, provide some standardization in markets where the taxonomy explicitly addresses transition, like Singapore. In markets with transition components to their taxonomy it should be clear whether corporate investments are Paris-aligned, transition-eligible, or not. Taxonomies mostly apply to individual bonds or loans; however, the company as a whole may or may not be following a suitable transition pathway such as one approved by a Science-based Targets Initiative (SBTi). Equity investors, therefore, need to proceed carefully when labeling a strategy as "transition investing." In public equities, investors must rely on disclosed information about transition pathways, targets, and corporate transition plans. Private equity investors, however, have more control over their portfolio companies and are in better position to ensure that plans for a transition are ultimately aligned with the Paris agreement.

TRANSITION INVESTING: INTERVIEW WITH EMILY WOODLAND AND HEIDI YIP, BLACKROCK

In conversation with James Cheo

James
How does BlackRock think about transition investing?

BlackRock
BlackRock's transition investing platform is slightly different. Whereas the sustainable platform buckets can apply to any number of environmental or social or governance characteristics, including combinations thereof, our transition investing platform was established more recently, in response to clients that are looking for a strong definition of transition investing.

We have defined transition investing as investing in issuers or assets that are either preparing for, aligned to, benefiting from, or contributing to the transition to a low-carbon economy. These are products that are focused exclusively on the low-carbon transition in their objectives. There is a lot of overlap with the products that are on our sustainable platform, but they are distinct as some products on the sustainable platform are not necessarily transition-focused, because they could be focused on other ESG factors. And then, we have some products on the transition platform that are not necessarily deemed to be within the classic understanding of what is green or sustainable today.

TRANSITION INVESTING: INTERVIEW WITH JEREMY HALL, BROOKFIELD

In conversation with James Cheo

James
How do you see the role of private markets in bringing about the sustainability transition?

Jeremy
Private markets are integral to the net-zero transition. We think it will pervade all sectors of the economy needing to adopt lower carbon emissions and a transformation of the energy mix to shift away from

where we are today, predominantly fossil fuels to clean energy. By our estimates, the transition to net zero will require US$200 trillion of investment by 2050. And when we think about private markets, which is the backbone of the global economy and one where we can bring our expertise and influence—to put that US$200 trillion in context, it will require an average annual investment of US$7 trillion per year for the next 25-plus years. That's roughly equivalent to 8% of current annual global GDP [gross domestic product] and more than triple the amount invested in 2021.[52]

James
What's the edge that Brookfield brings for decarbonization?

Jeremy
We talk about the term additionality, which is the way Brookfield can influence decarbonization and net-zero objectives. We are "going where the emissions are." Building out new green energy capacity is the place to start. But an incredible amount of work still needs to be done to reduce emissions and close the gap to achieve global decarbonization goals—work that can only be accomplished by actively engaging with the highest-emitting sectors and partnering with them to decarbonize their businesses.

Brookfield is a global leader in decarbonization. As a leading owner-operator of renewable power assets, we have an over 100-year history of owning, operating, investing, and developing renewable power and energy assets. Our renewables operations span five continents with ~5,000 operating employees and we are one of the world's largest renewables businesses with US$102 billion in AUM [assets under management] as of end-2023. We can leverage our operating capabilities, access to numerous decarbonization solutions, and our power marketing and commercial contracting experience to provide a full suite of decarbonization solutions to customers and partners.

James
What's the view on investing in the transition?

Jeremy
This is a hotly debated topic. Do you leave the dirty stuff, not touch it, and only focus on renewables? We often say that just more renewable

(Continued)

(*Continued*)

generation is not enough to support the net-zero transition. There's a lot of talk on negative screening. But our objectives are also aimed towards reducing the negative impact across sectors—mitigating the risk, helping potentially stranded assets, and improving a company's operations. I think it is important to define what we mean by sustainable investing from an impact investing context. Our definition is that we're helping these companies, either through our operational expertise and/or our capital transition, which allows us to contribute to sustainability impact targets alongside achieving a financial return. Our view is if left alone, they're not going to be able to do it themselves.

James
How do you think decarbonization can be tackled?

Jeremy
We need to go where the emissions are. Over 60% of the world's power sources are still running on fossil fuels. For every megawatt of electricity or heating produced with clean sources, less carbon is poured into the environment. However, through electrification, the transition will also increase overall demand for electricity—demand that utilities will need to meet with new, and clean, energy capacity. We expect utilities will have to increase their total clean energy capacity by around 19 times to both transition to net zero and meet increasing overall demand for electricity.[53] There's no way to get to net zero without tackling the problem from building new renewable capacity while actively decarbonizing and replacing existing carbon-intensive infrastructure in the utilities sector.

James
How do you decarbonize utilities?

Jeremy
Utilities companies are making emissions reduction and transformation plans. But most of the time their stated goals are underfunded. When we talk about additionality, we're going in to work with a utility company that may not have the actual operational expertise or the capital to transition from coal-fired energy production to renewables. For example, carbon-intensive thermal power generators, often built

20–30 years ago, are strategic infrastructure in well-located parts of the electricity grid. These assets often have transmission rights and offtakes that a transition investor can use to develop new, clean energy capacity.

Furthermore, these utilities' underlying assets were often built on land near population centers. Converting such sites to scaled-up clean energy hubs, while capital-intensive, can often be less costly, and quicker than working through the challenges of connecting new sites to the electricity grid. This can result in an acceleration in the energy transition. The investments we are targeting are where we can bring our operational expertise, influence, and financial commitment to bear to achieve an incremental impact on the path to net zero, hence that additionality.

James
So, there is a practicality to focus on where the emissions are?

Jeremy
Yes, you are right. Although new stand-alone capacity needs to be accelerated, it is often more practical and economical to start with using the network and infrastructure built around fossil-fuel-fired assets rather than constructing new transmission lines from scratch. Of course, new infrastructure will still be required for the transition to occur because not all fossil fuel generation was built in locations where natural resources, such as wind and solar, are abundant.

SUSTAINABLE INVESTING RETURNS

With all of these variations available, what level of financial performance should investors expect from sustainable investing? This is an important question for investors and a somewhat contentious one for academics with multiple perspectives to consider. One of the early studies of this topic was a paper published in 2009 looking at so-called "sin stocks," i.e., alcohol, tobacco, and gaming.[54] In the words of the authors:

> We hypothesize that there is a societal norm against funding opera-
> tions that promote vice and that some investors, particularly insti-
> tutions subject to norms, pay a financial cost in abstaining from
> these stocks. Consistent with this hypothesis, we find that sin stocks
> are less held by norm-constrained institutions such as pension plans

as compared to mutual or hedge funds that are natural arbitrageurs, and they receive less coverage from analysts than do stocks of otherwise comparable characteristics. Sin stocks also have higher expected returns than otherwise comparable stocks, consistent with them being neglected by norm-constrained investors and facing greater litigation risk heightened by social norms.[55]

Any investor holding sin stocks would expect to be compensated for the extra risk, meaning that, *ex ante*, the *expected* return for sin stocks should be higher than for nonsin stocks. Extending this thinking to other aspects of sustainability, companies facing a high degree of environmental or social risk would also have a higher expected return—otherwise, who would buy those stocks? To oversimplify by quite a bit, this line of reasoning follows what finance academics call *asset pricing theory*, i.e., a theory to explain the relationship between risk and expected return for different assets.

Flying in the face of asset pricing theory, between 2012–2020, US stocks with higher ESG ratings—which indicate lower exposure to ESG risks—*outperformed* their lower-rated counterparts. If asset pricing theory is correct, then how could this be the case? Another paper sought to explain these results by introducing factors that go beyond idiosyncratic, or single-stock risk. In the first part of their analysis the authors first showed the outperformance of "green" stocks (Figure 12.5, left). In Figure 12.5 (right), they introduced the concept of "green minus brown" (GMB) as a measure of the performance of green stocks relative to brown stocks. The analysis continued with an "industry-adjusted" return which captured how much of the stock price performance was due to the industry the company is in and not the company itself. For example, if Microsoft stock performs well, some of that performance may be attributable to the performance of software stocks more generally, instead of (or in addition to) unique characteristics of Microsoft. When the authors removed the effect of industry from the stock price performance, they found that the difference between green and brown stocks was much smaller (GMB [industry-adjusted]), but persistently non-zero.

What are investors to make of this seeming contradiction? On the one hand, asset pricing theory suggests that green stocks should underperform since they have lower risk. On the other hand, from 2013 to 2021 green US stocks handily outperformed their brown counterparts. The answer might come from another field of study, economics. Economists often express things in terms of supply and demand curves; where the curves intersect is a point of equilibrium. In the real world, however, markets are frequently out of equilibrium—either something is over/underproduced or there is higher/lower demand. In this case of green vs. brown stocks, if for some reason the demand was higher than the supply could support, then green stock prices

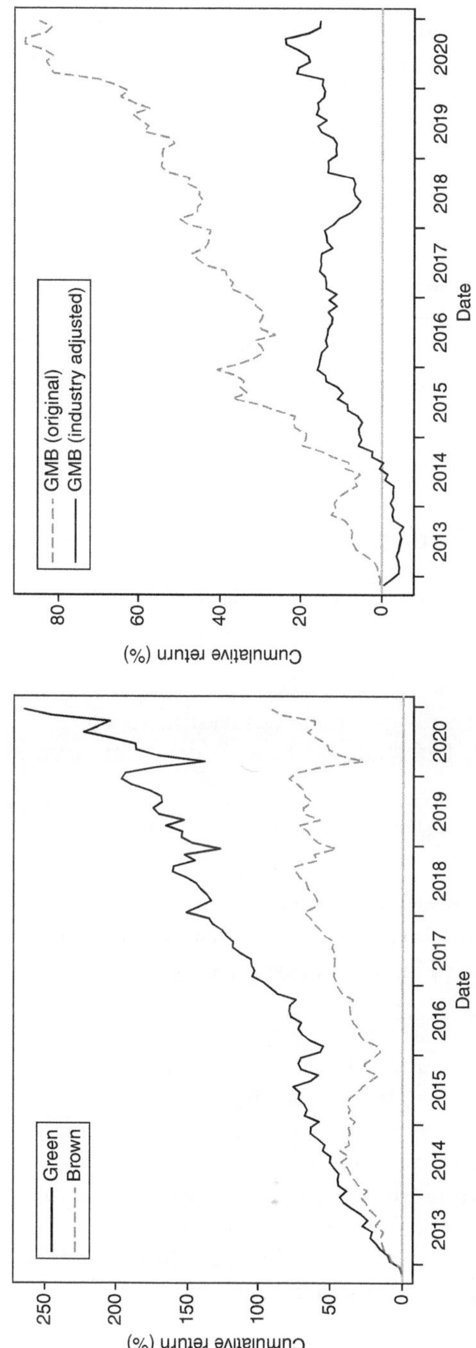

FIGURE 12.5 Performance of "green" and "brown" stocks.
Source: Pástor, L et al, 2022 / with permission of Elsevier.

would have gone up more than would have been expected at equilibrium. There is some evidence to suggest that this is what happened. A recent paper[56] analyzed trade-level data and concluded that without flows to ESG portfolios, green stocks would not have outperformed during 2012–2023.

Returning to the original question (what level of financial performance should investors expect from sustainable investing?), we are now better positioned to offer an answer: "it depends on what you believe is driving the market" is a reasonable response. If the market is in an environment where risk and reward are clearly linked in an easily observable manner, then asset pricing theory should hold and green stocks should *underperform* the market. However, if the market is driven by significant changes in supply and demand, then economics likely holds sway, bubbles can form (and persist), and green stocks might outperform.

ESG INVESTMENT: INTERVIEW WITH EMILY WOODLAND AND HEIDI YIP, BLACKROCK

In conversation with James Cheo

James
On ESG [environmental, social, and governance] investment returns and risks, is there a case that ESG factors show evidence of outperformance?

BlackRock
We need to start with how we define the term "ESG investment" in this context. Because as we've touched on already, there are different ways to approach sustainable investment, which can range from screened, to uplift, to thematic, and impact strategies. Some of it is just basic ESG integration.

When you look at the types of strategies we talked about in terms of the spectrum of sustainable investing, you should expect the performance case to change. One issue is that some academic literature will conflate the different types of strategies into one overall ESG investing bucket, which confuses the story around returns.

It would probably be more useful if that data was parsed into the different types of strategies. For example, screened strategies exclude entire sections of the investment universe, which potentially introduces short-term volatility vs. the benchmark, and you may be carving out entire sectors that outperform or underperform over a given time frame. Whereas thematic strategies may focus on sustainability-related themes that might have alpha tailwinds associated with those long-term sustainability related trends. So, you're investing in companies that actually are beneficiaries of some of the structural shifts that you're seeing in government policy and technological changes and shifts in consumer investor preferences, and, therefore, you can make a long-term performance case for those structural shifts. So, the short answer is it just really depends on what style of investing you're actually looking at. And in some cases, sustainability factors might be materially positive. In other cases, they might be agnostic.

Our goal is to seek the best risk-adjusted returns for our client portfolios. From the mandate that clients set for us, we help them manage the material risks and opportunities and how that could impact their portfolio. ESG integration is our base case for all our actively managed strategies, because we believe that looking at material factors like ESG factors, but also any other financial factors, is part of discharging our fiduciary duty to deliver the best risk-adjusted returns for clients. Asset managers should be taking on board all information that is material to getting the best risk-adjusted return to clients.

ESG INVESTMENT: INTERVIEW WITH MERVYN TANG, SCHRODERS

In conversation with James Cheo

James
What's your view [on] investment returns associated with ESG investing?

Mervyn
On ESG integration, a lot of people think it's just about investing in the best and most sustainable companies and not investing in the least sustainable companies. That is not necessarily true—ESG integration is about incorporating ESG information, and then considering it in

(Continued)

(Continued)

your evaluation, alongside all these other things in your investment process like valuation. And so, theoretically, if you take in more information and you analyze it correctly, you have opportunities for alpha. But that alpha is going to be on the quality of analysis of the information and how you apply it to your investment process, rather than ESG automatically adding alpha. It's an opportunity of using information to generate alpha. In the same way, when using financial data, if I just invest in the lowest price-to-equity (PE) ratio companies or the lowest price-to-book (PB) ratio companies, that doesn't mean that I generate alpha, but if I analyze that correctly, and I look at the catalysts that will drive potential revaluation in those companies, I could generate alpha with my financial analysis. ESG integration from my perspective doesn't automatically generate alpha but it is looking at information in a way that could.

James
Do sustainable funds generate alpha or have outperformance?

Mervyn
When I look at the variation of the performance of sustainable funds from Morningstar, in the global large-cap equity space, over the last year and then over the last five years, it is just as wide as nonsustainable funds.

One of the reasons is that there's lots of different sustainable fund methodologies, some that are more sector neutral, [and] some look at ESG leaders, and so they don't have tilts toward a certain way. You have climate funds that are very exposed to renewables and less exposed to energy that have been exposed to this cycle. You have thematic funds that are linked to health care, a few other different sectors that have a certain profile. So, the variation in sustainable fund performance is just as wide as the broader fund universe.

What we do see is that you do get the occasional, correlated exposures of sustainable funds. On average, more sustainable funds are underweight energy, tobacco, and alcohol, just because of the common use of different methodologies; more sustainable funds are overweight renewables, and even battery storage and climate solutions. And so, to the degree that certain sectors and regions have underperformed or outperformed in a particular market, you are going to get kind of systematic underperformance or outperformance over a time period.

So, if I looked [at] the last three years of how climate funds perform, they have underperformed, because climate has been slammed by the energy transition and stocks [of] alternative energy performed badly over the past few years. But then if I looked at five-to-ten-year returns it doesn't look so bad, and as a group at a similar level of performance as non-climate-related funds. And so, it is important to understand that sustainable funds have a certain set of exposures that are more likely to have overweights and underweights in certain sectors and markets. For climate transition funds, because a lot of the climate solution companies are concentrated in Europe, Canada, and the US, you may become more concentrated in those countries, and your performance is going to be linked to that.

It is not about sustainability necessarily adding alpha in that context, but you may end up having a set of exposures that you believe will be positive in the long term.

SUMMARY

The world of investing includes a variety of strategies with which to incorporate sustainability risks and opportunities. From relatively formulaic screening strategies to integration and active ownership, investment managers apply these strategies to create products that align with the objectives of specific sets of investors. When investors are conscious of sustainability and wish to do no harm or deliver benefits to stakeholders, while maintaining a market-rate return objective, there are many possible configurations of strategies to satisfy the sustainability preferences of investors. But what level of commitment to sustainability should we expect from investors? A recent paper[57] provides a somewhat sobering point of view. The authors interviewed over 500 equity portfolio managers from traditional and sustainable funds. The key takeaways suggest that investors may be less motivated to drive sustainability change than many would hope:

- The primary motivation for incorporating environmental and social (ES) factors is financial returns—even in sustainable funds.
- Very few investors will sacrifice returns for ES performance, citing their fiduciary duty.
- Only 5% of sustainable and 2% of traditional investors are willing to sacrifice more than 0.5% per year of financial performance.

- ES integration is driven more by whether fund managers believe in ES alpha than whether their fund has a sustainable label.
- Most investors think companies already manage ES well, rather than there being substantial underinvestment that would warrant large-scale engagement.
- Given (i) financial objectives and (ii) the belief that companies aren't systematically underinvesting in ES, asset managers are unlikely to lead the charge in transforming companies' ES. Not due to greenwashing, but because they're not set up to prioritize externalities over long-term value.

For those uncommon investors that plan to use their capital to solve problems, however, they may find themselves turning to an altogether different strategy: the subject of Chapter 13, impact investing.

CHAPTER 13

Impact Investing

The investment strategies discussed in Chapter 12 are all close relatives of traditional investing, from ESG integration to screening to active ownership and thematic investing. Impact investing, on the other hand, is sufficiently different from the other strategies to merit its own chapter. Rather than incorporating *sustainability* into investing, impact investing can feel like it's the other way around. After defining the strategy, Chapter 13 explores some of the characteristics that make it unique including establishing a theory of change for causality, defining and measuring impact, social return on investment, and the trade-off between impact and financial returns.

Despite its promise, impact investing is not without challenges and criticisms. Key issues include the difficulty of measuring impact, the risk of "impact washing"—where investments are marketed as impactful without substantiated benefits—and the tension between achieving financial returns and generating social good.

DEFINITION

The first use of the term "impact investing" dates to a meeting hosted in 2007 by the Rockefeller Foundation. According to the Global Impact Investing Network (GIIN), the term refers to investments which are "made with the intention to generate positive, measurable social and environmental impact alongside a financial return." Let's explore some of the key components of the definition.

Intention. At the core of impact investing is intentionality, which refers to the deliberate allocation of capital toward investments that aim to generate positive social or environmental benefits. Within this set of social or environmental benefits can be found a broad range of projects, from health care and education to renewable energy and sustainable agriculture. Unlike traditional investment approaches that may only consider financial returns, impact investing requires that positive outcomes are a primary objective, not an ancillary benefit.

Measurable. One of the most important aspects of impact investing is the measurement and management of impact itself. The GIIN[1] states that impact investing should be evidence-based and data-driven from the earliest stages of the investment process:

- Identify a social or environmental need aligned with empirical evidence or well-established science, as well as one expressed by the population or environmental community the investment seeks to serve.
- Use the best evidence accessible to:
  - Set targets about the investment's contribution to improvement of that need.
  - Design investment strategies based on solutions effective in addressing the needs identified and an understanding of potential negative impacts in the context of the investments.
  - Identify the qualitative and quantitative indicators used to gauge performance against targets.
  - Improve capacity to conduct impact analytics over time to improve the rigor of activities.

Financial Returns. Impact investments take numerous forms, especially debt instruments, but also equity, revenue-sharing agreements, and grants, among others. Impact investments are expected to generate financial returns; they are not philanthropy. Impact investing also does not demand a trade-off between doing good and earning profits. Many impact investors target market-rate returns while pursuing measurably positive impacts. Industry surveys consistently indicate that a substantial percentage of impact investors have met or exceeded their financial expectations. However, critics argue that the expectation of simultaneous financial gains and measurable impact may be unrealistic, particularly in high-risk environments. We will explore this further below.

Additionality. While not included in the official definition, additionality is another crucial principle of impact investing. In a high-additionality investment, the positive impact would not have occurred without the investor's involvement. Some impact investors prioritize high-additionality investments, highlighting the unique role that impact investors play in this segment of the investment landscape.

THEORY OF CHANGE

An important first step for many impact investors is establishing a *theory of change* (TOC). Originating in the fields of social science and organizational psychology, a TOC outlines the steps necessary to bring about desired social or organizational transformation, starting with a description of the *problem* one is trying to solve with detailed pathways of *inputs* and *actions* that the investee company would undertake. The *outputs* lead to change (the *outcomes*), which should ultimately lead to the desired long-term *impact*. This flow is described visually in Figure 13.1, taken from an impact-centric project in Nigeria from the 2010s:

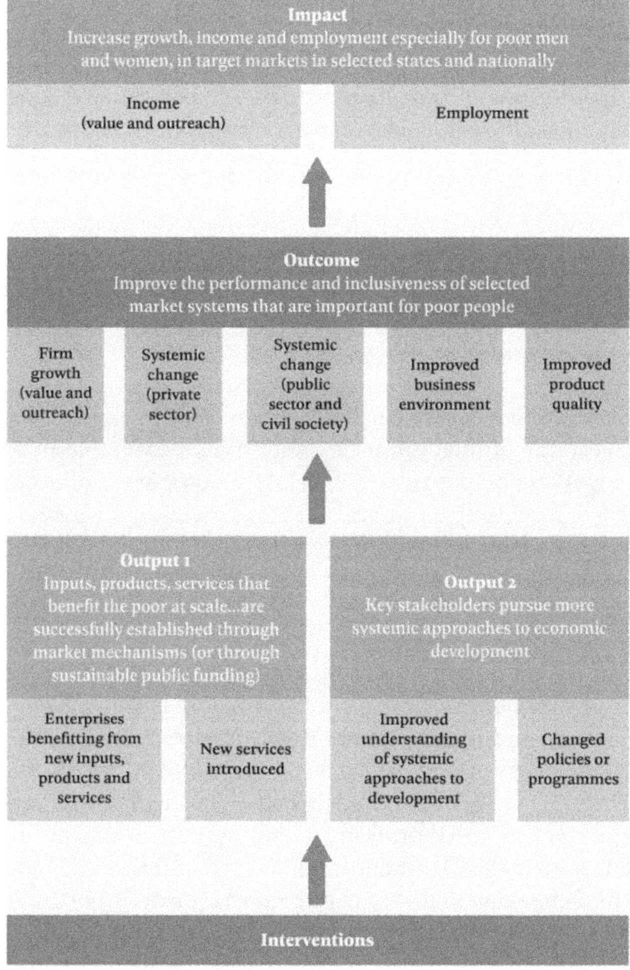

FIGURE 13.1 Theory of change (TOC).
Source: ITAD Limited / https://www.slideshare.net/slideshow/gems-me-handbook/29088360#1 / last accessed Aug 20, 2025.

In contrast, a very different type of TOC was prepared by an Asian investment manager in 2023[2]:

The problem
Countries in the Asia Pacific region accounted for 50% of global emissions; this was expected to increase as economic prosperity (highly correlated to carbon emissions) approached Global North levels. Countries in Asia Pacific set emission reduction targets through their Nationally Determined Contributions (NDCs), however, these targets were not ambitious enough. Given Asian listed companies' existing carbon footprints and their role in Asia Pacific's economic growth, unless these companies accelerated their pace of decarbonization, global efforts to tackle climate change would not succeed.

Intended long-term impact
The investor defined its ultimate goal as significantly mitigating this problem by empowering public companies to implement priority carbon reduction projects that would create significant and verifiable GHG emissions reductions.

Outcomes
The investor created a Theory of Change using backward mapping to connect the ultimate impact to specific, measurable outcomes. Achieving these outcomes would catalyze investors to allocate capital for enhanced impact at scale. Therefore, in line with SBTi and IPCC recommended reduction pathways, one of the outcomes for the investor was to identify, invest in, motivate, and assist listed companies to reduce their Scope 1, 2, and 3 carbon footprint by at least 40% in less than 10 years.

Inputs and activities
The activities and interventions of the investor were directly aimed at addressing the factors it believed contributed the most to the problem and where it believed it could wield the most influence through investor collaboration: providing patient capital, using a rigorous impact measurement framework to guide investment decisions, and engaging and supporting management of portfolio companies to accelerate and scale up carbon reduction projects.

To see a TOC from a public equity investor is unusual but important. Without one, it is challenging to make a convincing case that buying and selling stocks has any influence on the amount of impact the investment can generate. Even with a TOC, it's still a tall task, but when combined with a thoughtful plan for corporate engagement, a case can be made for impact in public equities.

IMPACT MEASUREMENT AND MANAGEMENT

Impact measurement and management (IMM) is a critical process through which investors and portfolio companies (e.g., social entrepreneurs) assess and report on the social and environmental benefits generated by their investments. IMM includes a range of methodologies such as materiality assessments, TOCs, selecting appropriate metrics, and continuously monitoring results, risks, and returns to optimize outcomes. Rigorous measurement practices support the belief that increasing allocations to impact investing are not diluting potential impact *or* returns.

How do impact investors measure impact? With help from a well-crafted TOC, investors will develop a set of metrics that capture how the operating entity expects to generate impact and how much impact is created by providing the product or service in question. Structured thinking is critical at this stage. As an example, imagine you are trying to identify the lowest-emissions way to prepare your morning coffee:

> The value chain, or life cycle, of a cup of coffee starts with the production of the coffee, which uses land and, in some cases, water for irrigation, and other inputs such as fertilizers and pesticides. Then, the coffee beans are de-pulped, washed, and dried to produce green coffee, which can be stored and transported over long distances. This is the state that coffee is in when it is purchased by brands to roast and grind to consumers' tastes. It is then packed, individually or in bulk, put on pallets wrapped in secondary and tertiary packaging, and then shipped to retailers and shops. When consumers buy and make a cup of coffee, they boil water or use a machine that uses energy, and pour the coffee into a cup, which will then either be discarded (paper/plastic cups) or washed (reusable materials).
>
> Considering the environmental impact along this value chain, packaging represents less than 20% of the total impact of making coffee in terms of impact indicators, such as climate change and air and water pollution. Most of the impact of a cup of coffee comes first from the production of the coffee itself at the farm in tropical

countries and second from the energy used to heat the water to brew the coffee, probably gas or electricity. All other activities and materials contribute only marginally to the overall impact of a cup of coffee.[3]

As recently as 2016, practitioner surveys indicated that many investors developed their own impact metrics for each investment. Today, however, valuable tools and resources are available that reduce the risk of "reinventing the wheel." The first is IRIS+,[4] a database of impact metrics crowdsourced from the community of impact investors. The website allows investors to search for terms related to the impact they plan to measure, generating a list of potential matches for consideration. This saves time but doesn't eliminate the need for careful thought and, potentially, some customization to suit the specific investment opportunity.

When impact investors reach the point of customization, either from an IRIS+ entry or from scratch, the second resource—Impact Frontiers' Five Dimensions of Impact—captures best practices in impact measurement. As shown in Table 13.1, working through the five dimensions helps investors think expansively about the types of impact that might be embedded within an investment.

TABLE 13.1   Impact Frontiers: Five Dimensions of Impact

What	"What" tells us what outcome the enterprise is contributing to, whether it is positive or negative, and how important the outcome is to the people and communities experiencing it, as well as to the planet.
Who	"Who" describes the people and communities experiencing the outcome across multiple characteristics such as gender, class, race, sexual orientation, and Indigenous status, and explores differences in outcomes based on these characteristics and/or unique intersections of these characteristics.
How much	"How much" tells us how many people experienced the outcome, what degree of change they experienced, and how long they experienced the outcome.
Contribution	"Contribution" tells us whether an enterprise's efforts resulted in outcomes that were likely better than what likely would have occurred otherwise.
Risk	"Risk" tells us the likelihood that impact will be different than expected.

Once the metrics are agreed and an investment is made, impact investors actively seek to improve the rigor of measurement and to increase the amount and quality of impact delivered:

- Embed feedback loops through the life of the investment as feasible.
- Identify risks to achieving stated impact goals and developing mitigation plans.
- Seek to mitigate any negative consequences from the activities.
- Disclose actual impact performance data to investors and investees, in as comparable a manner as possible.

This commitment to ongoing improvement is a characteristic of strong impact investing managers, rather than individual *funds*. It happens that, just like the Five Dimensions of Impact represent a best practice framework for measuring impact, there is a separate but related set of best practices for being an impact investment manager: the Operating Principles for Impact Management (OPIM) (Figure 13.2). As stated, "The Impact Principles provide an end-to-end framework of best practices that investors can use in the design, implementation and continuous improvement of their impact management systems and processes, ensuring that impact considerations are integrated throughout the investment lifecycle."[5]

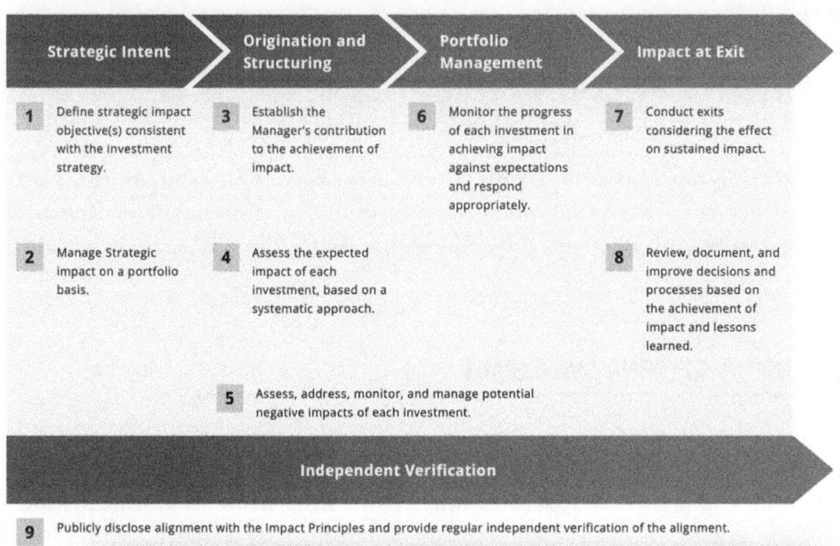

FIGURE 13.2 Operating Principles for Impact Management (OPIM).
Source: Global Impact Investing Network (GIIN) / https://www.impactprinciples.org/9-principles/ / last accessed Aug 20, 2025.

Finally, when an impact investor is ready to submit its IMM to external scrutiny, it will often turn to BlueMark, the leading independent verification firm for impact investing. Using the OPIM nine principles, the firm conducts a detailed assessment to benchmark the investor's current capabilities against accepted industry standards, then assigns a rating ("seal") that the investor can use in communications with prospects and clients.

SOCIAL RETURN ON INVESTMENT[6]

A final tool that many impact investors find useful (if occasionally somewhat simplistic) is called SROI, social return on investment. It takes the financial idea of return on investment (ROI) and makes adjustments that capture the estimated value of social (and environmental) benefits:

$$SROI = \frac{Social\ Value\ Created - Deadweight\ and\ Attribution}{Investment}$$

> **Social Value Created.** Total tangible and intangible benefits, e.g., improved health, employment, or environmental gains.
>
> **Deadweight.** Outcomes that would have occurred without the intervention.
>
> **Attribution.** Adjusting value to reflect the intervention's direct contribution.
>
> **Investment.** Total resources used, including money, time, and equipment.

Calculating SROI can help investors prioritize how they allocate their capital and identify the most important assumptions that should be stress-tested to make sure the SROI is as accurate as possible. It bears mentioning that SROI is not just an academic exercise. For example, Singapore-based impact investor IIX Global includes an SROI calculation in the prospectus for their series of Women's Livelihood Bonds (Table 13.2; see especially footnote 6).[7]

TRADING OFF RETURNS AND IMPACT

Finally, at the heart of arguments for and against impact investing is the perceived trade-off between financial returns and impact. The expectation of financial gain clearly separates impact investing from philanthropy, but so does impact measurement—most philanthropies cannot devote the resources necessary to rigorously measure impact in their program(s).

TABLE 13.2 IIX Global Women's Livelihood Bonds, Including Social Return on Investment (SROI)

Features		First Finance	Ananya	Dvara	Kinara Capital	Samunnati	Satya	Esta Dana	Lenana	EVN Finance
					Financial Institutions					
Issuer Exposure	Expected Loan Amount (US$)	10,000,000	8,000,000	14,400,000	14,400,000	9,000,000	11,400,000	7,000,000	12,000,000	10,000,000
	Proportion of Total %	10.40%	8.32%	14.97%	14.97%	9.36%	11.85%	7.28%	12.47%	10.40%
	Security	Unsecured	Client receivables	Client receivables	Client receivables	Client receivables	Client receivables	Unsecured	(a) Client receivables (b) Pledge over promoter shares (c) Promoter Guarantee (d) Pledge over Debt service reserve account (e) Promoter loans to be subordinated	Unsecured
	Country of Operations	Cambodia	India	India	India	India	India	Indonesia	Kenya	Vietnam
Operational Maturity	Legal Incorporation Status	Public Limited Company	Private Limited Company (Registered as NBFC-NDSI)	Private Limited Company (Registered as NBFC-NDSI)	Private Limited Company (Registered as NBFC-NDSI)	Private Limited Company (Registered as NBFC-NDSI)	Private Limited Company (Registered as NBFC-NDSI)	Private Limited Company	Private Limited Company	Joint Stock Company
	Years in Operation	15	14	15	27	9	6	9	9	15
	Number of Borrowers (active)	2,179	99,619	503,835	32,987	867[7]	975,808	243,873	28,544	237,132

(*Continued*)

TABLE 13.2 (*Continued*)

Features		First Finance	Ananya	Dvara	Kinara Capital	Samunnati	Satya	Esta Dana	Lenana	EVN Finance
						Financial Institutions				
Financial Stability[1][2]	Results as of Total Assets	FY 2022	FY Mar 2023	FY Mar 2023	FY Mar 2023	FY Mar 2023	FY Mar 2023	FY 2022	FY 2022	FY 2022
	(US$ millions) Net Loan Portfolio	$47.68	$61.83	$227.92	$304.89	$186.53	$567.16	$64.59	$31.42	$1,787.92
	(US$ millions) Net Profit	$35.26	$42.48	$194.33	$196.70	$127.18	$465.39	$51.32	$25.42	$1,015.04
	(US$ millions)	$0.33	$0.29	$1.57	$5.14	−$12.27	$6.63	$1.58	$3.65	$15.49
	Debt/Equity (×)[3]	1.71×	3.91×	4.86×	2.44× 3.29%	1.70×	4.38×	5.88×	0.47×	9.44× 2.22%
	PAR30[4][5]	2.98%	2.41%	4.18%	(PAR 90)	12.00%	1.67%	3.78%	2.06%	(PAR 90)
Impact	Expected Social Return on Investment [6]	~$3.25– 3.75	~$5.50–5.70	~$3.65–3.85	~$3.90–4.10	~$4.05–4.15	~$4.50–5.00	~$04.25– 4.50	~$4.75–4.95	~$3.20–3.40
	United Nations Sustainable Development Goals (SDG) Alignment	SDG 5, 6, 8, 10, 11, 13	SDG 1, 2, 5, 8, 10	SDG 1, 5, 6, 8, 10, 13	SDG 5, 8, 10	SDG 1, 2, 5, 13	SDG 1, 5, 6, 8, 10, 13	SDG 1, 5, 8, 10	SDG 1, 2, 5, 13	SDG 1, 5, 7, 8, 10, 13
	Total (Direct and Indirect) Female Beneficiaries Impacted by the WLB Loan	~1,300– 1,600	~130,000– 135,000	~85,000– 90,000	~3,000– 3,500	~84,000– 88,000	~140,000– 145,000	~240,000– 260,000	~50,000– 51,000	~147,000– 149,000

Source: WLB Asset VI Pte. Ltd / https://links.sgx.com/FileOpen/WLB6%20%20Final%20IM%20(8%20Dec%202023).ashx?App=Prospectus&FileID=61071, p17 / last accessed Aug 20, 2025.

(1) The financial statements of all Borrowers, except First Finance, are prepared in their local currencies. For each such Borrower, we present USD convenience translations of its financial information using the exchange rate specified under the heading "Selected Financial Information" in the discussion of such Borrower in "*The Borrowers*." First Finance's financial statements are presented in USD, which is its primary operating and reporting currency.

(2) The financial information of Ananya and Samunnati set forth in this table is provided on a standalone basis. For a discussion of the relevance of such information, please see the discussion of each such Borrower set forth in "*The Borrowers*."

(3) Debt/Equity refers to the ratio of indebtedness to total equity.

(4) PAR30 refers to the percentage (by value) of the Borrower's gross loan portfolio of client receivables which is overdue for more than 30 days as of the date of measurement.

(5) Kinara Capital and EVN Finance do not report PAR30. The data in this row for these two Borrowers instead represent their PAR90, i.e., the percentage (by value) of such Borrowers' gross loan portfolio of client receivables that is overdue for more than 90 days as of the date of measurement. I

(6) Social Return on Investment ("SROI") is a measure of how much social and environmental impact, in dollar figures, is created for every dollar invested into the organization and/or program. The SROI of each Borrower is calculated by dividing the social and environmental value of impact expected to be created as a result of the Loan through primary outcomes by the principal amount of the Loan to that Borrower.

(7) Represents number of active Farmer Producer Organization clients of the Borrower.

Investor motivation is an important contributor to this debate. At the risk of overgeneralizing, there are several categories of investors:

- Impact-agnostic investors are indifferent to impact.
- Impact-aware (investment-first) investors seek market-rate, risk-adjusted returns with impact as a secondary consideration.
- Impact-seeking (impact-first) investors are the most likely to accept concessionary returns, prioritizing social and environmental outcomes over financial performance.
- Catalytic investors are motivated to strengthen the impact investing ecosystem by participating in capability-building initiatives that deliver both impact and financial returns.

To properly assess how investors view the trade-off would require information that is inherently difficult to obtain. On the financial returns side, you would want to know the actual returns as well as what the investment would have returned if it had generated less (or more) impact. From an impact perspective, you would want to know how much impact was generated alongside the actual returns, and how much impact could have been generated under the counterfactual return scenarios. The lack of a multiverse in which to conduct experiments is a common frustration in social science research!

An alternative approach—with limitations—is to look at the choices made by institutional investors and impute a "willingness to pay" (WTP) for impact. An influential paper[8] from 2021 used data on venture capital investments, both impact and nonimpact, to estimate how much financial return investors were willing to sacrifice to invest in an impact fund. Their research showed that the aggregate WTP for impact was between 2.5% and 3.7% in expected internal rate of return (IRR). To put that in context, if a typical venture capital fund delivers 15–20% IRR, then impact investors were willing to forgo 12–24%[9] of the IRR in return for measurable impact.

SUMMARY

Impact investing is very different from the other sustainable investing strategies described in Chapter 12. Its definition provides clear direction: intent, positive, measurable, social and/or environmental benefits, financial return. Not every manager can create a fancy website and say they're an impact investor! It takes commitment to develop a TOC, craft the metrics that the investor and portfolio company will use together to track impact performance, and monitor ongoing performance with an eye toward continued refinement and improvement of the whole process.

The benefits for stakeholders can be profound; measuring SROI can help estimate the impact. But at the end of the day, investors in an impact investing fund must be prepared for some degree of sacrifice when it comes to financial returns.

CHAPTER 14

Sustainable Investing Across Asset Classes and Geographies

To this point in Part Four, the different investment strategies have been loosely aligned with one or more asset classes or geographies (typically, public equities). In practice, strategy selection and implementation may look very different across asset classes (think public equities vs. private credit) or geographies (think Indonesia vs. France). This brief chapter assumes the reader is familiar with the material in Chapters 11–13, and, after a quick refresher on asset classes, presents some of the unique aspects of sustainable investing across different asset classes and geographies. We will dive into the implications for *implementation* along these dimensions in Chapter 17.

ASSET CLASSES

Public companies are those which have elected to sell shares to the public, almost always through an initial public offering (IPO) process. For example, Rivian Automotive, an American electric vehicle manufacturer, went public at US$78 per share on November 10, 2021, raising nearly US$12 billion in one of the largest IPOs in US history. Following its market debut, Rivian's stock closed at US$100.73 per share, making pre-IPO (when Rivian was a *private* company) investors very happy. Investors who purchased shares *after* the IPO had a brief period in which to make money—the stock price collapsed shortly thereafter and currently trades around US$13 per share (−83.3% return) (Figure 14.1).

As we saw in Chapter 7, public companies also raise external capital by issuing debt; private companies can sell bonds as well, though this is far less common. Therefore, stocks and bonds are nearly always associated with public companies, and, together with cash, are collectively referred to as "traditional" investments.

Private companies or real assets, such as buildings, are commonly included in the portfolios of the largest investors. Among the most salient features of private assets is the fact that they are not required to publicly disclose financial results and are not traded very frequently, especially compared with publicly listed stocks and bonds. Private assets, therefore, are less

FIGURE 14.1   Rivian Automotive stock performance 2021–2025.
Source: Google, https://www.google.com/search?q=rivian+stock+price+chart&rlz=1C1GCEA_enSG1086SG1086&oq=rivian+stock+price+chart&gs_lcrp, retrieved July 30, 2025.

transparent when it comes to determining prices. Rather ather than a price based on daily trading volume (e.g., the price of LVMH updates every trading day) investors in private assets rely on what is called "mark-to-market" valuation.[1] Investors may invest in private companies or real assets directly or through pooled investment vehicles, most often private equity or venture capital funds which specialize in these types of investments.

SUSTAINABLE INVESTING ACROSS ASSET CLASSES

There are a few important differences between asset classes when it comes to sustainable investing. Some of the most common include the following:

- Public companies are subject to more regulations and reporting requirements than private companies, providing greater transparency for investors in sustainability matters, in addition to financial ones.[2]

- Stocks represent an ownership stake in the firm, so the sustainability characteristics of the stock are tightly linked to the sustainability characteristics of the firm. Bonds, on the other hand, represent a debt obligation over a fixed time period, e.g., a 15-year bond. The element of time adds an interesting twist to sustainability in fixed-income investing: bond investors are primarily concerned with sustainability risks that are expected to impact the firm's ability to meet its debt obligations *during the lifetime of the bond*. It follows, therefore, that sustainability-related risks, like climate change, will be more important to a 30-year bond than a 5-year bond.

- A generally accepted statement on the relationship between emissions and stock prices remains elusive. Multiple studies[3] have examined the issue with varying results depending on the specific emissions data and measure used. Heavily emitting firms in certain industries may be good candidates for private equity transition funds but should be evaluated on a case-by-case basis.

- Because private equity firms often own their portfolio companies (especially leveraged buyout [LBO] funds), their control creates greater opportunity to unlock value by acting on sustainability issues. One recent study stated that for some private equity investors, sustainability-related value creation led to ~6% revenue growth and ~6–7% multiple uplift in portfolio companies at exit.[4]

- Regardless of whether investing in public or private companies, stocks or bonds or funds, some industries are inherently more sustainable than others. Pharmaceuticals, education services, and renewable energy companies will always be considered more sustainable than fossil fuel, mining, and cement companies.

INVESTMENT RETURNS AND IMPACT: INTERVIEW WITH JEREMY HALL, BROOKFIELD

In conversation with James Cheo

James
How do you capture the investment returns and impact from decarbonization?

Jeremy
When going into an investment, we think about the financial return along with the contribution to sustainability impact targets and additionality that we can create.

(Continued)

(*Continued*)

Our strength is to implement successful transformation, and that requires sizeable and patient capital, an intimate understanding of power markets, and deep experience in the power and clean energy development sectors. Deep relationships with equipment suppliers, regulators, and other stakeholders in these sectors can help companies add value and de-risk their energy supply. Private markets are best suited for such transformation due to the longer-term investment horizon and the insulation of business plans from the pressures of short-term investor requirements such as quarterly results.

On investment returns of utility phaseouts and transformations, we need to consider, too, that utilities are diverse businesses with multiple assets. Utilities not only own energy infrastructure but, in some cases, have large customer books that provide investors like us ready and reputable offtakers. This substantially eliminates one aspect of development risk—finding a third-party contract/offtaker—and increases the certainty that renewable developments will proceed apace.

Some companies would prefer not to relinquish control, but they need the operational expertise and/or capital and want to partner with us. In some instances, we took a preferred equity position in the company and worked with them as a partner to decarbonize their businesses.

Private capital can bring in unified long-term investors and release utilities from the transition trap. It can help accelerate and expand on transition plans, capturing the returns that should accrue to those helping to fill the gap between clean energy demand and supply—while also reducing real economy emissions.

In quantifying the environmental impact, our Impact Measurement and Management framework is differentiated by its robust approach to measurement, through ongoing management of the impact targets by teams deeply experienced in developing and operating decarbonization assets, and through transparent reporting aligned with leading climate reporting standards and impact frameworks such as SBTi, TCFD, GHG Protocol. We are committed to supporting the goals of the Paris Agreement and accelerating the net-zero transition with an emphasis on measurable decarbonization.

At the same time, we strategically time capital deployment and target transactions at attractive valuations. Our global reach allows us to allocate capital across our target markets wherever we are seeing

> the most attractive opportunities. Our capabilities to originate and structure tailored, scaled, and creative transactions at attractive value entry points, combined with our operational capabilities and expertise, allows us to pursue many investments on a bilateral basis, which we believe enables us to earn attractive returns in the long term.

GEOGRAPHY

If sustainability takes a different shape depending on the asset class, it manifests differently in emerging markets (EMs) vs. developed markets (DMs). Historically, DM countries have been the largest contributors to global emissions; more recently, China and India have joined the list since burning coal has been the cheapest energy source to power their countries' rapid economic development. EM countries lack many public goods and services that people take for granted in DMs. Food, water, shelter, access to financial services, education, health care—one or all of these may be in short supply in the poorest countries in the world.

In EMs, therefore, environmental sustainability is inextricably linked to social issues. Investors must approach investments with both dimensions in mind (e.g., just transition), especially when pursuing environmental objectives. But the relative lack of institutional development in EMs creates opportunity as well. The bottom of the pyramid (BOP) can be an attractive market segment with the proper business model, and environment-focused investments can generate incremental value by taking the social issues into consideration at the same time. Typically, EM countries have large BOP populations and businesses can deliver profits even when selling prices are low—the BOP is a market segment, not a charity case. Under these circumstances, investing in EMs with social sustainability in mind increases the chances of generating meaningful impact while simultaneously achieving market-rate returns.

This is not to say that there is no need for social sustainability improvements in developed markets. Access to information and capital may be easier in Berlin than in Nairobi; differences in public infrastructure (food and water, shelter, health care, education) will lead to different needs for the local population. Because the context is different, the nature of the investments will be different as well.

GEOGRAPHIES: INTERVIEW WITH MITCH REZNICK, CFA, FEDERATED HERMES

In conversation with James Cheo

James

On the regional differences, when it comes to adoption of green bonds, standards, etc.—and of course, you know that most of the transition has to happen in emerging markets where regulation is looser—how do investors who are largely in developed markets invest into green bonds?

Mitch

A lot of the world's value chain sits in regions that are most vulnerable to climate change and biodiversity loss. The reality is that the only market that is scale outside of the US and Europe is China, particularly the local currency market in China. Maybe India could grow over time. In China, the local currency market for green bonds is about 10%. It's come off quite a bit because the Chinese debt markets have shrunk. There are concerns, but as companies get bigger and you want to finance meaningful amounts of capital, at some point you have to get to the hard currency markets. So, in certain jurisdictions, there are some weaknesses, but in the deep pools of capital, especially in the hard currency market, there are norms that protect against the greenwashing. The regulatory difference, over time, will converge and improve.

James

Why would sovereigns issue green bonds?

Mitch

The reasons for sovereigns to issue green bonds are not much different than corporates in the sense that sovereigns have made commitments through [the] Paris Agreement, the nationally determined contributions (NDCs) to decarbonize. There's a reputation around delivering the NDCs. So, issuing green bonds is to deliver on your commitment to the Paris Agreement, of which close to 200 countries did so. There is a need for financing going to the decarbonization projects and, perhaps, there is greenium they can capture as well, just like there might be for corporate treasuries.

EMERGING MARKETS: INTERVIEW WITH JEREMY HALL, BROOKFIELD

In conversation with James Cheo

James
Going to where the emissions are, how is Brookfield navigating opportunities in emerging markets?

Jeremy
Emerging markets generate 72% of global emissions and their demand for electricity is rising sharply. Although the decarbonization investment is surging globally, most emerging markets are receiving only a fraction of it. Significant growth in private climate finance, which has historically focused less on these markets, will be essential for the massive scale-up needed for the clean energy transition in emerging markets.

For the energy transition in emerging markets, there is a need for [an] unprecedented level of investments. In the early phases, private market investors are needed to catalyze other funding sources and crowd-in capital, including from multinational corporates intent on climate solutions for their emerging market-based operations.

When sizing up the emerging market transition investment opportunity, there is no one formula or approach. Each of these markets has different characteristics based on what it is trying to achieve relative to the current state of its overall power system and energy mix.

The good news is that there is tremendous opportunity for energy transition in emerging markets. First, there is significant potential to scale renewable energy investment in emerging markets due to rising demand for energy consumption. Second, renewables are becoming much more cost-effective. Wind and solar are now cheaper and less risky, on a capital expenditure basis, to fund and deploy than fossil fuel. Third, emerging markets have natural advantages in deploying renewables. They are generally in climates with higher solar and wind capture.

These advantages have made renewables cheaper than installing fossil fuel generators in emerging markets compared to developed market projects. On average, Brookfield estimates capital expenditures for these projects are about 40% less than equivalent-scale projects in the US or Europe.

(Continued)

(Continued)

However, there are challenges in investing in emerging markets. For instance, the rule of law and enforcement of contracts can be less predictable. Track records of local operators can be more limited, and the financial information of offtakers may be less transparent. Grid connection can be complicated by inefficiencies and regulatory risk. Currency repatriation is a risk given the long time frame for investments. Therefore, while the project cost of the emerging market energy transition may be 40% cheaper, the cost of sourcing that capital—the returns the average lender or investor demands for its risk—can be higher. For example, if the average cost of capital (including debt and equity) for a developed market solar project is around 5–6%, in an emerging market project that can be closer to 12%.[5]

Despite the risks, new capital structures are emerging to improve the risk/return profiles of these investments. In recent years, development banks and other public institutions have begun to team with large developed market financial corporations to blend the public and private investments to enable the transition in more creative and targeted ways. We have seen institutions and alternative managers start to focus on the emerging market transition opportunity and support these initiatives by "crowding in capital" and helping emerging markets with the transition to net zero.

SUMMARY

Chapters 12 and 13 on sustainable investing strategies and impact investing provided the building blocks for a further discussion of the importance of asset class and geography in sustainable investing. In Chapter 14, we recognized that private companies do not disclose the same information as public firms, making it more difficult for private markets investors to incorporate sustainability information into their analyses. We also saw that needs and investment opportunities will be different in EM and DM countries. Because of their relative lack of institutional and market development, EMs may offer a unique combination of financial returns alongside meaningful impact.

CHAPTER 15

Greenwashing and Investor Disclosure Regulations

In Part Three we learned that companies sometimes try to look more sustainable than they really are (greenwashing), whether it be in their advertising/marketing or in their financing decisions. As a result, governments and regulators have developed mechanisms to "encourage" desirable company behavior, from measurement and reporting to financing. When the encouragement isn't enough, fines and/or litigation are increasingly an option.

Investors also greenwash, though it takes a different form compared with "real economy" firms (and doesn't require nearly as much space to present). In the section on "Investor Greenwashing" we will review some of the ways that investment managers mislead their investors. The section that follows, "Investor Disclosure Regulations," describes regulatory initiatives in the European Union (EU) and the United Kingdom which are designed to curtail the amount of greenwashing in the investment management business and provide enhanced protection to retail investors.

INVESTOR GREENWASHING

At first glance, investment management may seem like an unusual industry to stand accused of greenwashing. After all, investment managers don't operate coal-fired power plants, dump toxic waste into the river, or displace Indigenous peoples.[1] But investment firms do make certain representations to their clients on their websites and in fund documents (e.g., factsheet, prospectus), and if not done with care there is a risk of making inconsistent or exaggerated claims. According to a 2023 report by the CFA Institute,[2] the most common potential missteps include:

- **Omission.** Omission is the failure to disclose a meaningful piece of information, such as changes to an investment strategy; details about investment and analytical methods, criteria, and processes; and definitions of metrics and key terms.

- **Unsubstantiated claim.** An unsubstantiated claim is a claim made without qualification or that is not supported with appropriate evidence. Unsubstantiated claims may or may not be true, but they can be potentially confusing because no evidence is presented that would allow for an evaluation of the claims. Unsubstantiated claims may be seen in the context of statements regarding real-world impact, comparisons to benchmarks, and alignment with or contribution to the Paris Agreement, the United Nations Sustainable Development Goals (SDGs), or other sustainability-related goals.
- **Inconsistency.** Inconsistency is a discrepancy of certain information. An inconsistency could be, for example, a discrepancy between the information presented in two different documents, a discrepancy between a fund's name and its investment objectives or strategy, or a discrepancy between stated investment policies and the measurement of outcomes.
- **Exaggeration.** Exaggeration is an overstatement of certain information. An example of exaggeration is when a fund claims that environmental, social, and governance (ESG) considerations are of primary importance in the investment process when ESG considerations are just one type of many similarly weighed considerations.

To date, the United States and Australia have levied fines and penalties on several investment managers for greenwashing (Table 15.1). The most significant case was brought in Germany and the United States against DWS after a whistleblower complaint; the day after the allegations were made public the chief executive officer resigned.

INVESTOR DISCLOSURE REGULATIONS

One of the interesting aspects of the DWS and similar incidents is that to properly evaluate the greenwashing claim requires insider information on the investment process—even with a list of holdings in hand, it may not be possible to know how the investment manager made the investment decision. This underscores the importance of setting clear expectations up front for what kind of information needs to be disclosed and how processes should be implemented.

Similar to its regulations for corporate sustainability,[3] the EU introduced the Sustainable Finance Disclosure Regulation (SFDR) requiring fund managers to measure and disclose important information about their ESG

TABLE 15.1 Significant Greenwashing Penalties

Firm	Fine/Penalty	Explanation
DWS (Deutsche Bank subsidiary)	€25 million (Germany)/ US$19 million (US)	Insider Desiree Fixler said the firm misrepresented in its annual report on the extent to which assets were invested using environmental, social, and governance (ESG) integration in the investment process. Separate fines imposed in US and Germany.
Invesco Advisers	US$17.5 million	Invesco Advisers told clients and stated in marketing materials between 2020 and 2022 that 70–94% of its parent company's assets under management were "ESG-integrated." However, according to the US Securities and Exchange Commission (SEC), those figures included a "substantial amount" of assets held in passive exchange-traded funds (ETFs) that did not take ESG factors into consideration in investment decisions.[a]
Goldman Sachs Asset Management	US$4 million	Several policy and procedure failures in their ESG research
WisdomTree Asset Management	US$4 million	Failing to comply with advertised ESG investment strategies
Vanguard Investments Australia	A$12.9 million	Making misleading claims about ESG exclusionary screens
Mercer Superannuation Australia	A$11.3 million	Made misleading statements about the sustainable nature and characteristics of some of its superannuation investment options
Active Super Australia	A$10.5 million	Invested in various securities that it had claimed were eliminated or restricted by its ESG investment screens

[a]https://www.ai-cio.com/news/invesco-pays-17-5-million-fine-to-settle-sec-greenwashing-charges/.

policies and processes. Most importantly, the SFDR introduces three fund classifications from which managers must choose the one that best represents the fund objectives:

- *Article 6* funds have no specific sustainability objectives or characteristics. Managers must disclose how sustainability risks are addressed in their decision-making process or explain why these risks are not considered relevant to the fund.
- *Article 8* ("light green") funds must promote specific environmental and/or social characteristics within their investment strategy and implement sustainability indicators that are systematically monitored and reported.
- *Article 9* ("dark green") funds must have an explicit sustainable investment objective as their primary objective, not just a consideration. Fund investments must contribute to an environmental or social objective, satisfy "do no significant harm" (DNSH) (which requires disclosure of Primary Adverse Impact [PAI] indicators), and demonstrate adherence to "good governance."

In addition to the SFDR, the European Securities and Markets Authority (ESMA) has issued separate fund naming rules using ESG and sustainability-related terms. The crux of the rules is that, in order to use terms like ESG, sustainability, green, or climate in a fund name, at least 80% of the assets should meet defined environmental or social characteristics, or sustainable investment objectives.

Across the English Channel, the UK Financial Conduct Authority (FCA) recently introduced its own regulation, the Sustainability Disclosure Requirements (SDR),[4] which incorporates both the labelling and naming elements from the SFDR and ESMA regulations. The four UK investment labels are:

- **Sustainability focus.** Comparable to the EU SFDR's Article 9 category which includes products with a sustainable investment objective.
- **Sustainability improvers.** Intended for products that don't currently deliver sustainability outcomes but have the potential.
- **Sustainability mixed goals.** Products with mixed sustainability and financial objectives.
- **Sustainability impact.** Products designed to achieve measurable positive impact.

From a fund-naming perspective, the SDR requires that funds with sustainability terms in the name must have 70% of investments following a sustainability objective, and all such funds shall use one of the four sustainability investment labels.

While the EU and United Kingdom are among the furthest along in addressing greenwashing by investment managers, other countries are moving in the same direction. For example, other countries have enacted their own regulations concerning naming of ESG funds, including Hong Kong, Japan, and Singapore.

SUMMARY

Investors must be careful when evaluating the sustainability claims of investment managers. Inconsistencies between marketing statements, fund documentation, and investment decisions—or any combination of the three—may qualify as greenwashing. In order to protect consumers, regulators in the EU, United Kingdom, and other jurisdictions are beginning to introduce regulations that require investment managers to disclose additional information about the sustainability goals and practices of their funds. Applying labels to funds wishing to present as a sustainable investment vehicle is a simple, visible step in the right direction.

Incorporating Sustainability into Your Portfolio

The journey from Part One to Part Five has been a long one, but patience and persistence are rewarded because now we talk about how you, the reader, can invest with sustainability in mind . . . to the extent you want to, of course.

And that's the first point, that investors have heterogeneous preferences for ESG. Your values, beliefs, and preferences belong to you, not your siblings or your neighbor. Depending on your financial position and what is most important to you, investment decisions might lean more toward returns or sustainability, toward climate leaders or health care, or toward a mix of financial-first liquid assets and sustainability-first private assets.

In Chapter 16, we begin with an exploration of individual preferences and the trade-off between financial and sustainability performance before discussing the actions investors can take with existing portfolios: replacing something you already have with a more sustainable version, divesting "bad" things, and adding "good" things.

Chapter 17 concludes with a "blank sheet of paper" approach, starting with an investment policy statement, then strategic and tactical asset allocation, and, finally, manager selection.

One final note: please remember that none of this material should be considered "investment advice." Do your own homework, and always consult a professional advisor if you have access to one.

CHAPTER 16

Selecting Sustainable Investments

several years ago, a student asked for help realigning her existing portfolio around some environmental, social, and governance (ESG) objectives. As we went through her holdings (in percentages, not value), we noted lots of opportunities to swap out of something she originally liked—say, a technology exchange-traded fund (ETF)—for an instrument with a clear sustainability mandate. But the questions quickly followed: "What do you care about the most?" "How important is tech exposure to you?" "Are you trying to feel less guilty or make a difference?"

Investing for sustainability is just as personal as any other kind of investment decision. Individuals, families, foundations, endowments, sovereign wealth funds, pension funds—they all have different values, beliefs, and/or preferences when it comes to sustainability. They will think differently about potential trade-offs between sustainability and financial performance, perhaps reflecting a faith-based or cultural perspective, or due to concerns about the ability to meet future obligations to retirees, or simply because they are at different life stages.

This chapter begins with a celebration of these differences, followed by a discussion of how investors navigate the trade-offs between risk, reward, and sustainability. In the section on "Adjusting an Existing Portfolio," we wrap it up with a process that individual investors can use to adjust their portfolios regardless of where they sit on the spectrum of sustainability objectives.

INDIVIDUAL PREFERENCES

We've mentioned the idea of varying individual preferences several times before in the book, most notably in the context of negative screening and impact investing strategies. A logical follow-up question is "preference for *what*?" There are many possible answers; none are wrong because these are individual preferences. Here are some common dimensions that investors should consider when contemplating a sustainability-aligned portfolio:

- Dimensions of traditional finance:
  - **Passive vs. active.** Depending on how much an investor believes in the efficient market hypothesis, portfolios may lean toward index ETFs or active funds, or even individual stock picking.
  - **Public vs. private.** A large part of this trade-off is based on the relative affluence of the investor and need for liquidity.
  - **Short(er) vs. long(er) term.** Investors who like to trade in search of short-term performance will have a very different appetite for sustainability than long-term investors.
- Dimensions of sustainability:
  - **Sustainability issues.** As we saw in Chapters 1–3, the list of sustainability issues is a long one. The degree to which someone cares about one issue more than another may be deeply personal. If your father died of lung cancer, you might avoid tobacco stocks. As an avid bird watcher, you might prioritize stocks with a positive stance toward biodiversity. You might care more about LGBTQ+ issues than the rights of Indigenous peoples, or vice versa, or skip those entirely to prioritize protections against child labor or human trafficking. The longer and more specific your list of *critical* sustainability issues, the harder it can be to find investment options aligned with that list.
  - **Solve problems vs. avoid harm.** Impact investors want to use their capital to create positive change in the world. Others just want to know that their investments aren't making the world any worse off than it is already. Both are valid perspectives, but creating positive change requires a higher burden of proof that investors may need to take into consideration.

All of these can be important, but it is likely that any individual cares more about one or two of these than the others. The highest priority preferences will be front-and-center in any portfolio rebalancing.

TRADE-OFF BETWEEN REWARD/RISK AND SUSTAINABILITY

Readers may have noticed a glaring omission in the bulleted list above: the potential trade-off between financial performance and sustainability performance. In fact, we give it this separate section because it is so important.

Investors are used to making trade-offs between return and risk. When presented with the following two investment options, most of us will have a clear preference:

- **Option 1.** Expected return of 4% per year, but the risk of a total loss is quite high.
- **Option 2.** Expected return of 20% per year, but it could be worth zero or it could triple in value.

In this case, the relationship between return and risk seems off in Option 1—high risk of losing everything, but the expected return is only 4%? At least with Option 2 the chance of losing everything is accompanied by a possibility of a +300% gain. This is how we might think about a trade-off between return and risk, like the two-dimensional chart in Figure 16.1 (top). Adding sustainability into the mix, however, is like adding a third dimension to the trade-off, as in Figure 16.1 (bottom).

The extra dimension makes it difficult to calculate the trade-offs in our head, but there are ways to simplify the process. For example, if we are already thinking about a particular asset with a return/risk profile, then we can compare investment options with roughly that same profile but different levels of sustainability—taking a slice out of the 3D map. Where it becomes especially challenging, however, is trying to decide how much financial performance (reward/risk) to sacrifice for improvements in sustainability. In our experience, there is no easy way to do this. As stated above, variables like income, wealth, and life stage play an important role in this decision for many investors. So, too, do the characteristics of the investment. You might be more willing to accept a larger trade-off for a fund run by a manager with a long track record and commitment to detailed measurement of impact, compared to a small fund from a new manager that lacks a certified process for impact measurement.

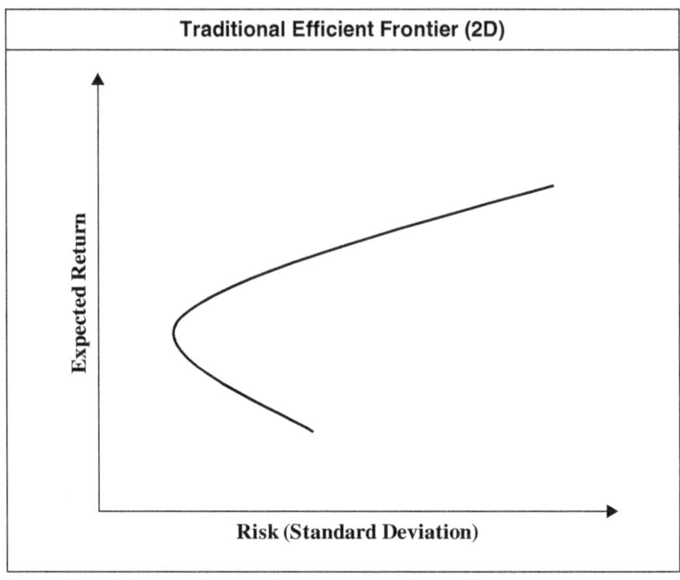

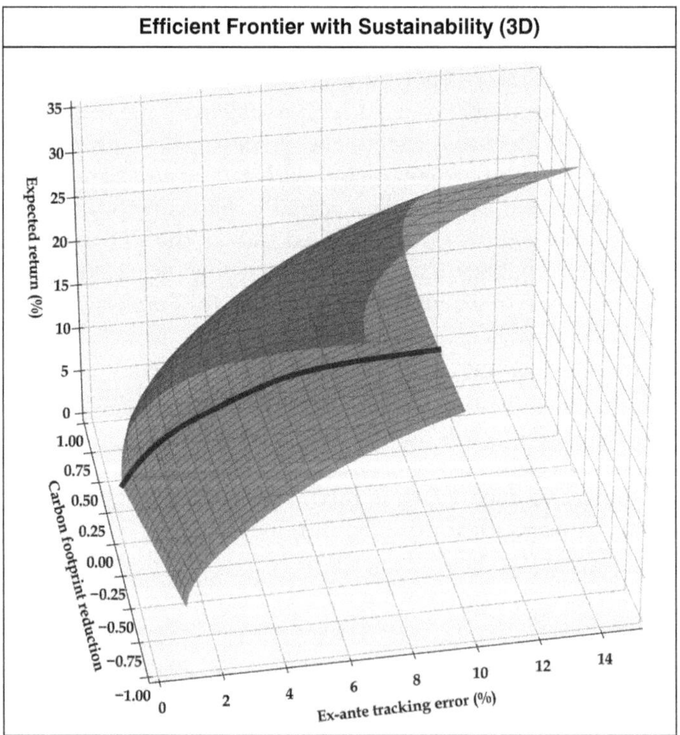

FIGURE 16.1 Visualizing the risk/reward tradeoff in traditional investing (top) and when sustainability is included (bottom).
Source: Copilot-generated images.

ADJUSTING AN EXISTING PORTFOLIO

The combination of sustainability preferences and willingness to accept trade-offs between sustainability and financial performance are challenging to navigate when transitioning an existing portfolio to a coherent sustainable investing portfolio. Such a transition can be made gradually and methodically through a combination of three potential changes:

- Upgrade existing investments with a more sustainable version, e.g., replace an S&P 500 ETF (NYSE: SPY) with a different S&P 500 ETF that incorporates exclusions aligned with your values (e.g., NYSE: EFIV). In this way you maintain your original exposure to the S&P 500 while improving the sustainability characteristics of your portfolio.
- Sell any "bad" things, e.g., if any of your existing investments are *misaligned* with your preferences, more than just *unaligned*, those investments are good candidates to be sold. For example, if you care strongly about biodiversity and one of your investments has been linked to deforestation, that might count as a *misalignment*.
- Add some "good" things, e.g., if you care deeply about a sustainability issue but lack exposure to investments working on that issue, look for ways to add that exposure through new investments. An investor with strong beliefs in access to financing might look for a stock associated with microfinance in emerging markets.

If these are the potential changes you could make, how should you get started? Here we suggest a step-by-step approach, emphasizing practical tactics to integrate ESG into a preexisting portfolio while keeping an eye on taxes, expenses, and tracking error.

Assess the Starting Portfolio and Investment Options

Begin by evaluating your current portfolio's ESG profile. If you hold individual stocks, assess alignment of the business and current practices with your sustainability preferences. For larger positions, read the company's most recent sustainability report. Do the same with mutual funds, unit trusts, and ETFs. Read the prospectus to learn how the strategy incorporates sustainability into the portfolio (more on that in Chapter 17) and check for allocations to sectors or stocks that are/are not aligned with your preferences. Some investment advisors can create a portfolio sustainability report summarizing your current state, e.g., "5% of your portfolio is in fossil fuel industries; your overall ESG rating is below average." This forms the baseline.

At the same time, identify options available to you that are better aligned with your preferences. Which markets and instruments are available through your broker(s)? If your provider offers a screening tool, use it to screen for stocks and funds aligned with your sustainability objectives. If your existing account relationships don't align well with what you are trying to achieve, can you switch your account to a different bank or broker with better alignment?

Set Environmental, Social, and Governance Goals and Priorities

Clarify what "success" looks like for the new portfolio. Is it complete elimination of certain industries? Achieving a certain average ESG score? Aligning a percentage of assets with a specific theme? Adding an allocation to impact-oriented investments? It may not be possible or wise to change everything at once, so prioritize according to what is most important to you. Where relevant, we suggest focusing first on transitioning out of the poorest-aligned investments, i.e., those holdings most misaligned with your values. By taking these steps first, your initial actions yield a meaningful improvement in the portfolio's sustainability profile.

Develop a Phased Transition Plan

Depending on your local tax environment, overhauling your entire portfolio all at once could trigger taxes and incur outsized transaction costs. Instead, implement changes in phases.

New Flows Make sure all *new investments* (fresh contributions, dividends, interest, etc.) are aligned with your sustainability preferences. For example, if you regularly invest US$500/month, channel this into new ESG-aligned funds instead of your old funds. Do the same thing with dividends and interest income. Following this approach, the portfolio's ESG allocation grows over time on a tax-efficient basis.

Optimize for Impact vs. Tracking Error Decide how much deviation from your original portfolio or benchmark you can tolerate. Some investors may want to stay tightly aligned with an index or target allocation, whereas others may prioritize reaching ESG alignment more quickly. A practical approach can be to first replace holdings where an ESG equivalent is available with similar risk/return (e.g., swap a conventional index fund for an ESG version of the same index fund), then later consider other sales and/or additions that might improve alignment at the cost of a bit more volatility.

Account for Taxes (as Appropriate)   If you are subject to high capital gain taxes, there are a few extra steps to consider when developing your plan:

- **Utilize tax-advantaged accounts first.** Viewing your taxable and non-taxable accounts together allow you to maintain overall asset allocation targets by adjusting sustainability exposures separately in the different accounts. For example, US investors might completely rebalance a tax-deferred individual retirement account (IRA) account for sustainability alignment this year with no/low tax impact. Even if you wait to adjust your taxable accounts, rebalancing the tax-deferred account quickly gets you closer to alignment while minimizing taxes.
- **Tax-loss harvesting.** The order and timing of stock sales matters when capital gains tax is involved. Review your taxable accounts for misaligned single-stock positions, targeting the highest cost-basis holdings for initial sales and using any losses to offset gains. For instance, suppose you own two energy stocks, one currently at a loss and the other at a gain. You can sell the position currently at a loss, exiting a misaligned position while getting a tax deduction.

Execute the Rebalancing

With the plan in place, start making changes while maintaining good records of your transactions, especially for tax lots sold. It may take several quarters or years to fully implement, and that's fine. A step-by-step execution plan might look like:

- **This quarter.** Sell three misaligned stocks (chosen for minimal gains) and use proceeds to buy an ESG equity ETF; swap a corporate bond fund for a green bond fund in the retirement account. Submit a redemption request to your misaligned private equity fund at the next opportunity.
- **Next quarter.** Redirect all monthly contributions to purchase more of the ESG ETF and green bond fund.
- **Mid-year.** Evaluate market conditions for opportunities to sell another chunk of profitable holdings. Redeem from the private equity fund and reinvest proceeds into something more ESG-aligned.
- **End of year.** Review the portfolio's new ESG profile vs. the goal, adjust the plan for next year accordingly.

Throughout, remain mindful of transaction costs. Remember to account for alternative investments which may have high exit fees or liquidity restrictions.

Monitor Exposures, Performance, and Refine

After implementing changes, track the financial and sustainability performance of the new portfolio; short-term underperformance or overperformance could just be noise. Track sector and factor exposures to avoid becoming *unintentionally* under/overweight in a certain industry. Often, ESG funds themselves are well-diversified, but double-check asset allocation after each round of changes. Most importantly, monitor if the portfolio now meets the intended ESG criteria. If these metrics are appropriate for your goals, use reports or tools to see metrics like carbon intensity, ESG ratings average, etc., and compare to your starting point. Celebrate the improvement, e.g., "We've reduced the portfolio's carbon footprint by 60%, and eliminated all exposure to tobacco and firearms."

If certain goals haven't been fully met, plan the next iteration of rebalancing to address them. As part of the long-term plan, be sure to stay up-to-date as new sustainable investment products come to market. For example, while a year ago your broker may not have offered a good ESG emerging markets bond fund, perhaps one is available today.

SUMMARY

Transitioning to a sustainable portfolio is much like any portfolio rebalancing exercise. It requires planning, prioritization, and ongoing management, but with the added dimension of achieving values alignment. Investors should recognize that their individual preferences may (or perhaps should) be different from their friends and family members. This is perfectly normal.

By proceeding methodically and using the tactics above, investors can rebalance in favor of ESG while still respecting practical constraints like taxes and maintaining sound diversification.

CHAPTER 17

Portfolio Construction and Risk Management

The previous chapter introduced preferences, trade-offs, and a process that individual investors can use to rebalance an existing portfolio toward a desired level of sustainability. In Chapter 17, we conclude with a look at what this process might look like for more sophisticated investors. Typically, sophisticated investors prepare and manage their portfolio by applying these concepts:

- **Objectives and constraints.** What's the end goal and what are the constraints on how the goal is reached.
- **Investment policy statement (IPS).** Clarifies and codifies the objectives, constraints, and other important issues for the investor, e.g., reporting requirements and tax considerations. Useful to share with lawyers, advisors, and other stakeholders and service providers.
- **Investment strategy.** How will investment decisions be made? This is a detailed document spelling out the philosophy (e.g., active vs. passive) and criteria (e.g., minimum analyst ratings) to be used to select and exit investments.
- **Strategic asset allocation (SAA).** Defines the target portfolio (assets and weights), taking into account the objectives and constraints prepared earlier, e.g., a 7.5% allocation to developed markets high yield debt.
- **Tactical asset allocation (TAA).** Taking into account market fluctuations and changes in valuation, TAA involves short-term adjustments to target allocations in an attempt to capture incremental performance.

But what happens when sustainability is added to this process? Objectives and constraints need to be adjusted, as will the IPS. The investment strategy will change to reflect the incremental use of sustainability information, as will the target portfolio. The opening section on "Modern Portfolio Theory and Environmental, Social, and Governance Issues" describes how modern portfolio theory (MPT)—a cornerstone of investment management since the 1950s—responds to this new information. With portfolio construction in mind, "Asset Selection with Sustainability" describes common approaches to asset selection, the final step in the process, with sustainability information.

MODERN PORTFOLIO THEORY AND ENVIRONMENTAL, SOCIAL, AND GOVERNANCE ISSUES

A fundamental concept in MPT is the efficient frontier, introduced by Harry Markowitz in 1952.[1] This frontier represents a set of optimal portfolios that provide the highest expected returns for a given level of risk or the lowest risk for a specified return. These portfolios are considered efficient because no additional returns can be obtained without taking on more risk, nor can more risk be assumed without the prospect of greater returns.

When environmental, social, and governance (ESG) issues are taken into account, they introduce new considerations into portfolio optimization. ESG factors, associated with nonfinancial elements such as environmental impact, social practices, and governance standards, are increasingly recognized as important to long-term financial performance. By integrating ESG criteria into their investment strategies, investors adapt the traditional efficient frontier to account for the potential risks and rewards associated with sustainable investing. A theory developed in 2020 combines these two concepts into what the authors call the ESG-efficient frontier,[2] outlining the trade-offs between costs and benefits when focusing on ESG factors. Exploring the ESG-efficient frontier starts with an assumption that there are three types of investors:

- **ESG-unaware investors.** Do not consider ESG scores and focus only on maximizing returns relative to risk.
- **ESG-aware investors.** Utilize ESG scores to adjust their assessments of a company's risk and potential returns while striving to balance both factors.
- **ESG-motivated investors.** Actively seek high ESG scores and may be willing to accept lower financial returns in favor of aligning their investments with their values.

The ESG-efficient frontier illustrates the best investment options for investors who prioritize both returns and ESG values. Expanding on the simple concept introduced in Chapter 16, the ESG-efficient frontier pinpoints the highest possible Sharpe ratio (SR)—a measure of return adjusted

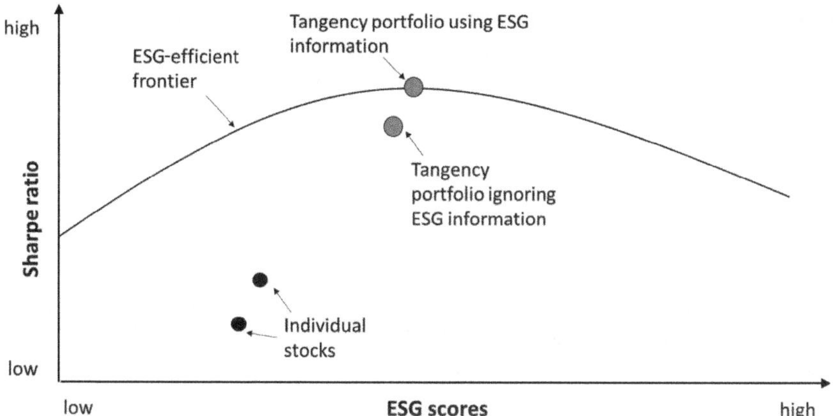

FIGURE 17.1 Environmental, social, and governance (ESG)-efficient frontier. The ESG–SR frontier, i.e., the maximum Sharpe ratio (on the y-axis) that can be achieved for all portfolios with a given ESG score (on the x-axis).[3]

for risk—across varying levels of ESG performance. Typically, incorporating ESG information results in a higher SR, improving risk-adjusted returns compared to portfolios that disregard ESG factors. However, an excessive focus on high ESG scores may lead to a marginal decrease in SR, reflecting the trade-off associated with prioritizing ESG issues.

The ESG-efficient frontier resembles a curve, peaking where the optimal balance between SR and ESG scores is attained (Figure 17.1). A portfolio developed without consideration of ESG factors may fall on the MPT-efficient frontier but will be inefficient—below the curve—from an ESG-efficient frontier perspective because ESG factors are not considered.

Note that adding constraints, such as excluding companies with lower ESG scores, will restrict available investment options, making it more difficult to achieve the highest SR for a given ESG level. The ESG-efficient frontier suggests that investors must be ESG aware and improve ESG performance in addition to risk-adjusted returns (SR) in the portfolio construction process.

ASSET SELECTION WITH SUSTAINABILITY

How should investors incorporate ESG into their portfolios, especially when following the "endowment model" (popularized by the late David Swensen at Yale University) with its sizeable allocations to alternative investments?[4] This section discusses how investors can approach the selection of traditional and alternative assets—everything from stocks and bonds, to private equity and venture capital, hedge funds and real assets— while incorporating sustainability information into the process.

Public Markets

Public markets, primarily equities (stocks) and fixed-income bonds, are the most common instruments for sustainable investing. In public markets, sustainable strategies can be executed through individual security selection (picking stocks/bonds) or collective investment vehicles like ESG-focused mutual funds and exchange-traded funds (ETFs). Below, we outline practical steps for implementing ESG in these asset classes.

Equities and Corporate Bonds When investing in individual stocks or corporate bonds, investors can incorporate ESG in several ways:

- **ESG data and analysis.** Notwithstanding their limitations, investors can usually access and review ESG ratings for individual companies (at least at a high level). Such information helps flag which holdings align with sustainability preferences or pose potential ESG-related risks. Many online brokerages and research platforms now embed these ESG ratings for easy reference. *A simple use case is to sell a low-ESG-rated stock and replace it with a higher-rated stock in the same industry, maintaining sector exposure while improving the portfolio's ESG profile.*
- **Screening and filters.** Apply inclusion/exclusion filters to the universe of securities. Online stock screeners increasingly allow filtering by ESG criteria, e.g., filtering out all companies with significant revenue from coal mining or filtering in only those with above-average emissions intensity. Data providers, like ISS ESG, offer screening services that let investors filter portfolios against dozens of customizable ESG criteria (controversial weapons, human rights violations, etc.). Similarly, specialized indices, like the FTSE4Good Index Series, identify companies with strong ESG practices; investors can use such indices as benchmarks or starting lists for stock selection. If managing a bond portfolio, investors might refer to indices of green bonds or use external labels (like *Climate Bonds Certified*) to find bonds funding sustainable projects.
- **ESG integration.** For equities, this could mean adjusting discount rates, growth assumptions, or cash-flow forecasts based on ESG performance. For example, a company with a poor environmental record

might be modeled with higher future costs due to potential carbon taxes or cleanup liabilities, reducing its fair value estimate. Bond investors can consider how ESG issues affect creditworthiness. Credit rating agencies and new ESG bond ratings can guide this; Moody's and S&P now incorporate ESG in credit ratings, and providers like MSCI offer separate ESG ratings for corporate bonds.

- **Active ownership.** For stock investors, active ownership means exercising the right to vote, especially voting in favor of ESG-focused shareholder resolutions, or joining investor coalitions. Some investors may even directly engage in dialogue with companies by writing to the chief executive officer (CEO) or participating in earnings calls to ask about ESG issues.
- **Green bonds and sustainability-linked bonds.** On the fixed-income side, public markets have growing segments of labeled sustainable debt. Investors implementing an ESG strategy in bonds can allocate a portion of their fixed-income portfolio to these labeled bonds to directly support sustainability initiatives. Market frameworks like the International Capital Market Association (ICMA) Green Bond Principles guide what qualifies as a green bond, emphasizing transparency in use of proceeds and reporting. Due diligence is needed to avoid greenwashing, but third-party certifications and ratings (e.g., from CICERO or Moody's Green Bond Assessments) can help validate a bond's credentials.

Incorporating ESG in public equity and bond investments relies on data and analysis. Investors should leverage the rich ESG datasets now available, choose securities that meet their sustainability criteria, and remain active stewards of those investments.

Environmental, Social, and Governance Mutual Funds, Exchange-traded Funds, and Indexes Investing through funds and ETFs is one of the most practical ways to build an ESG-aligned portfolio. Fund managers have created a wide variety of sustainable investing products that span asset classes, regions, and themes. Here's how to implement sustainable strategies using funds and indexes:

- **ESG-focused mutual funds/ETFs.** Many asset managers offer dedicated sustainable mutual funds and ETFs. Typically, these products apply some combination of the ESG strategies discussed (screening, integration, thematic focus) within a single vehicle. For example, there are broad-based ESG index funds that mimic standard benchmarks (like S&P 500 or MSCI All-Country World Index [ACWI]) but exclude certain industries and tilt toward ESG leaders. Other funds are thematic, such as clean energy ETFs, gender equality funds, or green bond funds. When choosing ESG funds, investors should examine the fund's prospectus and ESG methodology to understand detailed screens and methodologies used to embed sustainability in the fund. What metrics or ratings does it use? Morningstar's Sustainability Rating (the "globe" rating system) rates funds from 1 (lowest) to 5 (highest) globes based on the aggregate ESG risk of their holdings. Likewise, MSCI's ESG Fund Ratings grade funds AAA to CCC by evaluating the weighted average ESG score of the fund's holdings.

- **Fund screeners and databases.** Platforms like Morningstar, Bloomberg, and specialized organizations provide fund screener tools to find sustainable investments. The US SIF (Sustainable Investment Forum) publishes a database of sustainable funds, detailing each fund's ESG approach. Using these resources, an investor or advisor can compare funds' ESG strategies, performance, fees, and holdings side by side. Many fund screeners also incorporate ESG ratings. For example, an advisor might screen for all large-cap equity funds with at least 4-globe (above-average) sustainability ratings and no fossil fuel exposure, then evaluate that shortlist for performance and fees to pick suitable options for a client.

- **Passive investing.** There are now ESG versions of most major indices, e.g., the MSCI ACWI ESG Leaders Index selects top ESG companies globally, and FTSE4Good indices include companies meeting certain ESG criteria. If an investor prefers passive investing, they can simply choose ETFs that track specialized ESG indices or ESG versions of popular indices. One can also find bond indices focused on sustainability, like the Bloomberg MSCI Green Bond Index. By selecting the right indices, investors ensure at the design stage that their portfolio's constituents are more sustainable. Note that ESG indices vary in strictness; choose one that aligns with your preferences, and your financial objectives and constraints.

- **Multi-asset ESG portfolios and robo-advisors.** Opt for multi-asset solutions that are ESG-oriented. Some balanced mutual funds follow a sustainable mandate across stocks and bonds. Additionally, many robo-advisors provide socially conscious options, allowing investors to simply choose a "sustainable" or "climate" portfolio and have the

platform manage it automatically. Implementing through a robo-advisor is extremely practical for retail investors who want an ESG portfolio without selecting each fund themselves.
- **Monitoring fund holdings and engagement.** Even after selecting ESG funds, it's wise to monitor what they hold and how they exercise stewardship. Some so-called ESG funds have been critiqued for holding companies one might not expect, e.g., an "ESG" fund holding an oil company because it's best-in-class for that sector. Investors should read quarterly holdings reports to ensure no unwanted surprises. At the same time, read fund reports or stewardship disclosures to see if the manager is actively voting and engaging in line with your values.

*   *   *

A lingering question for investors interested in catalyzing changes in corporate behavior concerns the impact of ESG investing in public equities. Data suggests that sustainable equity mutual funds are more likely to be "greening their portfolios" than "greening the planet." A recent paper analyzed how funds changed their portfolios after the fund manager became a signatory to CDP (Carbon Disclosure Project) and found that the most common changes were reweighting of the portfolio rather than changing the names in the portfolio.[5] Unless the investor is able to review the complete portfolio for holdings in more impact-oriented companies, private market impact funds may be a better vehicle for catalyzing impact.

Overall, implementing sustainable investing through funds and indexes is about choosing vehicles that match your ESG objectives. It simplifies the process, but you must perform due diligence on the fund's strategy.

Private Markets

Sustainable investments in private markets (e.g., private equity, venture capital, private credit, real estate, and real assets) involves incorporating ESG into due diligence, selection of external managers/funds, and, sometimes, even direct project investments. While more upfront work may be required, such investments also offer opportunities for more direct impact since capital in private deals often directly funds new projects or companies. Below are key considerations for private markets.

Environmental, Social, and Governance Issues in Private Equity and Venture Capital

Private equity and venture capital invest in companies that are not publicly traded. In recent years, a robust ecosystem of impact-focused private equity/venture capital funds has emerged. To implement sustainable investing in this space:

- **ESG due diligence.** Even for mainstream private equity, ESG is increasingly woven into how deals are evaluated. When implementing an ESG policy in private markets, investors or fund managers perform ESG due diligence on target companies, assessing factors, like a target company's environmental compliance, labor practices, supply chain risks, or governance structure, as part of the investment decision. Confirm that the private equity firm identifies and tracks material ESG risks for each prospective investment and creates an ESG risk/opportunity memo that accompanies the investment committee decision. ESG integration in private equity means avoiding hidden ESG liabilities and identifying value creation opportunities—especially important in the many private equity transition funds launched recently.
- **Thematic investments.** Private markets enable investors to target very specific themes or regions, e.g., fintech start-ups that provide services to the unbanked or renewable energy projects in sub-Saharan Africa. Qualified investors can set aside an allocation for mission-driven thematic investments to serve as an extension of their charitable goals. Portfolios including thematic private assets should be monitored to ensure proper diversification and risk management.
- **Impact fund managers.** Impact-oriented investors can allocate to impact private equity/venture capital funds that align with their mission. Resources like ImpactBase from the Global Impact Investing Network (GIIN) have historically listed hundreds of private funds by theme. When performing due diligence, look at the fund's impact thesis and whether they track key impact metrics and report transparently. It's important to evaluate the fund manager's track record in both financial performance and impact performance.
- **Impact measurement.** Sustainable private funds, including many that do not follow a specific impact investing strategy, often report on impact metrics annually. As an investor, you should utilize these reports to monitor outcomes. Aligning impact metrics with a theory of change and broader frameworks, like the Impact Principles, adds credibility. As an investor implementing an impact strategy, one should ensure that impact is not only achieved but also transparently measured and communicated.

- **Private debt and microfinance.** In private markets, debt strategies can also have ESG goals. For instance, microfinance funds provide small loans to entrepreneurs in developing countries. Blended finance structures offer similar opportunities. For example, a pension fund might invest alongside public/philanthropic funds in a vehicle that provides climate adaptation loans to small businesses in climate-vulnerable regions.

*   *   *

In summary, private equity and venture capital offer avenues for high-impact investment but come with a unique set of considerations (liquidity, risk, high minimum investments, etc.). For those who can participate, carefully embedding ESG in every stage of the investment process is key to successful implementation. With increasing attention from institutions, investors should see improvements in impact measurement each year.

Real Assets and Real Estate

Real assets—infrastructure projects, real estate, and natural resources—are another important area for sustainable investing implementation. Here's how ESG can be integrated:

- **Real estate.** Real estate funds and real estate investment trusts (REITs) can be evaluated and managed for sustainability. Implementation involves focusing on properties that meet green building standards (e.g., Leadership in Energy and Environmental Design [LEED], Building Research Establishment Environmental Assessment Method [BREEAM], etc.), have high energy efficiency, and contribute positively to communities. An investor might choose a real estate fund that consistently scores well on GRESB (Global Real Estate Sustainability Benchmark), indicating the manager proactively addresses factors like building energy use, tenant well-being, and climate resilience. For direct real estate holdings, investors can retrofit buildings for efficiency, install renewable energy sources, and improve water conservation—environmental benefits which often reduce operating costs and increase property values.
- **Sustainable infrastructure.** Infrastructure investments (e.g., power plants, transportation systems, telecom networks) have long-term impacts and are well-suited for sustainable investing. This could involve investing in renewable energy projects, energy storage, smart grids, clean transportation, water treatment facilities, etc. Implementation requires careful due diligence on the project's feasibility, impact, and third-party technical and environmental assessments. Some investors

also consider "transition infrastructure," a variant on transition finance (see Chapter 7).

- **Natural capital.** Sustainable forestry, agriculture, land conservation, or other natural capital projects can generate returns while delivering environmental benefits. Such investments often apply standards like the Rainforest Alliance certification to ensure practices are truly sustainable. An example would be an investment in a sustainable timberland fund that harvests wood at a renewable rate and restores forest ecosystems, providing income alongside carbon sink benefits.

* * *

Implementing sustainable strategies in private markets generally requires more specialized knowledge and often partnerships with experienced fund managers or intermediaries. Unlike public markets where disclosure is more standardized, in private deals investors need to actively negotiate and set ESG expectations. Many institutional investors now include ESG clauses in limited partner agreements when committing to private funds, ensuring the general partner (GP) will incorporate ESG in managing the investments. The payoff is that private investments can align very tightly with an investor's sustainability mission—financing the *solutions* to ESG challenges, not just trading stocks of existing companies. However, investors should be cognizant of the higher risks, lower liquidity, and the necessity of rigorous impact measurement to ensure that promises translate into real outcomes.

SUMMARY

Professional investors tend to approach their investment process in a deliberate, systematic way. Beginning with a clear articulation of objectives and constraints, they will develop a target model portfolio (asset *allocation*) before selecting individual investments (asset *selection*). The ESG-efficient frontier shows that, compared to the classic Markowitz optimization and MPT which only considers return and risk, investors should incorporate ESG information into their portfolio construction process—which means that ESG information is needed for each of the assets that could be included in the portfolio.

The ease with which investors gather and analyze ESG information varies considerably across asset classes. In this chapter we explored these differences:

- In *public markets*, there is a lot of information available, thanks in part to ESG disclosure regulations of the sort described in Chapter 8. Relevant ESG data are available in corporate sustainability reports and aggregated online by information providers like Bloomberg or even yahoo!Finance. Armed with this information, investors can identify stocks and bonds that are more or less aligned with the investors' sustainability preferences and monitor changes in alignment over time. Investors without the resources to select individual assets on their own can choose from a long list of mutual funds, unit trusts, and ETFs with ESG characteristics. Especially interesting are the ETFs which combine the financial performance of a traditional index investment (e.g., NYSE: SPY) with additional ESG characteristics (e.g., NYSE: EFIV). The ESG versions of these passive ETFs can be substituted for the non-ESG versions to improve sustainability characteristics of a portfolio without significant changes to the financial performance objectives of the model portfolio.

- Sustainability information is harder to come by in *private markets*, including real estate and real assets, making asset selection more challenging for investors wishing to align their portfolios with their ESG preferences. Fund managers should clearly state how ESG considerations are integrated into the due diligence process. Thematic funds—and for certain investors, impact funds—can be used to allocate capital toward specific ESG issues and/or regions during portfolio construction, though attention should be paid to implications for diversification and liquidity. Where measurable impact is desirable, investors should check for evidence of a robust and transparent impact measurement and management process. Sustainability perspectives can also be applied to investments in private debt, real estate, infrastructure, and natural capital. Each offers a distinct opportunity for investors to align their capital with their ESG preferences, from climate change mitigation (retrofitting buildings) to access to water (urban water treatment facilities) or sustainable forest management solutions.

Armed with more information about the sustainability characteristics of different assets, investors have many opportunities to better align their portfolios with sustainability preferences. As demonstrated above, changes in portfolio construction or asset selection do not necessarily imply meaningful deterioration of financial performance. A deliberate, patient approach can lead to improved sustainability alignment over time, regardless of how significant the transition may be.

Conclusion: The Difference We Make

This book is the culmination of many hours of on-the-ground research, whether standing in front of the classroom or sitting next to clients. More than any book we know of, what you hold in your hands is the best summary-level, introductory text on sustainable finance—a thorough recap of the challenges we face, a review of the major international efforts to date, important theories and practice for companies and investors, common traps associated with greenwashing, key regulations in multiple markets, and practical advice for investors on how to incorporate sustainability into their portfolios. Our hope is that, after reading this book, you are better prepared to contribute to this important task: transitioning the existing model of financial markets to something more sustainable.

That we are still talking about the need to change is concerning, especially since the problems we face have been well known in scientific communities for decades, if not longer. The earliest recorded indication that people knew (or suspected) that burning fossil fuels would lead to a rise in temperature through the greenhouse effect dates back to the 19th century; internal documents reveal that scientists at the major oil companies knew about this as early as the 1950s. Social issues have been a recurring issue, too. Wars and slavery have been a fixture of history for thousands of years. More recently, changes in societal norms have shone a spotlight on social issues such as gender and racial equality, and access to education and health care.

If we have known about these problems, why haven't we fixed them? There are lots of good efforts under way, especially those under the umbrella of the United Nations which we reviewed in Chapter 4. These efforts are driven by well-intentioned people running well-designed programs that lead to lots of (small-ish) changes, but collectively have fallen short of the degree of transformation required. The problem is that we need the whole system to change, not just a handful of companies or countries. We know that any change is hard, personal or corporate, so *system change* must be that much harder!

To see why system change is so difficult, let's think about it from the perspective of the major stakeholders, starting with companies. As we discussed in Chapter 5, most companies are managed in a way that prioritizes shareholder interests more than other stakeholders. Some of this may be due to the influence of Friedman's shareholder value maximization theory, or because the Board of Directors has fiduciary responsibility to the owners of the firm. Whatever the reason, the implication is that companies will typically prioritize financial performance over sustainability performance. Of course, this is not always the case; some firms have chosen to prioritize sustainability even at the potential expense of profits. But the vast majority of companies in the world still make decisions based on the financials.

One way to address this problem could be to somehow encourage more companies to change their corporate charters. Professor Rebecca Henderson of Harvard University summarized the options well in her book *Reimagining Capitalism*[1]: B corporations, employee ownership, and cooperatives are just some of the structures that have allowed thousands of companies around the world to at least put sustainability on equal footing with financial performance. Navigating this trade-off between financials and sustainability would be even easier if there were more net present value (NPV)-positive investments for sustainability issues. For example, installation of solar panels is often cited as such an investment—so why isn't it even more prevalent? This leads us to the second set of stakeholders, the banks.

Many undergraduate discussions of the responsibility for climate change confront bank financing with some confusion; interestingly, there is usually less confusion among adult learners—particularly when there are bankers in the room! The conversation starts with something like "why don't banks just provide more financing to companies that are trying to reduce their emissions?" Of course, the vast majority of banks are for-profit, just like the companies they are financing, so they need to receive sufficient interest to compensate for the risk that a borrower is unable to make its payments. As a result, banks evaluate each potential borrower much in the same way as any other firm would evaluate an investment decision: with profit and risk in mind.

Consider two hypothetical firms looking for a loan to finance the installation of solar panels, one in a developed market like Austria, the other in an emerging market like Vietnam. One of the main factors behind any bank's decision to extend a loan, and the price of that loan, is the credit risk of the borrower. Let us further assume that the two firms are equally strong financially as measured by common financial ratios. If these two firms approach the same bank for the same loan, in all likelihood the bank will still charge the company in Vietnam a higher interest rate than the Austrian firm due to higher perceived *country* risk. This, in fact, is a common complaint in emerging markets—high financing cost—and one of the drivers of the Bridgetown Initiative mentioned in Chapter 7. If charging higher rates in emerging economies is common practice, should anyone be surprised if banks *don't* make a big push to lend to sustainability projects in emerging countries? And what about investments that are less certain to lead to material improvements in sustainability? Even a financially strong company in a developed market may not be able to arrange preferential financing for this type of project.

At the same time, banks *are* under a lot of pressure to "green their loan books" by increasing their lending to "green" companies and/or projects, and reducing their financing of "brown" industries like coal. That pressure might explain some of the critiques of sustainability-linked bonds (SLBs) and sustainability-linked loans (SLLs) we reviewed in Chapter 9. Should we expect banks to push back vigorously on key performance indicators (KPIs) and sustainability performance targets (SPTs) that are less-than-ambitious? Or should we expect banks to make commercial decisions that satisfy local regulations without an obligation to push companies to raise their climate ambition? Banks—like nearly every other type of company—default to a commercial mindset. If the bank can issue an SLL with remotely defensible KPIs and SPTs, it should probably do so, since the company and the bank both look good for entering into a "green" transaction.

If we can't count on companies to voluntarily improve their sustainability, and if banks won't act as the arbiter of ambition, what about other investors? With the wide range of sustainable investing strategies, shouldn't investors be able to drive corporate behavior? An answer appears in the "Summary" to Chapter 12: most investors feel constrained by fiduciary responsibility, to the point where they are largely unwilling to trade off financial for environmental and/or social (ES) performance. This doesn't mean that *all* investors think this way; some investment managers have a demonstrable focus on sustainable investing. Impact investing, even though it's a relatively small strategy, is laser-focused on creating positive, measurable changes in the world. But the survey results speak volumes; even the sustainability-minded investors have a hard time trading off financial performance for better ES performance.

At this point in a class discussion, the mood is relatively somber. What has the potential to change the attitudes of companies, banks, and investors? For one thing, risk. These stakeholders all care about risk, and if climate change leads to increased physical losses due to severe weather, or social unrest in local communities that keeps employees out of the factory, then perhaps these stakeholders will make different decisions *because the problems become more tangible.*[2] We are starting to see some of these kinds of effects in the insurance markets, where premiums in some areas for some risks are increasing to the point of being unaffordable—or disappearing altogether. Another important effect is risk of environmental, social, and governance (ESG)-related lawsuits filed against companies and countries, leading us to yet another stakeholder: lawyers.

Only once in tens of classroom discussions did someone mention "lawyers" as taking responsibility for saving the planet. However, they do have an important role to play. Some are working in the public interest at firms like ClientEarth, while others stand ready to advise clients on sustainability issues and others still wish to hold firms and nations accountable for their (in)action. However, if companies, banks, and investors aren't getting the job done by themselves, do lawyers have the reach to create system change on their own? Some lawyers will undoubtedly have a powerful impact, but for legal action to change the entire system will require a level of success in the courtroom that unequivocally puts a price on the legal risk of inaction. This will necessarily be difficult when considering the global nature of the problem.

Which leads us to the government. Class discussions always, *always*, come back to the idea that it is the government's responsibility to solve the sustainability problem. Even if we take that statement of responsibility to be true, why should we expect governments to *solve* the problem? For one, every government around the world functions in its own unique way. To say that "government" will solve the problem implies that the governments of Chile, Nigeria, Saudi Arabia, and Indonesia—to say nothing of China, the United States, the European Union, and India—act in a reasonably similar manner. This is unlikely at best. It also implies that each government will define the problem the same way, which we know will not be the case given the wide range of initial conditions affecting different countries around the world. On top of that, as someone once said about American politicians (but is probably true more broadly than that), the first job of a politician is to get reelected. Unless someone can make the case that investments in sustainability are good investments both financially and for people's lives, why should we expect politicians to solve the problem of their own accord? Should we expect punitive taxes on pollution and strict enforcement just because there's a negative externality to be addressed? That sounds like a stretch.

However, the good news is that there is some good news! Some companies are actively reducing their emissions and more generally improving their sustainability. Some banks are channeling more funds to sustainability-related activities, as are investors across all manner of asset classes. Some lawyers, like those who argued the case to the International Court of Justice mentioned in Chapter 5, fight in the courts so that other stakeholders will feel compelled to improve their sustainability lest they face legal action and financial penalties. And yes, some governments are taking action as well. Regulations for sustainability measurement and disclosure are a good start, as are taxonomies and a host of other actions described in Chapters 8–10 and 15. These are good first steps, but since, as of this writing, the 2030 emissions gap is flat or perhaps even widening (Figure C.1), it's probably fair to say that governments, too, need to try harder.

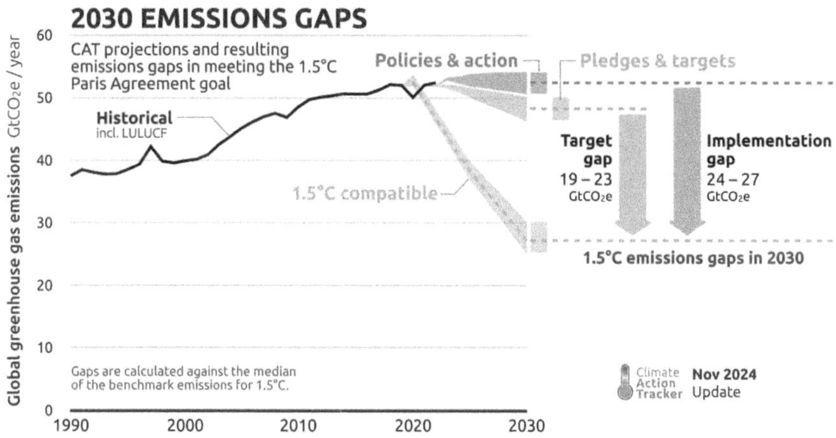

FIGURE C.1   2030 emissions gap.
Source: https://climateactiontracker.org/publications/mid-year-check-on-2035-climate-plans/, retrieved August 24, 2025.

Which brings us back to you, dear reader. What can YOU do? What can ANY of us do? First, we need to care. Figure out what you care most about, then go deeper to see what's being done and where the gaps are. We need to talk about these issues with our friends and colleagues, classmates and neighbors. As Canadian climate scientist Katherine Hayhoe writes in her book *Saving Us*,[3] the more we talk about climate change (and other issues), the more we realize that most people *do care*—but *they think that other people don't*. Talking about it is the first step toward collective action.

One of the great tools for talking about the impact of climate change is En-ROADS, a simulation available for free at https://en-roads.climateinteractive.org/ (Figure C.2). As they describe it, "[d]eveloped by Climate Interactive, MIT Sloan, and Ventana Systems, En-ROADS is a system dynamics model carefully grounded in the best available science…calibrated against a wide range of existing integrated assessment, climate, and energy models. En-ROADS runs on an ordinary laptop in a fraction of a second, is freely available online, offers an intuitive user-friendly interface, and is available in over a dozen languages."

We strongly encourage you to try En-ROADS for yourself. Adjust some of the slider bars at the bottom and see what kind of impact these changes have on expected temperature rise by the end of the century. They run an online training program a few times a year and its relatively easy to join the ranks of certified En-ROADS Climate Ambassadors, giving you a fact-based platform with which to take action through engagement in your community.

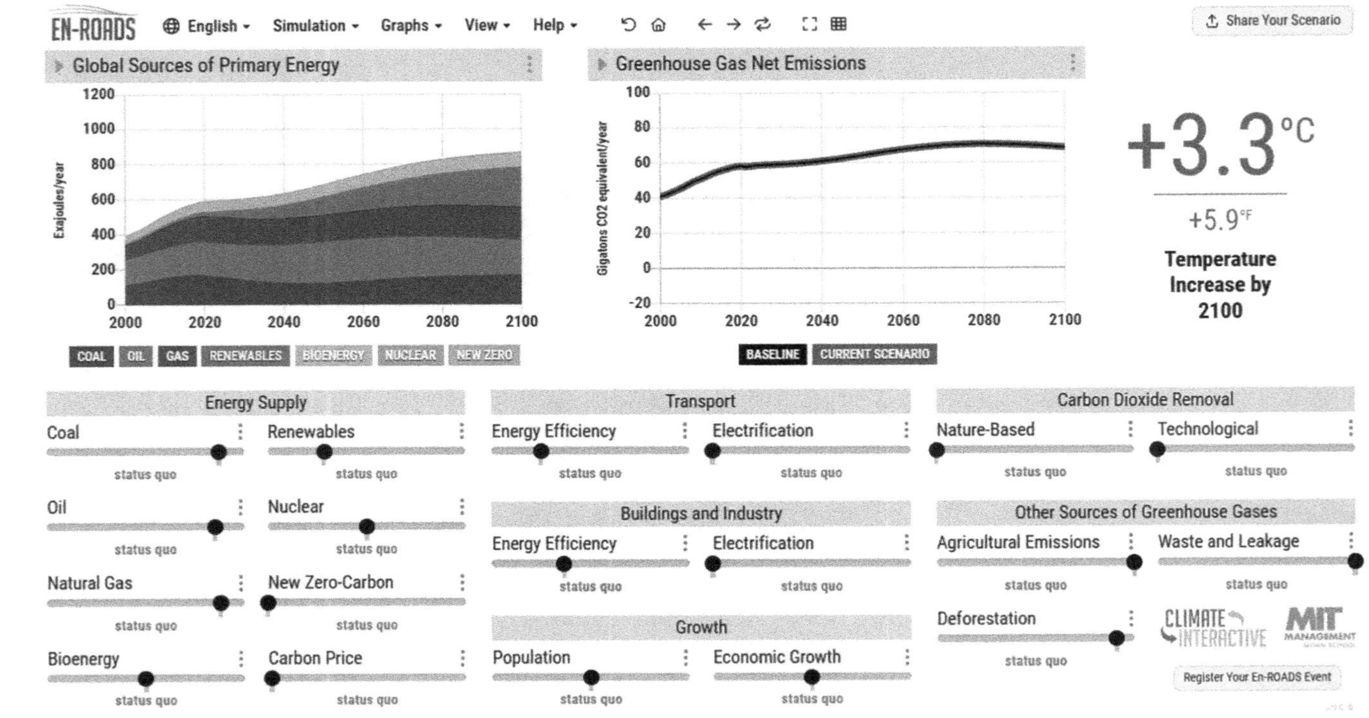

FIGURE C.2 En-ROADS scenario.
Source: https://en-roads.climateinteractive.org/.

Speaking of action, reading Chapters 16 and 17 provided you with many actionable ideas for how to incorporate sustainability into your investment portfolio, personal or professional. Whether you replace traditional index funds with their ESG counterparts, or allocate to the climate fund available in your retirement account, or just start reading the prospectus and sustainability reports for the funds and companies you own—all of these steps are reasonable, available to us right now, and make a (small) difference. If we all do them, the impact on the finance industry would be noticeable, though perhaps not itself enough to create the kind of change that is required across companies, banks, investors, and everyone else.

Ultimately Friedman may be right, not in how he said the social responsibility of the corporation is to maximize its profits, but rather that it should be the role of government to address negative externalities in the system. It seems like a stretch to expect capitalism in any of its current forms to self-reform in time and in magnitude to address the looming climate crisis; strong regulation (and enforcement) must be at the heart of any viable solution. And if you seriously expect government to take this kind of action, then consider whether you can expect your elected representatives to arrive at an enlightened policy position on ESG by themselves, or whether they need a nudge. Like executives, bankers, and investors, most officials probably need a nudge—so use your vote wisely.

If nothing else, by reading this book we hope that you are better informed about what the problems are, what's being done today, and what role finance has to play in creating a more sustainable future. Use this new knowledge to make a difference to the world.

List of Terms and Abbreviations

10-K, 10-Q	Mandatory financial filings for US public companies, annual (10-K) and quarterly (10-Q), as required by the Securities and Exchange Commission
501(c)(4)	Social welfare organizations which are tax-exempt in the United States; the term refers to the section of the Internal Revenue Code that describes such organizations
AANA	Australian Association of National Advertisers
ACRA	Accounting and Corporate Regulatory Authority (Singapore)
active	Investment strategy intended to outperform the benchmark through stock selection, market timing, or other means
ACWI	All-Country World Index
ADB	Asian Development Bank
additionality	A positive outcome that otherwise would not have happened without the impact investment
AGM	annual general meeting
Article 6	In the Paris Agreement, a framework for voluntary cooperation between countries to meet their climate targets
ASEAN	Association of Southeast Asian Nations
ASRS	Australian Sustainability Reporting Standards
AUM	assets under management
B Corporation	Benefit corporation, a for-profit organizational form certified by B Lab to meet rigorous standards, often including a legal commitment by the Board to consider purpose alongside profit
biomass	Organic material that can be used as a fuel source
blended finance	A structuring approach that uses catalytic capital from public or philanthropic sources to increase private sector investment in sustainable development
BOD	Board of Directors

BOP	bottom of the pyramid; base of the pyramid
BREEAM	Building Research Establishment Environmental Assessment Method
BRSR	Business Responsibility and Sustainability Report (India)
carbon allowance	A legal permit to emit one metric ton of CO_2e
carbon credit	A tradeable instrument representing one metric ton of CO_2e avoided, reduced, or removed from the atmosphere
carbon offset	The act of using a carbon credit to compensate for a company's own emissions ("offsetting")
CBAM	Carbon Border Adjustment Mechanism
CBI	Climate Bonds Initiative
CCfD	Carbon Contracts for Difference
CCPA	Central Consumer Protection Authority (India)
CDP	Carbon Disclosure Project
CFA	Chartered Financial Analyst
CFPP	coal-fired power plant
civil law	Legal system that relies on legal codes; recent origins in continental Europe
climate justice	Recognizing that climate change disproportionately impacts low-income communities and communities of color around the world
CO_2e	carbon dioxide equivalent
common law	Legal system that relies on past judicial decisions and precedent; recent origins in England
COP	Conference of the Parties
cost of capital	Minimum rate of return a company must earn to satisfy its investors, both equity and debt; often WACC, or weighted-average cost of capital
CPA	Certified Public Accountant
CSDDD	Corporate Sustainability Due Diligence Directive
CDSB	Climate Disclosure Standards Board
CSR	corporate social responsibility
CSRD	Corporate Sustainability Reporting Directive
DAC	direct air capture

DCF	discounted cash flow
DDT	dichloro-diphenyl-trichloroethane
DEI	diversity, equity, and inclusion
DFI	development finance institution
DMA	day moving average, e.g., 200 DMA
DNSH	do no significant harm
EBA	European Banking Authority
EESG	economic, environment, social, governance; as used by City Developments Limited (Singapore)
efficient frontier	The set of portfolios providing the highest expected return for a given level of risk (or lowest risk for a given return)
EFRAG	European Financial Reporting Advisory Group
EMH	efficient-market hypothesis
ES	environment and social
ESG	environment, social, governance
ESGC	ESG controversy
ESMA	European Securities and Markets Authority
ESRS	European Sustainability Reporting Standards
ETF	exchange-traded fund
ETM	Energy Transition Mechanism
ETS	Emissions Trading System
EV	electric vehicle
externality	Unintended costs or benefits experienced by third parties when a good or service is produced or consumed
fast fashion	Rapid mass production of trendy clothing at a low cost
FDIC	Federal Deposit Insurance Corporation
fiduciary duty	A legal or ethical obligation to act in the best financial interests of another party
FTSE	Financial Times Stock Exchange
FX	foreign exchange
G20	Group of Twenty, comprising 19 countries plus the European Union and African Union; represents roughly 85% of global gross domestic product (GDP)

GAAP	Generally Accepted Accounting Principles
GFANZ	Glasgow Financial Alliance for Net Zero
GHG	greenhouse gas
GICS	Global Industry Classification Standard
GIIN	Global Impact Investing Network
GLP-1	glucagon-like peptide-1
GMB	green minus brown
Great Pacific Garbage Patch	The world's largest accumulation of floating ocean plastic, located in the North Pacific Ocean
greenium	The difference in interest rate between a conventional bond and a green bond, for bonds from the same issuer, at similar size and duration
greenwashing	Where a company falsely tries to appear more environmentally friendly or "greener" than it really is
GRESB	Global Real Estate Sustainability Benchmark
GRI	Global Reporting Initiative
GSIA	Global Sustainable Investing Alliance
ICE	internal combustion engine
ICMA	International Capital Market Association
IFRS	International Financial Reporting Standards
IIRC	International Integrated Reporting Council
ILO	International Labour Organization
IMM	impact measurement and management
IMO	International Maritime Organization
IMP	Impact Management Project
impact-washing	Where a company falsely tries to appear like it creates more positive environmental and/or social impact than is really the case
intangibles	Nonphysical resources that provide an economic benefit
intentionality	In impact investing, an investor deliberately seeking to generate positive, measurable environmental and/or social benefits
IOSCO	International Organization of Securities Commissions
IPCC	Intergovernmental Panel on Climate Change
IPO	initial public offering

IPS	investment policy statement
IRR	internal rate of return
ISS	Institutional Shareholder Services
ISSB	International Sustainability Standards Board
ITMO	International Transferred Mitigation Outcomes
KPI	key performance indicator
Kyoto Protocol	International treaty (1997) committing industrialized countries to reduce greenhouse gas emissions
LBO	leveraged buyout
LEED	Leadership in Energy and Environmental Design
leverage ratio	A measure of the amount of debt a company carries relative to its assets or equity, e.g., debt-to-equity ratio
mark-to-market	Valuation of assets by using the most recent market price for the asset or an equivalent
MAS	Monetary Authority of Singapore
materiality	Information which is significant enough to influence the decision of a reasonable person or investor
MBS	mortgage-backed securities
MiFID	Markets in Financial Instruments Directive
MPF	Mandatory Provident Fund (Hong Kong)
MPT	modern portfolio theory
NBS	nature-based solutions
NDC	nationally determined contribution
net zero	The state where human-generated GHG emissions are balanced by an equal amount of emissions removed from the atmosphere
NFRD	Non-Financial Reporting Directive
NGO	nongovernmental organization
NPV	net present value
OECD	Organisation for Economic Co-operation and Development
Omnibus	A package of proposed changes to European Union (EU) sustainability regulations, put forth in February 2025, that proponents believe would enhance EU competitiveness
OPIM	Operating Principles for Impact Management

options	Types of financial contracts whose value is derived from another asset, e.g., call options give the buyer the right but not the obligation to purchase the asset at a predetermined price
Paris Agreement	International treaty (2015) with the goal to limit global warming to well below 2°C, preferably 1.5°C, above pre-industrialized levels
passive	Investment strategy intended to replicate the performance of a benchmark as closely as possible, usually for a relatively low fee
PCAF	Partnership for Carbon Accounting Financials
PE	private equity
PES	payment for ecosystem services
planetary boundaries	Thresholds for nine terrestrial systems and processes that, if crossed, may increase the risk of large scale and/or irreversible environmental changes
PM	Particulate matter; the most harmful type is less than five microns in size, referred to as PM5
PRI	Principles for Responsible Investment
price-to-book value	A measure of how expensive or cheap a company is, market value per share/book value per share
ratings	A third-party measure of attractiveness, as in bond ratings, analyst ratings, and ESG ratings
REDD+	Reducing emissions from deforestation and forest degradation in developing countries
REIT	real estate investment trust
RFP	request for proposal
RSPO	Roundtable on Sustainable Palm Oil
SAA	strategic asset allocation
SAC	Sustainable Apparel Coalition
SASB	Sustainability Accounting Standards Board
SBTi	Science-based Targets Initiative
SDG	Sustainable Development Goal
SEC	Securities and Exchange Commission (US)
SECR	Streamlined Energy and Carbon Reporting (UK)
SFC	Securities and Futures Commission (UK)

SFDR	Sustainable Finance Disclosure Regulation (EU)
Sharpe ratio	A measure of risk-adjusted return, with higher Sharpe ratio indicating a better return for the amount of risk
SLB	sustainability-linked bond
SLL	sustainability-linked loan
SMA	separately managed account
SME	small- and medium-sized enterprise
SPT	sustainability performance target
SROI	social return on investment
SRS	Sustainability Reporting Standards (UK)
swaps	Financial contracts where two parties agree to exchange cash flows over a specific period, based on a notional principal amount, e.g., currency swaps
TAA	tactical asset allocation
taxonomy	A classification system defining which economic activities are aligned with specific environmental or other sustainability objectives, to be used in determining eligibility for specialized financing
TCFD	Task Force on Climate-related Financial Disclosures
TDR	triple dividend of resilience
TNFD	Task Force on Nature-related Financial Disclosures
TOC	theory of change
tracking error	Deviation between a portfolio's returns and the returns of its benchmark, over time
triple bottom line	A sustainability framework that includes profit, people, and planet
UDHR	Universal Declaration of Human Rights
UN	United Nations
UN PRB	United Nations Principles for Responsible Banking
UN PRI	United Nations Principles for Responsible Investment
UNEP	United Nations Environment Programme
UNEP FI	United Nations Environment Programme—Finance Initiative
UNGC	United Nations Global Compact

use of proceeds	Statement in a financial document that details how the company plans to spend money raised from investors
value Chain	Activities directly or indirectly involved in the creation and deliver of a product or service; in emissions reporting, 15 upstream and downstream activities are included in Scope 3
VC	venture capital
VCM	voluntary carbon markets
vesting	In employee compensation, the process whereby an employee gradually earns ownership of an asset, e.g., stock options
VRF	Value Reporting Foundation
WACI	weighted-average carbon intensity
WHO	World Health Organization
WMO	World Meteorological Organization
WRI	World Resources Institute
WTP	willingness to pay

Endnotes

INTRODUCTION

1. See https://www.stockholmresilience.org/research/planetary-boundaries.html (accessed August 27, 2025).
2. Imagine if people demanded that kind of precision before deciding to wear a seatbelt or stop smoking. We know not wearing seatbelts and smoking can both kill you, we just don't know if or when.
3. Disclaimer: Insights shared represent the views of individual speakers and may not necessarily reflect those of their employers. All the information provided here is for educational and informational purposes only and does not constitute, and should not be construed as, an offer to sell, or a solicitation of an offer to buy, any securities or related financial instruments.
4. If you aren't familiar with the term "Skynet," stop what you are doing and watch *The Terminator* (1984) (https://en.wikipedia.org/wiki/The_Terminator), directed by James Cameron. Thank us later.

PART ONE   Challenges Ahead

1. See https://www.oed.com/dictionary/sustainability_n?tab=meaning_and_use# 19473065, 2b (accessed August 28, 2025).
2. Hayat, U., Orsagh, M., Schacht, K.N. et al. (2015). *Environmental, Social, and Governance Issues in Investing: A Guide for Investment Professionals*. Charlottesville, VA: CFA Institute. https://www.cfainstitute.org/sites/default/files/-/media/documents/article/position-paper/esg-issues-in-investing-a-guide-for-investment-professionals.pdf (accessed August 27, 2025).

CHAPTER 1   Environmental Issues

1. This material is well described by the Intergovernmental Panel on Climate Change (IPCC) which will be described in Chapter 4. As with any scientific research, statistical uncertainty means we cannot be 100% certain of our measurements or forecasts; a small (but vocal) minority still contests the significance of human contributions to global warming. Climate change sceptics may visit https://skepticalscience.com (accessed September 22, 2025).
2. It is important to distinguish between two terms: according to the Oxford English Dictionary, climate refers to the general weather conditions *usually*

found in a particular place [emphasis added], while weather refers to the conditions in the air above the Earth, such as wind, rain, or temperature, especially *at a particular time over a particular area* [emphasis added].

3. Lindsey, R. (2023, August 22). Climate change: Global sea level. NOAA Climate .gov. https://www.climate.gov/news-features/understanding-climate/climate-change-global-sea-level (accessed August 27, 2025).

4. Gettelman, A., Christensen, M.W., Diamond, M.S. et al. (2024). Has reducing ship emissions brought forward global warming? *Geophysical Research Letters* 51 (15): e2024GL109077. https://doi.org/10.1029/2024gl109077.

5. AFP (2013). Palm oil companies behind Singapore smog, Greenpeace says. https://phys.org/news/2013-06-palm-oil-companies-singapore-smog.html (accessed August 27, 2025).

6. World Health Organization (WHO) (2024, October 24). Ambient (outdoor) air pollution. https://www.who.int/news-room/fact-sheets/detail/ambient-(outdoor)-air-quality-and-health (accessed August 27, 2025).

7. Broughton, E. (2005). The Bhopal disaster and its aftermath: a review. *Environmental Health* 4 (1): 6. https://doi.org/10.1186/1476-069x-4-6.

8. Gatmatyan, D.B. (2023). Brockovich–PG&E case. EBSCO. https://www.ebsco .com/research-starters/law/brockovich-pge-case (accessed August 27, 2025).

9. U.S. Fish & Wildlife Service. (2021). Bald eagle. The Environmental Protection Agency banned the use of DDT and some related pesticides in the United States in 1972, which laid the foundation for the bald eagle's recovery. The bald eagle population has since recovered.

10. Veolia Environnement SA (VIE.PA) had a market capitalization of approximately US$22.2 billion as of July 1 2025. Data retrieved from Yahoo Finance. https://finance.yahoo.com/quote/VIE.PA/. Waste Management, Inc. (WM) has a market capitalization of approximately US$92.1 billion as of July 1 2025. Data retrieved from Yahoo Finance. https://finance.yahoo.com/quote/WM/.

11. Ritchie, H., Samborska, V., and Roser, M. (2023, November 1). Plastic pollution. Our World in Data. https://ourworldindata.org/plastic-pollution (accessed August 27, 2025).

12. The Ocean Cleanup. (2025, June 24). The Great Pacific Garbage Patch. https://theoceancleanup.com/great-pacific-garbage-patch/#what-are-the-effects-on-marine-life-humans-and-ecosystems (accessed August 27, 2025).

13. National Oceanic and Atmospheric Administration (NOAA) (n.d.). What are microplastics? https://oceanservice.noaa.gov/facts/microplastics.html (accessed August 27, 2025).

14. Kokutse, F. (2024, November 23). As fast fashion's waste pollutes Africa's environment designers in Ghana are finding a solution. *AP News.* https://apnews .com/article/ghana-fashion-waste-clothing-pollution-0809f25605722a53658 bf21d7d9b1548 (accessed August 27, 2025).

15. See Organisation for Economic Co-operation and Development (OECD) (2022). Global plastics outlook. https://thesustainableagency.com/blog/recycling-facts-and-statistics/ (accessed August 27, 2025), and https://businesswaste.com/waste-types/textile-waste/textile-waste-facts/ (accessed August 27, 2025).

16. Shavanov, M.V., Magomadov, A.S., and Slavkina, V.E. (2022). Factors affecting arable agriculture in the future. *IOP Conference Series: Earth and Environmental Science* 979: 012116.

17. See https://www.worldwildlife.org/publications/2024-living-planet-report (accessed August 27, 2025).

18. Brown, B.E., Dunne, R.P., Somerfield, P.J. et al. (2019). Long-term impacts of rising sea temperature and sea level on shallow water coral communities over a ~ 40 year period. *Scientific Reports* 9 (1): 8826. https://doi.org/10.1038/s41598-019-45188-x.

19. As mentioned previously, melting of polar ice caps due to rising temperatures is already linked to sea-level rise.

CHAPTER 2   Social Issues

1. See https://docs.un.org/en/A/RES/64/292 (accessed August 29, 2025).

2. See https://echale.mx/en (accessed August 29, 2025) and https://www.mahindralifespaces.com (accessed August 29, 2025).

3. See https://www.enezaeducation.com (accessed August 29, 2025) and https://www.khanacademy.org (accessed August 29, 2025).

4. See https://www.halodoc.com (accessed August 29, 2025).

5. See https://www.gpfi.org (accessed August 29, 2025).

6. See https://www.m-pesa.africa (accessed August 29, 2025) and https://international.nubank.com.br/about (accessed August 29, 2025).

7. Edmans, A. (2011). Does the stock market value intangibles? Employee satisfaction and equity prices. *Journal of Financial Economics* 101 (3): 621–640. https://doi.org/10.1016/j.jfineco.2011.03.021.

8. Boustanifar, H. and Kang, Y.D. (2021). Employee satisfaction and long-run stock returns, 1984–2020. *Financial Analysts Journal* 78 (3): 129–151.

9. Edmans, A., Pu, D., Zhang, C. et al. (2023). Employee satisfaction, labor market flexibility, and stock returns around the world. *Management Science* 70 (7): 4167–4952. http://dx.doi.org/10.2139/ssrn.2461003.

10. See https://www.merriam-webster.com/dictionary/diversity%2C%20equity%20and%20inclusion accessed June 27, 2025.

11. The reports are available at https://www.mckinsey.com/capabilities/people-and-organizational-performance/our-insights/why-diversity-matters (2015) (accessed August 29, 2025), https://www.mckinsey.com/capabilities/people-and-organizational-performance/our-insights/delivering-through-diversity (2018) (accessed August 29, 2025), https://www.mckinsey.com/featured-insights/diversity-and-inclusion/diversity-wins-how-inclusion-matters (2020) (accessed August 29, 2025), and https://www.mckinsey.com/featured-insights/diversity-and-inclusion/diversity-matters-even-more-the-case-for-holistic-impact (2023) (accessed August 29, 2025).

12. See the discussion in Green, J. and Hand, J.R. (2024). McKinsey's Diversity Matters/Delivers/Wins Results Revisited. *Econ Journal Watch* 21 (1): 5–34.

13. See https://diversityproject.com/resource/dp-cognitive-diversity-full-research/ (accessed August 29, 2025).

14. For more information on climate justice, see https://www.un.org/sustainable development/blog/2019/05/climate-justice/ (accessed August 29, 2025) or https://centerclimatejustice.universityofcalifornia.edu/what-is-climate-justice/ (accessed August 29, 2025).

CHAPTER 3   Governance Issues

1. See https://www.investopedia.com/terms/e/enron.asp (accessed August 29, 2025).

2. See https://www.ft.com/content/284fb1ad-ddc0-45df-a075-0709b36868db (accessed August 29, 2025).

3. See https://www.sec.gov/enforcement/foreign-corrupt-practices-act (accessed September 22, 2025).

4. See https://www.govinfo.gov/content/pkg/COMPS-1883.pdf/COMPS-1883.pdf (accessed September 22, 2025).

5. See https://www.govinfo.gov/content/pkg/COMPS-9515.pdf/COMPS-9515.pdf (accessed September 22, 2025).

6. See https://en.wikipedia.org/wiki/Nick_Leeson (accessed August 29, 2025).

7. The original report is still available online at https://documents1.worldbank. org/curated/en/280911488968799581/pdf/113237-WP-WhoCaresWins-2004. pdf (accessed August 29, 2025).

8. See https://rpc.cfainstitute.org/sites/default/files/-/media/documents/article/ position-paper/corp-governance-listed-companies-2005-1st-edition.pdf (accessed September 22, 2025).

9. See https://permutable.ai/nestle-esg-score-an-in-depth-analysis-and-look-at-its-impact-on-the-industry (accessed August 29, 2025).

10. See https://www.motorfinanceonline.com/features/tesla-finds-itself-trailing-behind-shell-on-esg-scores-why (accessed August 29, 2025).

11. A useful reference on this topic is available at https://www.bakermckenzie.com/-/ media/files/insight/publications/2020/03/the-revival-of-dual-class-shares.pdf (accessed August 29, 2025).

12. But not enough concern to avoid investing in the IPO! Because the owner of Snapchat was a "hot" IPO, investors turned a blind eye to whatever feelings they might have had about the implications for corporate governance. See https:// blogs.cfainstitute.org/marketintegrity/2017/04/18/snapchat-ipo-whats-wrong-with-this-picture/ (accessed August 29, 2025) for more information.

13. See https://www.cnbc.com/2017/08/01/sp-500-to-exclude-snap-after-voting-rights-debate.html (accessed August 29, 2025).

14. For a good review of the academic literature, see https://diversityproject.com/ wp-content/uploads/2025/06/DP-Cognitive-Diversity-Full-Research-Paper.pdf (accessed August 29, 2025).

15. See https://www.epi.org/publication/ceo-pay-in-2023/ (accessed August 29, 2025).

16. Faulkender, M., Kadyrzhanova, D., Prabhala, N. et al. (2010). Executive compensation: An overview of research on corporate practices and proposed reforms. *Journal of Applied Corporate Finance* 22 (1): 107–118. https://doi.org/10.1111/j.1745-6622.2010.00266.x.
17. Badawi, A.B. and Bartlett, R (2024). ESG Overperformance? Assessing the Use of ESG Targets in Executive Compensation Plans. Stanford Law and Economics Olin Working Paper No. 592, Rock Center for Corporate Governance at Stanford University Working Paper No. 257, European Corporate Governance Institute – Finance Working Paper No. 1025/2024, Stanford Public Law Working Paper. http://dx.doi.org/10.2139/ssrn.4941016.
18. Ibid.
19. Badawi, A.B. and Bartlett, R (2024), p. 4.
20. A summary of the Netflix poison pill appears at https://sites.law.berkeley.edu/thenetwork/2012/11/16/netflix-good-governance-and-poison-pills/ (accessed August 29, 2025).
21. See https://www.sec.gov/Archives/edgar/data/1065280/000119312512452184/d435273dex41.htm Annex B paragraph 2 (accessed August 29, 2025).
22. See https://www.investopedia.com/terms/d/dodd-frank-financial-regulatory-reform-bill.asp (accessed August 29, 2025).
23. See, for example, https://www.npr.org/2021/10/05/1043377310/facebook-whistleblower-frances-haugen-congress (accessed August 29, 2025).

CHAPTER 4 Mobilizing for Action

1. John Muir is well known for founding the Sierra Club (https://en.wikipedia.org/wiki/Sierra_Club) in 1892.
2. Today this modeling language is referred to as "system dynamics" and is still taught at MIT.
3. See https://www.unep.org/resources/annual-report-2024 (accessed September 4, 2025).
4. See https://www.ozone.unep.org/treaties/montreal-protocol (accessed September 4, 2025). Adoption of the Montreal Protocol is often cited as an example of how governments can collaborate to address urgent climate issues.
5. See https://www.ipcc.ch/assessment-report/ar6/ (accessed September 22, 2025).
6. See https://www.hks.harvard.edu/sites/default/files/centers/mrcbg/programs/senior.fellows/2021-22/Chris%20Skidmore%20COP-Out%20A%20Brief%20History%20of%20the%20UN%20COP%20process.pdf (accessed September 4, 2025) for more detail.
7. See https://www.hks.harvard.edu/sites/default/files/centers/mrcbg/programs/senior.fellows/2021-22/Chris%20Skidmore%20COP-Out%20A%20Brief%20History%20of%20the%20UN%20COP%20process.pdf (accessed September 4, 2025) for more detail.
8. See https://www.unep.org/resources/annual-report-2024 (accessed September 4, 2025).

9. See https://www.worldbank.org/en/news/feature/2022/05/17/what-you-need-to-know-about-article-6-of-the-paris-agreement (accessed September 4, 2025) for more information.

10. Liang, H., Sun, L., and Teo, M. (2022). Responsible hedge funds. *Review of Finance* 26 (6): 1585–1633. https://doi.org/10.1093/rof/rfac028.

11. The MDGs are not as well-known as the SDGs; learn more at https://www.un.org/millenniumgoals/ (accessed September 4, 2025).

12. See https://rspo.org (accessed September 4, 2025).

13. Luke Combs, a wildly popular country music artist as of this writing, received the 2023 Country Music Association Award for Song of the Year for his recording of "Fast Car." The original 1988 recording by Tracy Chapman won a Grammy for Best Female Pop Vocal Performance.

CHAPTER 5 The Relationship Between Companies, People, and Planet

1. This clearly ignores the large number of people who either work for themselves (including small family businesses) or survive in the informal economy. Both of these groups are especially important in emerging market economies, but are unlikely to be large drivers of greenhouse gas emissions.

2. See https://www.theguardian.com/environment/2024/apr/09/human-rights-violated-inaction-climate-echr-rules-landmark-case (accessed September 4, 2025).

3. See https://www.hrlc.org.au/case-summaries/un-human-rights-committee-finds-australia-violated-torres-strait-islanders-human-rights-over-climate-inaction/ (accessed September 4, 2025).

4. See https://statecourtreport.org/our-work/analysis-opinion/montanas-climate-change-lawsuit-may-see-sequels-across-america (accessed September 4, 2025).

5. See https://www.msn.com/en-us/news/world/world-s-top-court-says-major-polluters-may-need-to-pay-reparations-for-climate-harm/ar-AA1J9sHu (accessed September 4, 2025).

6. Sato, M., Gostlow, G., Higham, C. et al. (2024). Impacts of climate litigation on firm value. *Nature Sustainability* 7: 1461–1468. https://doi.org/10.1038/s41893-024-01455-y. The authors find negative 3-day cumulative abnormal returns around filing or decision date, especially for carbon majors.

7. We refer to these as "public companies" even though they are part of the private sector.

8. This is referred to as "divestment." The actual impact of divestment is a contested topic in investing circles and will be discussed in Part Four.

9. "There is one and only one social responsibility of business—to use it resources and engage in activities designed to increase its profits so long as it stays within the rules of the game, which is to say, engages in open and free competition without deception or fraud" Friedman, M. (1970). The Social Responsibility of Business is to Increase its Profits. *New York Times Magazine, September 13*, 122–126.

10. See https://www.epi.org/publication/ceo-pay-in-2023/ (accessed September 4, 2025).

11. Freeman published his landmark book in 1984: Freeman, R.E. (1984). *Strategic Management: A Stakeholder Approach*. Boston, MA: Pitman.

12. See https://news.darden.virginia.edu/2024/05/16/stakeholder-how-ed-freemans-vision-for-responsible-business-moved-from-theory-to-reality/ (accessed September 4, 2025).

13. See https://carbonpricingdashboard.worldbank.org for a summary of current carbon taxes around the world. Most are well below the level believed sufficient to compel companies to make investments in emissions reduction.

14. A good academic review of the development of CSR is Latapí Agudelo, M.A., Jóhannsdóttir, L., and Davídsdóttir, B. (2019). A literature review of the history and evolution of corporate social responsibility. *International Journal of Corporate Social Responsibility* 4 (1). https://doi.org/10.1186/s40991-018-0039-y.

15. Carroll, A.B. (2016). Carroll's pyramid of CSR: Taking another look. *Journal of Sustainable Business* 1: 3. https://jcsr.springeropen.com/articles/10.1186/s40991-016-0004-6 (accessed September 22, 2025).

16. Wood, D.J. (1991). Corporate social performance revisited. *Academy of Management Review* 16 (4): 691–718.

17. Hart, O.D. and Zingales, L. (2022). The new corporate governance. NBER Working Paper No. 29975, JEL No. G3,K22,L21, Harvard University and University of Chicago.

18. Hart and Zingales (2022).

19. The formula states $-s_i\delta(1-\lambda_i) + \lambda_i(h-\delta) > 0$. Assume each shareholder i has a preference for the welfare of others, λ_i where $\lambda[0,1]$, between pure self-interest ($\lambda_i = 0$) and pure selflessness ($\lambda_i = 1$). For a corporate proposal with a cost δ and a welfare value of h, a shareholder with an ownership stake of s_i will vote in favor of the proposal if the welfare value is greater than the cost $(h-\delta)$, as long as the cost to the shareholder is less than the total welfare generated, after adjusting for the shareholder's preference for the welfare of others.

20. See https://www.blackrock.com/corporate/about-us/investment-stewardship/blackrock-voting-choice (accessed September 5, 2025).

21. See https://corpgov.law.harvard.edu/2024/02/24/technology-advances-facilitate-pass-through-voting/ (accessed September 5, 2025).

22. Hart and Zingales (2022), see section 5.3.

23. Hart and Zingales (2022), see section 5.2 for a more detailed description.

24. For more information on these legal systems see "Common Law and Civil Law Traditions" by the University of California, Berkeley School of Law. https://www.academia.edu/30065462/Common_Law_Civil_Law_Traditions (accessed September 22, 2025).

25. Liang, H. and Renneboog, L. (2017). On the foundations of corporate social responsibility. *The Journal of Finance* 72: 853–910. https://doi.org/10.1111/jofi.12487.

26. IVA indices measure a company's environmental and social risks and opportunities, plus the extent to which a company develops CSR strategies designed to manage those risks and opportunities.

27. The material in this section is based on Chang, X., Fu, K., Jin, Y. et al. (2022). Sustainable finance: ESG/CSR, firm value, and investment returns*. *Asia Pacific Journal of Financial Studies* 51: 325–371. https://doi.org/10.1111/ajfs.12379.

CHAPTER 6　Sustainability Measurement and Reporting

1. See https://dictionary.cambridge.org/dictionary/english/materiality (accessed September 8, 2025).
2. Entire courses and books are dedicated to sustainability accounting; the material presented here is necessarily at a summary level only and designed to introduce readers to the main concepts.
3. The list includes industry specialists (Extractive Industries Transparency Initiative, Forest Stewardship Council, Marine Stewardship Council, Textile Exchange, Sustainable Agriculture Initiative) and other specialized players (Natural Capital Accounting and Valuation of Ecosystem Services, Social & Human Capital Protocol, Water Footprint Network).
4. See https://www.globalreporting.org/ (accessed September 8, 2025).
5. See https://ghgprotocol.org/ (accessed September 8, 2025).
6. See https://www.cdp.net/en (accessed September 8, 2025).
7. See https://www.ifrs.org/sustainability/climate-disclosure-standards-board/ (accessed September 8, 2025).
8. See https://integratedreporting.ifrs.org/the-iirc-2/council/ (accessed September 8, 2025).
9. See https://sasb.ifrs.org/ (accessed September 8, 2025).
10. See https://sciencebasedtargets.org/ (accessed September 8, 2025).
11. See https://www.fsb-tcfd.org/ (accessed September 8, 2025).
12. See https://tnfd.global/ (accessed September 8, 2025).
13. The major economies that do not follow IFRS accounting are the United States (Generally Accepted Accounting Principles [GAAP]), China (China Accounting Standards), India (India Accounting Standards), and Japan (Japanese GAAP). All but the United States are making efforts to converge with IFRS.
14. Source: https://stockanalysis.com/quote/sgx/C09/market-cap/ and https://stockanalysis.com/quote/sgx/u11/market-cap/ (accessed July 24, 2025).

CHAPTER 7　Financing Sustainability: Green, Social, and Sustainability Bonds and Other Instruments

1. To address liquidity challenges in Small Island Developing States (SIDS), like Barbados, the Bridgetown Initiative proposed several solutions, such as a large-scale Climate Mitigation Trust and a US$1 trillion credit expansion across the multilateral development banks, to reduce the high cost of capital in emerging markets. See https://www.globalpolicy.org/en/news/2024-06-05/bridgetown-initiative-30-released-whats-news (accessed September 9, 2025).

2. Prompt: "Construct four investment examples showing the following scenarios: (i) negative NPV; (ii) positive NPV but IRR<10%; (iii) positive NPV and IRR > 10%; and (iv) NPV is lower than scenario (iii) but the IRR is higher."

3. Drawn from the 2025 Green Bond Principles, p. 3, available at https://www .icmagroup.org/assets/documents/Sustainable-finance/2025-updates/Green-Bond-Principles-GBP-June-2025.pdf (accessed September 9, 2025). The additional point (i) was originally Green Bond Frameworks but has been generalized here since it applies equally to various forms of sustainable financing.

4. For example, Singapore-listed real estate developer City Development Limited (CDL) shares its Sustainable Finance Framework at https://cdlsustainability. com/pdf/Sustainable%20Finance%20Framework_20Jun2022.pdf (accessed September 9, 2025).

5. Green bonds are the most frequently analyzed since there are more of them and they have a longer history, i.e., greater data availability.

6. Henisz, W. J., & McGlinch, J. (2019). ESG, Material Credit Events, and Credit Risk. Journal of Applied Corporate Finance, 31(2), 105–117. https://doi.org/ 10.1111/jacf.12352.

7. Research refers to this as a "matched pair," where the two bonds are issued by the same firm on the same date for the same notional amount, term, and interest rate. Only a few pure matched pairs exist, so researchers have mostly agreed on a methodology used to identify close pairs by gradually relaxing some of those constraints.

8. See Flammer, C. (2021). Corporate green bonds. *Journal of Financial Economics* 142 (2): 499–516, for a good (but not the only) scientific analysis of green bonds.

9. Flammer (2021). The risk measure is the E rating from an ESG rating agency, a concept which will be discussed in Chapter 11.

10. Lam, P. and Wurgler, J.A. (2024). Green bonds: New label, same projects. See https:// doi.org/10.2139/ssrn.4951223 (accessed September 9, 2025).

11. See https://www.climatebonds.net/files/documents/publications/Climate-Bonds-Initiative_Global-State-of-the-Market-Report_May-2025_2025-06-18-123430_mejk.pdf, p. 17 (accessed September 9, 2025).

12. See https://www.thaiunion.com/en/newsroom/press-release/1397/thai-union-launches-thailands-first-sustainability-linked-bond (accessed September 9, 2025) and the section on KPIs/SPTs is available at https://investor.thaiunion.com/ sustainable.html (accessed September 9, 2025).

13. Because green bonds require proceeds go toward qualifying green projects, the risk of greenwashing is lower—but not zero, as we will discuss in Chapter 8.

14. Even though renewable energy (solar, wind, etc.) is lower in emissions than traditional fossil fuel-based energy, there are issues within the value chain such as mining for rare earths, waste disposal at end of life, and the like.

15. Chapter 8 discusses actions by governments and regulators, one of which is referred to as a "taxonomy" that defines which business activities can be considered green.

16. The Climate Bonds Initiative published a guide for corporates wishing to explore transition financing, available at https://www.climatebonds.net/files/documents/ publications/Financing-the-Corporate-Climate-Transition-with-Bonds.pdf (accessed September 9, 2025).

17. See https://files.wri.org/d8/s3fs-public/2022-11/triple-dividend-climate-finance .pdf (accessed September 9, 2025). This report also provides a systematic overview of scientific research on adaptation projects, including many references to studies of projects around the world.

18. See https://www.unep.org/resources/adaptation-gap-report-2024 (accessed September 9, 2025).

19. See https://www.wri.org/research/climate-adaptation-investment-case (accessed September 9, 2025).

20. Note the report uses two new measures of return in the last two columns of the table: BCR (benefit-to-cost ratio) and EIRR (economic IRR that incorporates nonfinancial returns). As with NPV, bigger positive numbers are better.

21. See https://www.nortonrosefulbright.com/en-sg/knowledge/publications/ 9713e070/blue-bonds-making-a-splash-in-the-capital-markets (accessed September 9, 2025).

22. Bosmans, P. and De Mariz, F. (2023). The blue bond market: a catalyst for ocean and water financing. *Journal of Risk and Financial Management* 16: 184. https:// doi.org/10.3390/jrfm16030184. See also https://www.systemiq.earth/wp-content/ uploads/2024/06/Blue-Bonds-Report.pdf (accessed September 9, 2025), for an even longer list.

23. See https://www.conservation.org/pres.-releases/2025/01/15/us-35-million-u.s.- and-indonesia-debt-for-nature-swap-finalized (accessed September 9, 2025).

24. Vanilla bonds incur issuing costs associated with preparing documents and speaking with investors. Issuing a sustainability bond carries additional costs, e.g., the external review and annual reporting.

25. Di Tommaso, C., Pacelli, V., and Povia, M.M. (2025). Green loans and bank risk: Navigating the path to sustainable finance. *International Review of Economics & Finance* 101: 104138. https://doi.org/10.1016/j.iref.2025.10.138.

26. See https://www.uobgroup.com/sustainability/sustainable-banking/net-zero- commitment.page (accessed September 9, 2025).

27. An authoritative resource on blended finance can be found at https://www .convergence.finance (accessed September 9, 2025).

28. See https://www.convergence.finance/blended-finance#market-size (accessed September 9, 2025).

29. See https://sustainablefutures.linklaters.com/post/102j64w/germany-initiates- first-tenders-for-carbon-contracts-for-difference (accessed September 9, 2025).

30. See https://unfccc.int/climate-action/momentum-for-change/financing-for- climate-friendly-investment/payments-for-environmental-services-program (accessed September 9, 2025).

PART THREE   Regulations and Companies

1. This will have the additional benefit of being more up-to-date than is possible with this book. Artificial intelligence (AI) tools, like ChatGPT, Claude, and others, are useful for such follow-up research.

CHAPTER 8　Corporate Disclosure Requirements

1. Another entity with the ability to impose disclosure requirements are stock exchanges. In Singapore, even though the Singapore Exchange (SGX) is itself a public company (like NASDAQ and the London Stock Exchange, among others), SGX policies are closely aligned with government priorities. To this end, the SGX, not the government regulator (the Monetary Authority of Singapore), is the entity imposing reporting requirements on listed companies. See the specific section "Singapore," below, for more information.

2. See https://finance.ec.europa.eu/capital-markets-union-and-financial-markets/company-reporting-and-auditing/company-reporting/corporate-sustainability-reporting_en#legislation (accessed September 10, 2025) for a comprehensive overview of EU corporate sustainability regulation. Note that another regulatory element, the Carbon Border Adjustment Mechanism (CBAM), will be discussed in Chapter 10.

3. See https://www.efrag.org/en (accessed September 10, 2025) for more information.

4. See https://eur-lex.europa.eu/legal-content/EN/TXT/?uri=CELEX:32022L2464 (accessed September 10, 2025) for more information.

5. See https://www.efrag.org/en/sustainability-reporting/esrs-workstreams/sector-agnostic-standards-set-1-esrs (accessed September 10, 2025) for more information.

6. See https://commission.europa.eu/business-economy-euro/doing-business-eu/sustainability-due-diligence-responsible-business/corporate-sustainability-due-diligence_en (accessed September 10, 2025) for more information.

7. This section draws heavily on the analysis available at https://www.mayerbrown.com/en/insights/publications/2025/02/european-commission-presents-omnibus-simplification-package-with-amendments-to-csrd-csddd-cbam-and-taxonomy (accessed September 10, 2025).

8. See SEC.gov | SEC Votes to End Defense of Climate Disclosure Rules (accessed September 10, 2025).

9. See https://www.china-briefing.com/news/china-unveils-basic-standards-for-corporate-sustainability-esg-disclosure/ (accessed September 10, 2025).

10. See https://ecovadis.com/regulations/india-business-responsibility-and-sustainability-reporting-brsr/#:~:text=The%20Securities%20and%20Exchange%20Board,human%20rights%20or%20environmental%20protection (accessed September 10, 2025).

11. See https://www.brightest.io/uk-sustainability-reporting (accessed September 10, 2025).

12. See https://kpmg.com/au/en/home/insights/2024/09/24ru-12-australian-sustainability-reporting-standards-legislation-finalised.html (accessed September 10, 2025).

13. See https://www.allenandgledhill.com/sg/publication/articles/29209/ifrs-sustainability-disclosure-standards-to-be-incorporated-into-sgx-climate-reporting-rules-from-fy-2025 (accessed September 10, 2025).

CHAPTER 9 Defining Green: Greenwashing and Taxonomies

1. Or as some biologists or cognitive scientists might ask, when the photoreceptors in my eyes send signals to my brain indicating that I "see" the color "green," how do I know you see the same color?

2. This chapter is directed toward *corporate* greenwashing and regulation. Investment managers may also be guilty of fraud, e.g., Bernie Madoff and Madoff Securities, as well as greenwashing. This will be covered in Chapter 15.

3. See https://www.ft.com/content/78b3c741-1ab8-48f5-92a8-4e98dfa230ab (accessed September 10, 2025).

4. See https://www.ul.com/insights/sins-greenwashing (accessed September 10, 2025).

5. Nemes, N., Scanlan, S.J., Smith, P. et al. (2022). An integrated framework to assess greenwashing. *Sustainability* 14 (8): 4431. https://doi.org/10.3390/su14084431. The original table stretches over six pages; this version omits several columns for simplification. See the paper at https://www.mdpi.com/2071-1050/14/8/4431#app1-sustainability-14-04431.

6. See https://www.koreaherald.com/article/2592136 (accessed September 22, 2025).

7. See https://www.slrconsulting.com/insights/the-risk-of-greenwashing-a-global-perspective/ (accessed September 10, 2025).

8. See https://greenclaims.campaign.gov.uk (accessed September 10, 2025).

9. See https://www.lawrbit.com/article/guidelines-for-prevention-regulation-of-greenwashing-or-misleading-environmental-claims-2024/ (accessed September 10, 2025).

10. See https://aana.com.au/self-regulation/codes-guidelines/environmental-claims/ (accessed September 10, 2025).

11. Available at https://climatecasechart.com (accessed September 10, 2025).

12. See https://www.clientearth.org/latest/press-office/press-releases/historic-win-against-greenwashing-as-klm-s-advertising-ruled-illegal/ (accessed September 10, 2025).

13. Full text available at https://eur-lex.europa.eu/legal-content/EN/TXT/?uri=celex%3A32020R0852 (accessed September 10, 2025). Note that the Taxonomy is focused on environmental issues; technical criteria for social and governance issues are not (yet) included.

14. See https://eur-lex.europa.eu/legal-content/EN/TXT/?uri=celex%3A32020R0852, Article 18, point (1) (accessed September 10, 2025).

15. Lam, P. and Wurgler, J.A. (2024). Green bonds: New label, same projects. (September 09, 2024). http://dx.doi.org/10.2139/ssrn.4951223.

CHAPTER 10 Taxes and Carbon Markets

1. See https://www.investopedia.com/terms/e/externality.asp (accessed September 15, 2025).

2. See https://climate.mit.edu/posts/mit-alumnus-william-nordhaus-wins-nobel-prize-economic-sciences-modeling-global-interplay (accessed September 15, 2025).

3. For more on CBAM see https://trade.ec.europa.eu/access-to-markets/en/news/carbon-border-adjustment-mechanism-cbam (accessed September 15, 2025).

4. The six industries are iron/steel, cement, fertilizers, aluminum, hydrogen, and electricity.

5. See https://climate.ec.europa.eu/eu-action/eu-emissions-trading-system-eu-ets/eu-ets-emissions-cap_en (accessed September 15, 2025).

6. See https://carbonpricingdashboard.worldbank.org (accessed September 15, 2025) for comprehensive data on carbon markets.

7. Probst, B.S., Toetzke, M., Kontoleon, A. et al. (2024). Systematic assessment of the achieved emission reductions of carbon crediting projects. *Nature Communications* 15: 9562. https://doi.org/10.1038/s41467-024-53645-z.

8. In 2023, the head of the UN Trillion Trees Campaign had to backtrack on his own 2019 claims that the Earth could hold an additional 1.2 trillion trees which would absorb up to two-thirds of historical carbon emissions, because tree planting was being used to avoid the hard work of real emissions reductions (greenwashing). See https://www.wired.com/story/stop-planting-trees-thomas-crowther/ (accessed September 15, 2025) for details.

9. Singapore doesn't have access to hydroelectric power like Brazil, or large tracts of land like many other countries that could be used for solar or wind farms. Instead, it is working with neighboring countries to build solar farms overseas and import renewable energy via cable—even as far away as Australia (https://www.suncable.energy). Singapore is also exploring the possibility of geothermal energy and may consider advanced small modular reactor designs for nuclear power in the future.

10. See https://www.carbonmarkets-cooperation.gov.sg/introduction/ (accessed September 15, 2025).

PART FOUR   Sustainable Investing

1. We would have preferred to keep the symmetrical structure of the book by putting Chapter 15 into Part Five, but there isn't enough material to justify additional chapters like Chapters 8–10.

CHAPTER 11   Interpreting Corporate Sustainability Disclosures: Environmental, Social, and Governance Ratings

1. Analysts typically focus on a set of stocks within a single sector, e.g., automobile manufacturers. This is called "covering" the stocks in the sector.

2. For more information on what research analysts do, see https://www.investopedia.com/articles/personal-finance/082815/day-life-equity-research-analyst.asp (accessed September 16, 2025). Also, it may be behind a paywall but Opinion columnist Matt Levine offers an excellent tongue-in-cheek description of equity research in the following piece: https://www.bloomberg.com/opinion/articles/2025-01-09/it-s-tough-to-be-a-research-analyst (accessed September 16, 2025).

3. Yahoo Finance. (n.d.). Thai Airways International Public Company Limited (TAWNF). https://finance.yahoo.com/quote/TAWNF/ (accessed January 8, 2025).

4. Cbonds. (n.d.). Thai Airways International Bonds. https://cbonds.com/bonds/350551/ (accessed January 8, 2025).

5. Bloomberg News. (2024, September 26). Thailand risks credit rating downgrade, opposition warns. *Bangkok Post*. https://www.bangkokpost.com/business/general/2872578/thailand-risks-credit-rating-downgrade-as-debt-mounts-opposition-peoples-party-deputy-leader-sirikanya-tansakun-warns (accessed September 16, 2025).

6. Berg, F., Kölbel, J.F., and Rigobon, R. (2022). Aggregate confusion: The divergence of ESG ratings. *Review of Finance* 26 (6): 1315–1344. https://doi.org/10.1093/rof/rfac033.

7. See https://www.investopedia.com/terms/c/covered-stock.asp (accessed September 16, 2025) for some of the considerations of equity coverage.

8. This is not always the case. There is a small portion of the equity market where companies—usually very small firms—pay for equity research coverage. See Billings, B.K., Buslepp, W.L., and Huston, G.R. (2014). Worth the hype? The relevance of paid-for analyst research for the buy-and-hold investor. *Accounting Review* 89 (3): 903–931. https://doi.org/10.2308/accr-50681, for more on this part of the market.

9. National Bureau of Economic Research. (2018, August). Evaluating the role of credit ratings in the 2008 crisis. *The Digest*. https://www.nber.org/digest/aug18/evaluating-role-credit-ratings-2008-crisis (accessed September 16, 2025).

10. Musk, E. [@elonmusk]. (2022, May 19). Exxon is rated top ten best in world for environment, social & governance (ESG) by S&P 500, while Tesla didn't make the list! ESG is a scam. It has been weaponized by phony social justice warriors. [Tweet]. Twitter. https://twitter.com/elonmusk/status/1526958110023245829 (accessed September 16, 2025).

11. Kuh, T. (2024). The story of the first ESG index. *Morningstar*. https://www.morningstar.com/sustainable-investing/story-first-esg-index (accessed September 16, 2025).

12. Refinitiv (2022). Environmental, Social and Governance Scores from Refinitiv. London Stock Exchange Group. https://www.lseg.com/content/dam/lseg/en_us/documents/media-centre/press-releases/2019/refinitiv-esg-scores-methodology.pdf (accessed September 16, 2025).

13. Sustainalytics (2024). The ESG Risk Ratings: Methodology Abstract (Version 3.1). Sustainalytics. https://www.sustainalytics.com/docs/knowledgehublibraries/default-document-library/sustainalytics_-esg-risk-ratings_-version-3-1_-methodology-abstract_-june-2024.pdf (accessed September 16, 2025).

14. Mauer, W.P.G. (2024). ESG Ratings: An Overview of Providers and Upcoming Regulations. Mauer WPG. https://www.mauer-wpg.com/en/insights/esg-ratings-an-overview-of-providers-and-upcoming-regulations (accessed September 16, 2025).

15. CDP (n.d.). About Us. CDP. https://www.cdp.net/en/about (accessed September 16, 2025).

16. ISS (n.d.). Sustainability solutions. ISS. https://www.issgovernance.com/esg/ (accessed September 16, 2025).

17. FTSE Russell (n.d.). FTSE4Good Index Series. London Stock Exchange Group. https://www.lseg.com/en/ftse-russell/indices/ftse4good (accessed September 16, 2025).

18. GRESB (n.d.). GRESB: ESG benchmark for real assets. GRESB. https://www.gresb.com/nl-en/products/real-benchmarks-members/ (accessed September 23, 2025).

19. Berg, F., Kölbel, J.F., and Rigobon, R. (2022).

20. Mitch may be right to be concerned. A recent paper looked at ties between credit ratings agencies and their ESG ratings arms: "Using the acquisitions of Vigeo Eiris and RobecoSAM by Moody's and S&P as shocks to the commercial ties between ESG rating agencies and their rated firms, we show that, after their acquisitions by the credit rating agencies (CRAs), ESG rating agencies issue higher ratings to existing paying clients of the CRAs. This effect is greater for firms that have more intensive business relationships with the CRAs, but weaker for firms with more transparent ESG disclosures or higher long-term institutional ownership. The upwardly biased ESG ratings help client firms issue more green bonds and enable the CRAs to maintain credit rating business." See Li, X., Lou, Y., and Zhang, L. (2024). Do commercial ties influence ESG ratings? Evidence from Moody's and S&P. *Journal of Accounting Research* 62: 1901–1940. https://doi.org/10.1111/1475-679X.12582.

21. See https://www.reuters.com/business/finance/wells-fargo-asset-cap-likely-be-lifted-next-year-sources-say-2024-11-26 (accessed September 16, 2025) for more information.

22. Simpson, C., Rathi, A., and Kishan, S. (2021). The ESG mirage. *Bloomberg.* https://www.bloomberg.com/graphics/2021-what-is-esg-investing-msci-ratings-focus-on-corporate-bottom-line/ (accessed September 16, 2025).

23. Ramakrishnan, S. (2024, August 27). Failed sale, appraisal delays behind first loss on a AAA bond since 2008 crisis. *Reuters.* https://www.reuters.com/markets/us/failed-sale-appraisal-delays-behind-first-loss-aaa-bond-since-2008-crisis-2024-08-27 (accessed September 16, 2025).

24. Berg, F., Kölbel, J.F., and Rigobon, R. (2022).

25. U.S. Securities and Exchange Commission. (2003). *Litigation complaint: SEC v. Henry McKelvey Blodget.* U.S. Securities and Exchange Commission. https://www.sec.gov/litigation/complaints/comp18115b.htm (accessed September 16, 2025).

26. See https://www.investor.gov/introduction-investing/investing-basics/glossary/fair-disclosure-regulation-fd (accessed September 16, 2025).

27. Council of the European Union. (2024, November 19). Environmental, social and governance (ESG) ratings: Council greenlights new regulation. Council of the European Union. https://www.consilium.europa.eu/en/press/press-releases/2024/11/19/environmental-social-and-governance-esg-ratings-council-greenlights-new-regulation/ (accessed September 16, 2025).

CHAPTER 12   Sustainable Investing Strategies

1. See https://blogs.cfainstitute.org/investor/2024/08/30/market-efficiency-vs-behavioral-finance-which-strategy-delivers-better-returns/ for an entertaining analysis of EMH vs. Behavioral Finance as implemented by investment managers most closely related to the respective ideals, Dimensional Fund Advisors (EMH, Eugene Fama) and FullerThaler (Behavioral Finance, Richard Thaler).

2. Fama, Eugene (1970). "Efficient Capital Markets: A Review of Theory and Empirical Work". Journal of Finance. 25 (2): 383–417. doi:10.2307/2325486

3. See Dearth, M. and Ku, S.-Y. (2023). *Getting Started in Alternative Investments.* Hoboken, NJ: Wiley, pp. 169–170.

4. For a description of short selling see https://www.investopedia.com/articles/investing/111313/multiple-strategies-hedge-funds.asp (accessed September 17, 2025).

5. See https://www.investopedia.com/terms/a/assetclasses.asp (accessed September 17, 2025).

6. For an approachable overview of alternative investments, see Dearth, M. and Ku, S.-Y. (2023). *Getting Started in Alternative Investments.* Hoboken, NJ: Wiley.

7. This concept of diversification leading to reduced risk was first formalized by Harry Markowitz in 1954. Today when people speak of portfolio construction or portfolio optimization, assets with low correlation (more properly, low *covariance* assets) and diversification are the fundamental building blocks.

8. Less common than technical trading in these markets but may also be included as part of a macro strategy.

9. Some have tried to incorporate quantitative techniques to venture investing with mixed results. One apparent success is Hatcher+ (https://hq.hatcher.com/), a Singapore-based investment advisor which analyzes data on thousands of companies from accelerators and incubators to identify investment opportunities.

10. The presence of disclosure requirements does not eliminate the possibility of fraud (e.g., Enron), but lowers it considerably.

11. One of the authors recalls a faith-based institution that required its investment managers to avoid stocks of companies that produce contraception.

12. This practice is called "divestment"; we will review the pros and cons of divestment later in the chapter.

13. Principles for Responsible Investment (2024, October 21). An Introduction to Responsible Investment: Screening and Exclusions. https://www.unpri.org/introductory-guides-to-responsible-investment/an-introduction-to-responsible-investment-screening-and-exclusions/12727.article (accessed September 17, 2025).

14. Atta-Darkua, V., Glossner, S., Krueger, P. et al. (2023). Decarbonizing institutional investor portfolios: Helping to green the planet or just greening your portfolio? *Swiss Finance Institute Research Paper No. 25-42* 20: http://dx.doi.org/10.2139/ssrn.4212568.

15. See www.unglobalcompact.org (accessed September 17, 2025) and https://www.oecd.org/en/publications/oecd-guidelines-for-multinational-enterprises-on-responsible-business-conduct_81f92357-en.html (accessed September 17, 2025).

16. See https://rpc.cfainstitute.org/-/media/documents/article/industry-research/guidance-for-integrating-esg-information-into-equity-analysis-and-research-reports.pdf (accessed September 17, 2025).

17. Much sustainability-related data updates only annually. For quantitative investing, it is preferable to use more data, and from longer periods of time, to improve the predictive power of the analysis.

18. See https://www.unpri.org/case-studies/22641.more?navcode=1854 (accessed September 17, 2025) for UN PRI case studies.

19. See https://www.gsi-alliance.org/wp-content/uploads/2023/12/GSIA-Report-2022.pdf (accessed September 17, 2025) for a description of the methodology, and https://www.gsi-alliance.org/members-resources/ (accessed September 17, 2025) for the library of reports.

20. Global Sustainable Investment Alliance (2021). Global Sustainable Investment Review 2020, p. 11. https://www.gsi-alliance.org/wp-content/uploads/2021/08/GSIR-20201.pdf (accessed September 17, 2025).

21. Global Sustainable Investment Alliance (2022). Global Sustainable Investment Review 2022, p. 8. https://www.gsi-alliance.org/wp-content/uploads/2023/12/GSIA-Report-2022.pdf (accessed September 17, 2025).

22. MFS Investment Management (n.d.). Responsible Investing Policy Statement. MFS Investment Management. https://www.mfs.com/en-us/individual-investor/insights/sustainability/responsible-investing-policy-statement.html (accessed September 17, 2025).

23. Nordea Asset Management (2025). Responsible Investment Policy. Nordea Asset Management. https://www.nordea.com/en/doc/nordea-responsible-investment-policy-january-2025.pdf (accessed September 17, 2025).

24. See https://en.wikipedia.org/wiki/Global_Industry_Classification_Standard (accessed September 17, 2025).

25. See https://www.ubs.com/us/en/wealth-management/insights/article.2047675.html (accessed September 17, 2025).

26. Actively managed funds may also be thematic, but there are more examples of ETFs since the investment process is more systematic and easier to scale.

27. Wellington and BlackRock created "impact" funds in public equities, leading the Global Impact Investing Network (GIIN) to develop guidance to equities fund managers on how to deliver credible impact (available for download at https://thegiin.org/publication/research/listed-equities-working-group/ [accessed September 17, 2025]). Readers interested in this topic may also wish to read about Singapore-based investment manager Panarchy Partners and their proposal for the Asia Gigaton Fund. https://hbsp.harvard.edu/product/NTU372-PDF-ENG (accessed September 17, 2025).

28. Traditionally, debtholders may have had less of a dialogue with management about topics that were not related to debt repayments. More recently, some fixed-income investors are actively engaged with company managements on sustainability-related topics because they believe these topics pose material financial risks to the company.

29. Larcker, D.F., Tayan, B., and Copland, J.R. (2018, June 14). *The big thumb on the scale: An overview of the proxy advisory industry*. Harvard Law School Forum on Corporate Governance. https://corpgov.law.harvard.edu/2018/06/14/the-big-thumb-on-the-scale-an-overview-of-the-proxy-advisory-industry/ (accessed September 17, 2025).

30. Legal & General Investment Management (2024). Active Ownership Report 2023, p. 4. Legal & General Investment Management. https://cms.lgim.com/globalassets/lgim/_document-library/responsible-investing/active-ownership-report-2023---full-report.pdf (accessed September 17, 2025).

31. Governance Institute of Australia (2018). Shareholder Resolutions: Is There a Case for Change? p. 12. https://www.cgiglobal.org/media/4d1llzyy/shareholder_resolutions_is_there_a_case_for_change.pdf (accessed September 17, 2025).

32. Aggarwal, R., Erel, I., Ferreira, M. et al. (2011). Shareholder voting and corporate governance around the world. *Review of Financial Studies* 24 (7): 1967–2025. https://doi.org/10.1016/j.jfineco.2010.10.018.

33. See https://www.lgim.com/asia/en/responsible-investing/investment-stewardship/ (accessed September 18, 2025).

34. See https://esgscores.lgim.com/en/uk/institutional/ (accessed September 18, 2025).

35. See https://www.lgim.com/landg-assets/lgim/_document-library/responsible-investing/active-ownership-report-2023---full-report.pdf (accessed September 18, 2025).

36. See https://www.lgim.com/landg-assets/lgim/responsible-investing/esg-impact-reports/q2-2024-engagement-report.pdf (accessed September 18, 2025).

37. See https://am.landg.com/asset/4a19da/globalassets/lgim/_document-library/climate-impact-pledge/cro_cip-2024-final-8de7.pdf (accessed September 23, 2025).

38. See https://www.lgim.com/landg-assets/lgim/_document-library/responsible-investing/active-ownership-report-2023---full-report.pdf (accessed September 18, 2025).

39. See https://blog.lgim.com/categories/esg-and-long-term-themes/lgims-voting-intentions-for-2024/ (accessed September 18, 2025).

40. See https://www.lgim.com/asia/en/responsible-investing/climate-impact-pledge/ (accessed September 18, 2025).

41. See https://www.lgim.com/asia/en/responsible-investing/climate-impact-pledge/ (accessed September 18, 2025).

42. For this and many of the following references please see https://www.lgim.com/landg-assets/lgim/_document-library/responsible-investing/active-ownership-report-2023---full-report.pdf (accessed September 18, 2025).

43. See https://www.lgim.com/landg-assets/lgim/lgim-human-rights-policy-004_v2.0-1.pdf (accessed September 18, 2025).

44. See https://www.lgim.com/landg-assets/lgim/_document-library/climate-impact-pledge/lgim.climate_impact_pledge_2021.pdf (accessed September 18, 2025).

45. See https://www.lgim.com/landg-assets/lgim/_document-library/climate-impact-pledge/climate-impact-pledge-report-2023.pdf (accessed September 18, 2025).

46. Robert Bosch Stiftung (2024, June 26). Annual Report 2023. Robert Bosch Stiftung. https://www.bosch-stiftung.de/en/annual-report-2023 (accessed September 18, 2025).

47. Transition finance currently applies to greenhouse gas (GHG) emissions rather than other environmental factors. Social issues are important to consider as well but are not subject to technical screening criteria like the emissions issues.

48. Monetary Authority of Singapore and McKinsey & Company. (2023, September). Accelerating the early retirement of coal-fired power plants through carbon credits, p. 3. https://www.mas.gov.sg/-/media/mas-media-library/publications/monographs-or-information-paper/sg/accelerating-the-early-retirement-of-coal-fired-power-plants-through-carbon-credits---september-2023.pdf (accessed September 18, 2025).

49. Asian Development Bank (n.d.). Energy Transition Mechanism (ETM). https://www.adb.org/what-we-do/energy-transition-mechanism-etm (accessed September 18, 2025).

50. Climate Investment Funds (2024, June 4). Climate Investment Funds endorses $500m Philippines' coal transition plan. https://www.cif.org/news/climate-investment-funds-endorses-500m-philippines-coal-transition-plan (accessed September 18, 2025).

51. Asian Development Bank. (2024 September 20). ADB approves policy loan to support Indonesia's energy transition. https://www.adb.org/news/adb-approves-policy-loan-support-indonesia-energy-transition (accessed September 18, 2025).

52. See https://www.brookfield.com/news-insights/insights/going-there-why-investors-need-get-their-hands-dirty-fight-against-climate (accessed September 23, 2025).

53. See https://bep.brookfield.com/press-releases/bep.brookfield-and-microsoft-collaborating-deliver-over-105-gw-new-renewable-power (accessed September 23, 2025).

54. Hong, H. and Kacperczyk, M. (2009). The price of sin: The effects of social norms on markets. *Journal of Financial Economics* 93 (1): 15–36.

55. Hong, H. and Kacperczyk, M. (2009).

56. van der Beck, P. (2021). Flow-Driven ESG Returns Swiss Finance Institute Research Paper No. 21-71, Winner of the Swiss Finance Institute Best Paper Doctoral Award 2022. http:// doi.org/10.2139/ssrn.3929359.

57. Edmans, A., Gosling, T., and Jenter, D. (2024). Sustainable Investing in Practice: Objectives, Constraints, and Limits to Impact. FEB-RN Research Paper No. 18/2024, HKU Jockey Club Enterprise Sustainability Global Research Institute - Archive, European Corporate Governance Institute – Finance Working Paper No. 1028/2024. http:// doi.org/10.2139/ssrn.4963062.

CHAPTER 13   Impact Investing

1. See https://thegiin.org/publication/post/core-characteristics-of-impact-investing/ (accessed September 23, 2025).

2. The following example is taken from Asia Gigaton Fund: Public Equities Investing for Impact, available at https://hbsp.harvard.edu/product/NTU372-PDF-ENG (accessed September 18, 2025).

3. Vionnet, S. (2023). *Impact Thinking: Learn Critical Thinking Skills to Make Better Decisions that Create Societal Value.* https://a.co/aD5Nxbc (accessed September 18, 2025).

4. See https://iris.thegiin.org (accessed September 18, 2025)—also a helpful reference for students during class projects.
5. See https://www.impactprinciples.org/ (accessed September 18, 2025).
6. A good resource on SROI is available at https://socialvalueuk.org/resources/a-guide-to-social-return-on-investment-2012/ (accessed September 18, 2025).
7. Read about this remarkable series of publicly traded impact bonds at https://wlb.iixglobal.com (accessed September 18, 2025).
8. Barber, B.M., Morse, A., and Yasuda, A. (2021). Impact investing. *Journal of Financial Economics* 139 (1): 162–185. https://doi.org/10.1016/j.jfineco.2020.07.008.
9. Calculated as 2.5/20 to 3.7/15.

CHAPTER 14   Sustainable Investing Across Asset Classes and Geographies

1. See https://www.investopedia.com/terms/m/marktomarket.asp (accessed September 19, 2025).
2. This is changing, e.g., the European Union's Corporate Sustainability Reporting Directive (CSRD) will require large private companies to measure and report sustainability information. See Chapter 9.
3. For example, see Aswani, J., Raghunandan, A., and Rajgopal, S. (2024). Are carbon emissions associated with stock returns?: Reply. *Review of Finance* 28 (1): 111–115. https://doi.org/10.1093/rof/rfad020.
4. See the Principles for Responsible Investment (PRI) Sustainability Value Creation guide, available at https://www.unpri.org/private-markets/sustainability-value-creation/13332.article (accessed September 19, 2025).
5. See https://www.brookfield.com/news-insights/insights/what-it-takes-catalyze-transition-emerging-markets#brazil-and-chile (accessed September 23, 2025).

CHAPTER 15   Greenwashing and Investor Disclosure Regulations

1. Directly, anyway. Here we are closer to the idea of financed emissions discussed in Chapter 7.
2. See https://rpc.cfainstitute.org/research/reports/2023/greenwashing-risks-in-investment-fund-disclosures (accessed September 19, 2025).
3. The Sustainable Finance Disclosure Regulation (SFDR) is considered part of the EU Green New Deal, alongside the European Sustainability Reporting Standards (ESRS), the Corporate Sustainability Reporting Directive (CSRD), and the Corporate Sustainability Due Diligence Directive (CSDDD) (Chapter 8); and the Carbon Border Adjustment Mechanism (CBAM) (Chapter 10). See https://finance.ec.europa.eu/sustainable-finance/disclosures/sustainability-related-disclosure-financial-services-sector_en (accessed September 19, 2025) for more information.
4. This section is drawn from https://www.fca.org.uk/consumers/sustainable-investment-labels-greenwashing (accessed September 19, 2025).

CHAPTER 17   Portfolio Construction and Risk Management

1. Markowitz, H. (1952). Portfolio Selection. *The Journal of Finance* 7 (1): 77–91. https://doi.org/10.2307/2975974.
2. Pedersen, L.H., Fitzgibbons, S., and Pomorski, L. (2021). Responsible investing: The ESG-efficient frontier. *Journal of Financial Economics* 142 (2): 572–597. https://doi.org/10.1016/j.jfineco.2020.11.001.
3. Pedersen, L.H., Fitzgibbons, S., and Pomorski, L. (2021).
4. See https://caia.org/sites/default/files/2_investing_11-13-17.pdf (accessed September 19, 2025) for a discussion of the endowment model and benefits associated with outsized allocations to alternative investments like venture capital.
5. Atta-Darkua, V., Glossner S., and Krueger P. et al. (2023). Decarbonizing Institutional Investor Portfolios: Helping to Green the Planet or Just Greening Your Portfolio? Swiss Finance Institute Research Paper No. 25-42. http://doi.org/10.2139/ssrn.4212568.

CONCLUSION   The Difference We Make

1. See https://reimaginingcapitalism.org/ (accessed September 23, 2025).
2. Some believe that, since our mitigation efforts are too small and too slow, the rising rate of environmental disasters due to climate change will require governments to shift their focus to *adaptation*, putting a halt to even those feeble mitigation efforts and consigning the fate of humanity to an ever-warming environment.
3. See https://www.simonandschuster.com/books/Saving-Us/Katharine-Hayhoe/9781982143848 (accessed September 23, 2025).

Academic References

Aggarwal, R., Erel, I., Ferreira, M. et al. (2011). Shareholder voting and corporate governance around the world. *Review of Financial Studies* 24 (7): 1967–2025. https://doi.org/10.1016/ j.jfineco.2010.10.018.

Aswani, J., Raghunandan, A., and Rajgopal, S. (2024). Are carbon emissions associated with stock returns?: Reply. *Review of Finance* 28 (1): 111–115. https://doi.org/10.1093/rof/rfad020.

Atta-Darkua, V., Glossner, S., Krueger, P. et al. (2023). Decarbonizing institutional investor portfolios: Helping to green the planet or just greening your portfolio? *Swiss Finance Institute Research Paper No. 25-4220*: http://dx.doi.org/10.2139/ssrn. 4212568.

Badawi, A.B. and Bartlett, R (2024). ESG Overperformance? Assessing the Use of ESG Targets in Executive Compensation Plans. Stanford Law and Economics Olin Working Paper No. 592, Rock Center for Corporate Governance at Stanford University Working Paper No. 257, European Corporate Governance Institute–Finance Working Paper No. 1025/2024, Stanford Public Law Working Paper. http://dx.doi.org/10.2139/ssrn.4941016.

Barber, B.M., Morse, A., and Yasuda, A. (2021). Impact investing. *Journal of Financial Economics* 139 (1): 162–185. https://doi.org/10.1016/ j.jfineco.2020.07.008.

Berg, F., Kölbel, J.F., and Rigobon, R. (2022). Aggregate confusion: The divergence of ESG ratings. *Review of Finance* 26 (6): 1315–1344. https://doi.org/10.1093/ rof/ rfac033.

Billings, B.K., Buslepp, W.L., and Huston, G.R. (2014). Worth the hype? The relevance of paid-for analyst research for the buy-and-hold investor. *Accounting Review* 89 (3): 903–931. https://doi.org/10.2308/accr-50681

Bosmans, P. and De Mariz, F. (2023). The blue bond market: a catalyst for ocean and water financing. *Journal of Risk and Financial Management* 16: 184. https://doi.org/10.3390/jrfm16030184.

Boustanifar, H. and Kang, Y.D. (2021). Employee satisfaction and long-runstock returns, 1984–2020. *Financial Analysts Journal* 78 (3): 129–151.

Broughton, E. (2005). The Bhopal disaster and its aftermath: a review. *Environmental Health* 4 (1): 6. https://doi.org/10.1186/1476-069x-4-6.

Brown, B.E., Dunne, R.P., Somerfield, P.J. et al. (2019). Long-term impacts ofrising sea temperature and sea level on shallow water coral communities overa ~ 40 year period. *Scientific Reports* 9 (1): 8826. https://doi.org/10.1038/s41598-019-45188-x.

Carroll, A.B. (2016). Carroll's pyramid of CSR: Taking another look. *Journal of Sustainable Business* 1: 3. https:// jcsr. springeropen. com/ articles/10.1186/ s40991-016-0004-6 (accessed September 22, 2025).

Chang, X., Fu, K., Jin, Y. et al. (2022). Sustainable finance: ESG/CSR, firm value, and investment returns. *Asia Pacific Journal of Financial Studies* 51: 325–371. https://doi.org/10.1111/ajfs.12379.

Di Tommaso, C., Pacelli, V., and Povia, M.M. (2025). Green loans and bank risk: Navigating the path to sustainable finance. *International Review of Economics & Finance* 101: 104138. https://doi.org/10.1016/j.iref.2025.10.138.

Edmans, A. (2011). Does the stock market value intangibles? Employee satisfaction and equity prices. *Journal of Financial Economics* 101 (3): 621–640. https:// doi.org/10.1016/j.jfineco.2011.03.021.

Edmans, A., Gosling, T., and Jenter, D. (2024). Sustainable Investing in Practice: Objectives, Constraints, and Limits to Impact. FEB-RN Research Paper No. 18/2024, HKU Jockey Club Enterprise Sustainability Global Research Institute -Archive, European Corporate Governance Institute–Finance Working Paper No. 1028/2024. http://doi.org/10.2139/ssrn.4963062.

Edmans, A., Pu, D., Zhang, C. et al. (2023). Employee satisfaction, labor market flexibility, and stock returns around the world. *Management Science* 70 (7): 4167–4952. http://dx.doi.org/10.2139/ssrn.2461003.

Faulkender, M., Kadyrzhanova, D., Prabhala, N. et al. (2010). Executive compensation: an overview of research on corporate practices and proposed reforms. *Journal of Applied Corporate Finance* 22 (1): 107–118.https://doi .org/10.1111/j.1745-6622.2010. 00266.x.

Flammer, C. (2021). Corporate green bonds. *Journal of Financial Economics* 142 (2): 499–516.

Freeman, R.E. (1984). *Strategic Management: A Stakeholder Approach*. Boston, MA: Pitman.

Friedman, M. (1970). The Social Responsibility of Business is to Increase its Profits. *New York Times Magazine, September*, 13: 122–126.

Gettelman, A., Christensen, M.W., Diamond, M.S. et al. (2024). Has reducing ship emissions brought forward global warming? *Geophysical Research Letters* 51 (15): e2024GL109077. https://doi.org/10.1029/2024gl109077.

Green, J. and Hand, J.R. (2024). McKinsey's Diversity Matters/Delivers/Wins Results Revisited. *Econ Journal Watch* 21 (1): 5–34.

Hart, O.D. and Zingales, L. (2022). The new corporate governance. NBER Working Paper No. 29975, JEL No. G3,K22,L21, Harvard University and University of Chicago.

Henisz, W. J., & McGlinch, J. (2019). ESG, Material Credit Events, and Credit Risk. *Journal of Applied Corporate Finance*, 31(2): 105–117. https://doi.org/10.1111/ jacf.12352-based on the correction this will be added as end note in chapter 7.

Hong, H. and Kacperczyk, M. (2009). The price of sin: the effects of social norms on markets. *Journal of Financial Economics* 93 (1): 15–36.

Kölbel, J.F. and Lambillon, A.P. (2022). Who pays for sustainability? An analysis of sustainability-linked bonds. Swiss Finance Institute Research Paper, 23.

Lam, P. and Wurgler, J.A. (2024). Green bonds: New label, same projects. See https://doi.org/10.2139/ssrn.4951223 (accessed September 9, 2025).

Larcker, D.F., Tayan, B., and Copland, J.R. (2018, June 14). *The big thumb on the scale: An overview of the proxy advisory industry*. Harvard Law School Forum on Corporate Governance. https://corpgov.law.harvard.edu/2018/06/14/the-big-thumb-on-the-scale-an-overview-of-the-proxy-advisory-industry/

Latapí Agudelo, M.A.,Jóhannsdóttir, L., and Davídsdóttir, B. (2019). A literature review of the history and evolution of corporate social responsibility. *International Journal of Corporate Social Responsibility* 4 (1). https://doi.org/10.1186/s40991-018-0039-y.

Li, X.,Lou, Y., and Zhang, L. (2024). Do commercial ties influence ESG ratings? Evidence from Moody's and S&P. *Journal of Accounting Research* 62: 1901–1940. https://doi.org/10.1111/1475-679X.12582.

Liang, H. and Renneboog, L. (2017). On the foundations of corporate social responsibility. *The Journal of Finance* 72: 853–910. https://doi.org/10.1111/jofi.12487.

Liang, H., Sun, L., and Teo, M. (2022). Responsible hedge funds. *Review of Finance* 26 (6): 1585–1633. https://doi.org/10.1093/rof/rfac028.

Markowitz, H. (1952). Portfolio Selection. *The Journal of Finance* 7 (1): 77–91. https://doi.org/10.2307/2975974.

Nemes, N., Scanlan, S.J., Smith, P. et al. (2022). An integrated framework to assess greenwashing. *Sustainability* 14 (8): 4431. https://doi.org/10.3390/su14084431.

Pedersen, L.H., Fitzgibbons, S., and Pomorski, L. (2021). Responsible investing: The ESG-efficient frontier. *Journal of Financial Economics* 142 (2): 572–597. https://doi.org/10.1016/j.jfineco.2020.11.001.

Probst, B.S., Toetzke, M., Kontoleon, A. et al. (2024). Systematic assessment of the achieved emission reductions of carbon crediting projects. *Nature Communications* 15: 9562. https://doi.org/10.1038/s41467-024-53645-z.

Sato, M., Gostlow, G., Higham, C. et al. (2024). Impacts of climate litigation on firm value. *Nature Sustainability* 7: 1461–1468. https://doi.org/10.1038/s41893-024-01455-y.

Shavanov, M.V., Magomadov, A.S., and Slavkina, V.E. (2022). Factors affecting arable agriculture in the future. *IOP Conference Series: Earth and Environmental Science* 979:012116.

van der Beck, P. (2021). Flow-Driven ESG Returns Swiss Finance Institute Research Paper No. 21-71, Winner of the Swiss Finance Institute Best Paper Doctoral Award 2022. http://doi.org/10.2139/ssrn. 3929359.

Wood, D.J. (1991). Corporate social performance revisited. *Academy of Management Review* 16 (4): 691–718.

Index